The Farmhouse Tree

The Farmhouse Tree in the 1920s

THE FARMHOUSE TREE

by David Hill

Jayde Design

London

The Farmhouse Tree
by David Hill.

First published in Great Britain
in 2013 by Jayde Design,
21, Honor Oak Road,
Honor Oak,
London,
SE23 3SH.

3 5 7 9 10 8 6 4

A C.I.P. catalogue record for this
book is available from the British
Library.

I.S.B.N.: 978-0-9575764-1-4.

Printed and bound
by CPI Group (UK) Ltd,
Croydon,
CR0 4YY.

www.JaydeDesign.com
JaydeDesign@CompuServe.com

Dedicated to the memory of:

John Hill 1901–1963
Annie Hill 1909–1989
Nellie Hill 1893–1972

CONTENTS

FOREWORD

by Philip Bowern

W HEN DAVID HILL first submitted an article to the *Western Morning News* for publication in our 'Country Notebook' slot, launched three years ago, it was clear we had stumbled upon a rare talent.

A lot of people believe they can write; almost as many who reach "a certain age" and think they can write about the past. In truth, few can do so in a vibrant and compelling way that both brings the past to life and reveals something about the present in doing so.

At first glance David's writing appears to be a rather gentle take on nostalgia. Thoughtful, descriptive and affectionate it lures you in and encourages the reader to believe he or she is in for a pleasant meander down memory lane.

But read on and David reveals himself to be both a stylist of rare ability who uses words and phrases with an almost musical, poetic quality, and an extremely thought-provoking purveyor of ideas and emotions that have as much currency today as they did in the 1950s he writes about.

The poetry shines through in his descriptions of the countryside, the farming practices and the daily trials and tribulations of ordinary life. You feel his emotions, his pains and his pleasures growing up in the 1950s and you can relate to them, not only as you would to a character in some dim and long since departed past, but as if they were happening in the here and now.

That is because David remembers so well the embarrassments, the awkwardness, the delights and the discoveries of boyhood and puts them across with a freshness and a directness that is difficult to beat.

The past, they say, is another country and there is much in David's writing that reveals the sheer strangeness to the modern reader of rural Devon in the 1950s.

You quickly realise, as you read his work, that so much has changed. But even as modernity was encroaching upon and often improving the lives of ordinary people in other parts of the country through the middle years of the twentieth century, life on the farm owed as much, in 1950s Devon, to the previous century as it did to the century to come.

For readers who remember those days, David's articles bring back memories so powerfully and so sharply focused that they are often deeply moved.

We have had readers call us and write to us at the *Western Morning News* with hugely positive responses to what they have read, precisely because David's recollections match their own and reawaken their own memories so vividly.

But younger readers are fascinated too, both with the precisely drawn details that give them an insight into just how much has changed in sixty years, and the human observations that David makes which underline how little has altered about the way we feel and respond to life.

From the poignant and moving to the laugh-out-loud funny, David knows how to construct a piece of writing, whether it is 300 words or closer to 3,000. He builds in light and shade, always tells a story and has the knack of asking questions which are always resolved by the end of the piece.

David Hill is a writer of rare polish. I once joked to him, as a bit of a hack writer myself, that I would "dash out a piece" to fill a gap in the *Western Morning News*. That, after all, is what most journalists do. David was askance.

Modesty prevented him from revealing just how much care he takes with his own work, but the effort is substantial because he is a craftsman with words. To many of us who work in the churn-factory of daily newspapers yesterday's news, to coin a phrase, is tomorrow's fish-and-chip papers.

David, on the other hand, produces work that succeeds on the newspaper page but also has longevity. It never feels laboured, never loses its freshness and always leaves the reader feeling that he or she has learned something and truly 'felt' something.

One of the marks of a good writer is his or her ability to inform on an intellectual level and move on an emotional one. David Hill does both, as the pieces in this collection show.

Read and enjoy. You will not, I promise, be disappointed.

Philip Bowern,
Head of Content,
Western Morning News,
June 2013.

INTRODUCTION

by Michael Moorcock

I WAS NEVER evacuated from London during the War, though my mother took us away a couple of times, returning after the Blitz but before the V-bombs started to fall on our neighbourhood (the most V-bombed area of England). Like many Londoners she found country life too boring to be tolerable and preferred the risks of the German bombs. I do remember, however, being taken by my father to stay with his mother's relatives who were Browns from Exeter. I still have powerful memories of their smallholding, one of whose main attractions for me was a big limousine going to seed in their lovely apple orchard. I had many great imaginary adventures in that car when I wasn't playing on near-deserted Devon beaches defended by barbed wire. I remember their farmhouse mainly as the residence of dozens of cats which would leap down from all sorts of hiding places at feeding time. Those were happy days for me when I suppose my parents were going through the 'difficulties' which ended when my dad walked out of our house soon after VE Day and rode his mighty motorbike off to where his new lady waited for him.

My Devon relations are the nicest relatives I remember from my early childhood. I think they were childless themselves and so tended to dote on me, their only direct descendant. When, many years later, my father showed me their somewhat battered family bible, I offered to get it rebound for him. It cost a small fortune to have done but at last I brought it back, handsomely restored. He wasn't greatly impressed and he told me to keep it. I had forgotten how unsentimental he could be. I thought he should hold on to it and I would have it after he died. Somewhat typically he later told me he'd passed it on to a cousin (not related to the Browns) because I "didn't seem to want it". I had actually wanted it very much, it being the only connection I had to my Devon family, and regretted not accepting it when my dad offered it! I remember the Browns with great affection. Those times spent in Devon were some of my happiest, the subject of my earliest poems.

David Hill's wonderful memoir vividly brought back those happy days. My great-uncle had been chauffeur to a local bigwig and had retired by the time I began to visit. In spite of the war, they were very happy and peaceful times for me. I've always had a special fondness for the West Country and eventually set one of my fantasy sequences there, deriving a lot of inspiration from a Cornish–English dictionary I bought during a very wet holiday in Marazion.

My mother and I would eventually move to a corrugated iron 'cottage' in Mitcham, not far from the little terraced cottage where she had been born, when the area was still pretty rural, mostly famous for its vast lavender fields and a huge travelling fair, the largest in England, which would set up twice a year on the nearby Common. Heated by a big coke-fired kitchen range and lit by oil lamps, our cottage was the only more or less habitable building belonging to a large house which had probably fallen into ruin even before the war started. We had a flush toilet but it was attached to the nearby stables across a cobbled courtyard. I remember, in the winter of 1947, walking on a pathway between walls of snow higher than my head in order to use that toilet. Primitive as it was, our cottage was a peaceful retreat for us with the bombing stopped and life beginning to return to normal.

David's book had a tremendous effect on me, recalling some of my sweetest memories and bringing his own life into sharp perspective, offering the best kind of reminiscence. My life became very different after the war but I was lucky enough to grow up in a part of South London which was still partially rural. Woods and commons were all around us yet the centre of the city was only twenty minutes away by train, so it isn't hard to identify with David's life and family. They seem to exemplify some of the best in people at a time when we were all just as uncertain about our lives as we are today. On one level, having emerged from a terrible war, we were simply glad to be alive and anxious to return to the rhythms of work and leisure we had known before everything we cared about was threatened. But, as David describes in this moving memoir, the economic forces which would make our lives so different to that of a previous generation were already in play, and inevitably began to change our world at once into a better place as well as a worse one. Much that we cared about – including small farms, self-sufficient villages and a sense of unchanging ways of life from generation to generation – faded away to be replaced by a more complicated understanding of a world where it was no longer possible to exist contentedly in a microcosm, in happy ignorance of what went on in the former British colonies, say, or in the American South.

As we became more conscious of what was going on in a larger world it was not always as easy to take pleasure in the smaller one.

Massive changes came about. Slowly our humanity extended to embrace people of different races and places, different lifestyles or sexual orientation, and our sense of justice and the law grew to allow us concern for millions of people our parents had hardly known existed.

David Hill's book reminds us how small can be beautiful and yet continue to embrace the larger, more complex world. He shows us that simplicity can be sustained and itself prove sustaining while informing us how to live rich, loving lives when everything around us changes. In these anecdotes of his childhood on his family farm, he movingly brings to life a time which has not so much vanished as slipped out of sight. Only a few years have passed since I lived in rural Yorkshire where some neighbours still used horses for ploughing and a farmer might tramp for an hour or so across the fells to enjoy a pint before turning around and tramping home again. David makes it clear that where and when we live can make a difference as to how we live, our environment and our time do not necessarily determine either our humanity or the pleasure we take in living, while our intelligence and sensibility are no less sophisticated whether we live in a rural hamlet or a major metropolis.

This is a wise book, full of love for a way of life, a respect for people of all kinds and a great relish for the physical world. David Hill has a generous spirit and a vivid memory. He reminds us that, while times might change dramatically, our common humanity rarely does. I found his book moving, informative and above all heartening. I think you will, too.

Michael Moorcock,
Rue St Maur, Paris,
June 2013.

PROLOGUE

The Roots of the Farmhouse Tree

"WELL, WHAT DO you think of the old farmhouse?" asked my aged maiden aunt one rainy afternoon as we were sitting on the double bed in the spare room at the far end of the landing, listening to Charles Penrose on the wind-up gramophone.

The question caught her nine-year-old nephew totally by surprise, but before I could reply she added, "One day it'll be all yours and all the sixty acres of land. When you're a lot older, that is." I stared at her. How could it possibly be mine when it belonged to my father?

"It's good fun, Auntie," I blurted out finally, "and it's so old that sometimes I imagine I'm living in a tree. It just seems to grow out of the earth like an oak tree. And each room and each outbuilding are branches, and the cob walls are the trunk." The words came out in a rush, and as soon as I'd uttered them I could feel my face going red. I hadn't meant to reveal my secret thoughts, but they'd slipped out in my confusion.

She smiled. "A farmhouse tree. You and your fanciful ideas and notions. Whatever will you come out with next? Mind you, it's well over two hundred years old, and oak trees grow to a great age."

"Auntie, it won't fall down, will it?"

"And whatever put that idea into your head?"

"Yesterday, when I was standing by the back kitchen wall I accidently pulled a small piece of the cob out, and Dad said if I wasn't careful it would all come tumbling down around our ears."

"Did he indeed? Well he was just pulling your leg. It's good for another two hundred years at least. Outlast all of us, and others too I expect."

From the gramophone came the final guffaw of the laughing policeman. Lifting the silver arm she carefully removed the needle, dropped it into an empty matchbox, replaced it with a new one from a small blue-and-yellow tin and returned the record to its brown paper sleeve. Finally, she closed the two doors at the front of the cabinet, removed the handle and slotted it into the compartment at the base of the gramophone.

"We'll let him go off duty now," she said with a smile. I gave a sigh of relief. She wasn't going to play 'The Old Rugged Cross'. Today the crackling rendition wouldn't reach a climax with His Master's Voice coming out in a slow drawl, with the wooden cross creaking and groaning as it leaned precariously, the hidden mechanism in the gramophone grinding to a halt.

Today there would be no mild rebuke concerning my blasphemous behaviour as I tried in vain to stifle my giggles, while my aged maiden aunt cranked the handle to get the record to revolve at the correct speed to upright the cross.

Getting up from the bed she said, "Now if you come along with Auntie she might just be able to put her hand on a bag of barley sugars for us to enjoy... Farmhouse tree indeed. Whatever next?"

Leaving the spare room we walked along the landing to her bedroom. Pausing at the door she said, "We won't tell anyone about your farmhouse tree. It'll be our little secret. Just between us. Me and you. Now let's see where Auntie has put those sweets. Seconds later I heard the rustle of cellophane as she found them, and I knew there'd be one, perhaps even two as she sealed her promise.

David's aged maiden aunt, Aunt Nell, in 1964

THE FARMHOUSE TREE

Cuckoo

FROM THE DAY that I was first carried into the farmhouse tree in the autumn of 1947, I had two mothers – my real mother aged thirty-eight and my father's sister, my aged maiden aunt aged fifty-four. Having never married, Aunt Nell had lived on the farm since her birth in 1893, a provision in her parents' will leading to an understanding that she should live on the family farm for as long as she wished. And she did, living on a small annual allowance left to her, and her old age pension which she was paid in the 1950s.

There was a period when I took on the appearance of a nestling cuckoo. I had only to sit up in my carriage-sized pram-nest, flap my arm-wings, open my mouth-beak and give off a loud squawking cry. Immediately two mother birds flew down and began thrusting particles of nourishing food into my upturned beak.

In those early years both women saw it as their daily duty, working in harmony, to ensure that their baby, which both women had waited sixteen years to arrive, was given the best possible nourishment they could provide which included cod liver oil, orange juice and fresh farm milk.

Both gave me physical sustenance, and at the same time both formulated my spiritual well-being, my mother from a Church of England viewpoint and my aged maiden aunt from a Methodist John and Charles Wesley pulpit. They saw to it that as sowers, the seeds of faith were planted and nurtured in a rich soil with no tares or stones – unsuitable comics such as the *Beano* and *Dandy* to name but two – to inhibit and prevent the process. In their eyes the best nutrients were Sunday school and the children's page of the *Christian Herald*.

There was no escape as two great-aunts were responsible for running both the Sunday school and the chapel. Any absence would have been duly noted and reported. There was none.

"God answered our prayers in His own good time, even if I do say it was a long time. But He moves in a mysterious way, His wonders to perform," said my aged maiden aunt as she straightened my tie (with cowboys on) before I set out for Sunday school.

To which my mother added, as she dabbed a smut from my cheek with the corner of her handkerchief moistened with her spittle, "Now we must bring you up to follow in those ways and tread the path of righteousness." And tread the straight and narrow path I most certainly did, at times with very unwilling footsteps.

A Spiritual Diet with the Roughage Removed

MINE WAS A Methodist family; mother, father, an aged maiden aunt, Jim and Derek my two imaginary friends and me. No farm work on Sunday except for the milking. No knitting, no sewing, no darning, no washing, no ironing, no preparation of vegetables for the Sunday roast dinner. Everything prepared on Saturday night and the weekly milk- or rice-pudding made and placed in the Calor gas oven.

If the main ingredients of my religious diet were hymns, prayers, grace, Sunday school and chapel, my mother and aged maiden aunt took it upon themselves to remove all roughage from my rich binding diet, which meant I was always bound up on a Sunday. Roughage being games, toys, comics, books and sweets. All were removed on the seventh day.

My aged maiden aunt, five feet two in her stockinged feet, knew her Bible inside out. "Remember the Sabbath day to keep it holy. Six days shalt thou labour and do all thy work, play games, eat sweets and read comics. But the seventh is the Sabbath of the Lord thy God."

No books, no papers, no comics on Sunday. "Is that the *Beano* I see in your hand behind your back? God doesn't read comics on a Sunday, especially not the *Beano*. A comic for the heathen children, like that Kenneth Harris. Them that hath not seen the light. Those living across the sea where the sun is hot. Give it here, please."

Only the Bible and the weekly *Christian Herald* on Sunday with its Golden Star Brigade page for all God's young earthly bodies shining with a pure celestial light. "Wear your badge that I sent away for with pride, now that you're a member of God's club," she instructed as she pinned it on my blazer lapel just before I set out for Sunday school. "And in future no more *Beano*s. The *Swift*, *Enid Blyton Magazine* and the *Children's Newspaper*, yes. Good wholesome reading. And finally remember you're always in His holy sight. God is always watching you. Immortal, invisible, God only wise. And He'll see if you're reading the *Dandy* as well."

The very thought of being viewed by a pair of invisible all-seeing eyes, my every action duly noted, including going to the lavatory indoors or behind the beech tree outside, sent a shiver of chill fright tingling up and down my spine. Together with my imaginary friends I searched the farmhouse tree from the attic to the cellar, hunting high and low. He wasn't lurking in the 'ood shed, or the shippen or the sty. He wasn't in the cob-walled stable, under my bed or kitchen table. At midnight when the floorboards creaked and shadow monsters roamed the candlelit walls, I hid beneath the sheets in my brass-and-iron double bed mumbling words for Him to hear. A cry for help, a silent plea: "Please God, keep on watching and I promise I'll be good tomorrow." But on Monday morning I removed my Golden Star Brigade badge and replaced it with the Bisto Kids' badge which I wore with pride as I showed off to my mates.

One Sunday I thought of a way to read the *Beano*. But my cunning wheeze was quickly foiled. "Is that the *Beano* sticking out from between the pages of the *Christian Herald*? Give it here, please. That Kenneth Harris you'm mixing with at school is a bad influence. Young heathen, leading you astray. Leading you off the straight and narrow path. Paint the picture, learn the text and enjoy the earthly story with a heavenly meaning and then you'll shine as bright as any star. You won't be dim like that Kenneth Harris."

As I worked my way through the moral tale I wondered to myself why Dennis the Menace didn't have the same cross to bear.

Each Monday at the crack of dawn just as the golden cockerel was crowing his notes across the sky from his eastern perch, my aged maiden aunt crossed the road to pick up the *News of the World* from the blacksmith's wife. "Just to see what the heathens read and get up to, you understand."

Spreading it out on the breakfast table, she read it as fast as she was able, poring over every word and picture, until at last she announced, "What wickedness, what sin. What a world we'm living in. The shameless hussy and him a vicar too. Roman Catholic though. Good job we'm all Methodists."

When the paper had been thoroughly devoured, the pages were drawn, quartered and hung on a nail on the outside lavatory pine door. "There, that's all it's fit for. Whatever will they print next week?"

No Dinky, Matchbox or Corgi toys, snakes and ladders, ludo, snap or tiddlywinks on Sunday.

"Are those marbles I see clenched in your hand? Give them here, please. You can have them back tomorrow."

Handing them over I waited for her homily and I wasn't disappointed. "The Lord blessed the Sabbath and hallowed it, and hallowed doesn't mean playing with marbles. Rest, yes; marbles, no." Pausing she gave me the knowing look I knew so well. "And before you ask, God doesn't play with marbles either... Not on a Sunday or any other day of the week."

No sweets or chocolate on Sunday unless it was Christmas Day or Easter Day when an exception was made to the unwritten rule. On Easter Sunday she always presented me with a super-duper boxed chocolate egg, and once a rare pink-and-white sugar egg. Yum, yum, pig's bum.

"Doesn't God eat sweets?" I once asked her when feeling very brave, assuming my all-seeing, all-hearing deity who had created the world in six days could create the finest sweetshop imaginable, crammed with His home-made liquorice bootlaces, aniseed balls and gobstoppers, in the twinkling of an eye.

"God doesn't need to eat on Sunday or any other day of the week. And He certainly wouldn't chew bubblegum. A filthy habit. A heathen habit. Now spit yours out, wrap it up and throw it away. God eating sweets indeed. Whatever will you come out with next?"

A few minutes later as I was colouring in the picture in the *Christian Herald*, a hand reached over my shoulder. "A barley sugar for you. You'm allowed a barley sugar. Auntie likes them too. A medicinal sweet. Good on coach outings or car journeys." She sucked hers as she ruffled my curly hair. "No, God doesn't object to barley sugars on Sunday, or any other day of the week." In my mind's eye, God with a big pink bubble stuck in His long white beard.

No strong liquor on Sunday, Monday, Tuesday, Wednesday or any other day of the week. Cider at hay harvest time to wash away the dust and grime from sun-scorched throats, but only for the heathen men, those raking swathes of newly mown hay or shooking sheaves of barley, wheat or oats beneath the glare of a summer's day. "Ration them to two pints each, then keep the firkin out of reach. Well hidden down a rabbit hole. Strong liquor rots the body, kills the soul. Just for the heathen men who sit in the Masons Arms and not their homes of a night."

We even crossed the road on our way to chapel when we approached the house of ill repute. Walking on the other side of the pub until we were well past.

At Christmas time, Stone's ginger wine, 14% proof but never viewed as alcohol or the devil's water. For me a bottle of fizzy Corona limeade pop delivered by the Corona pop lorry man. The explosion of bubbles from the fluorescent green liquid bursting up my nose. The big loud burp. My father laughing: "Where ere you be let the wind go free. In church or chapel let it rattle..."

In the corner cupboard of front room, a special bottle – BRANDY. "Strictly medicinal, you understand. Don't know what they see in it myself. Shock, a death, a cold or flu. Mind you, I will say this. You know when you've had some. Warms where goes."

Yes, mine was a Methodist family with a touch of Anglican thrown into the diet by my mother just to be on the safe side, a belt-and-braces procedure. Sunday was the worst day of the week. Hymns, hymns, hymns and yet more hymns and lessons of Holy Scripture, prayers and a sermon.

From early in the morning the farmhouse tree resounded with religious music. Sandy MacPherson on his organ in his personal chapel in the valley. As to where this valley was located, no-one could tell me. "It's just there," said my aged maiden aunt. "Why do you have to question everything so?"

Later, the wireless service. "But not if it's Roman Catholic," said my aged maiden aunt as she twisted the knob.

"Thank you, all-seeing and all-hearing God," I whispered, "for making Roman Catholics."

"There, you'll be able to read the story in the *Christian Herald* again," she added. "No need for all that dressing up and waving tins around filled up with smoke. Good job we'm all Methodists."

In the afternoon, Sunday school and the chapel service. To round off the rest of the unhappy toyless, comicless, sweetless day, hymn singing around the wireless set, our voices sending hymns and prayers winging to our Methodist God with a touch of Anglican, all-seeing, all-hearing God high up in the sky. With the congregation from a far-off town or city, we thanked Him for His bounteous gifts. "But not if it's Roman Catholic."

Every Sunday no bars of chocolate licked, no sweets sucked, no toffees chewed, no bubbles blown. Every Sunday I was drunk on psalms and psalters and prayers and the hangover lingers with me still. My aged maiden aunt kept taking a once-in-a-while, strictly-medicinal brandy tot and lived well past her allotted biblical span of three-score years and ten.

Yes, mine was a Methodist family, with all the roughage removed on a Sunday.

Attic

BRANCHES OF THE farmhouse tree were never referred to as *the* attic or *the* kitchen. 'The' was never used. Attic was a place shrouded in mystery and cobwebs. Hanging from the rafters during the daylight hours were pipistrelle and long-eared bats which escaped at twilight through the gaps between worm-eaten planks in the boarded-up window frames which were wedged into position by an iron ball. This had once been used to anchor the corner of a tarpaulin rick sheet. Once airborne, the bats flitted across back court and the meads. The floor was made up of ill-fitting wooden boards, through the gaps of which the floor of back kitchen could be glimpsed below.

Occasionally there would be a frantic scrabbling above my brass-and-iron double bed. Mice had invaded again and I snuggled down deep into my snug den beneath blankets, quilt and eiderdown. Attic, out of bounds to me but not to a rat which one afternoon crept uninvited through the half-open back door and up the rickety stairs. He squatted for a couple of days, during which time he gnawed at my father's seed potatoes and then left in a wire-cage trap and was drowned in the hogshead water butt in an explosion of diamond bubbles, squirming paws and a frantic coiling and uncoiling of tail.

In winter, biting winds blowing in from Exmoor entered through the plank gaps, and gaps under the slates, freezing the water in the lead pipes. Hot-water bottles quickly filled with water from the stream, which had been boiled in the black iron kettle over the open fire, were pressed against the pipes until water gurgled through the taps.

Once, to satisfy my curiosity, after a constant "Can I, Dad? Can I look up there, Dad? Can I?", I was allowed to follow him up the stairs, my penlight torch lighting up the gaps between the rough-hewn stair boards. Stored in the blackness and glimpsed for the first and last time, apples for the winter laid out on sheets of the *Western Times* and smudged with bat droppings which my tut, tut, tutting head-shaking aged maiden aunt wiped off with a damp dishcloth before peeling and turning them into dumplings, pies and tarts.

In the beam of light, family objects from three generations including stirrups, a side saddle, spurs and a whip. A Gladstone bag, leather cases, a metal hoop, a catgut tennis racquet, headless lead soldiers, a bundle of old *Christian Herald*s and a piano accordion. Much later in life I discovered it had last been played by an uncle, who in his youth had been very musical, but at the age of fourteen had contracted meningitis and had died almost forty years later in a public mental home in Exeter.

Attic, a dark place. Back down the stairs, curiosity satisfied. Closing the door on my hidden fears. Closing the door on the place of memories, seldom recalled and then only in hushed tones when old photographs and funeral cards were taken out from a drawer in front room at Christmas.

A Lovely Neck

"YOUR DAD HAD a lovely neck," laughed my mother one afternoon when I was visiting her in the nursing home where she spent her final years. "I was seventeen and he was in his mid-twenties. I'd sit behind him in church and look at his neck. Always scrubbed clean it was, just above his Sunday best collar."

When she was twenty-one and he was twenty-nine they were married and she moved into the farmhouse tree and ran the house with her sister-in-law for the next thirty-plus years.

Until the death of her husband in 1963, she walked through the village each day delivering milk either in Lucozade bottles or billycans, and fresh butter, cream and eggs. During the 1930s she walked four miles to the local station at East Anstey where the butter she had churned, and the cream separated by my father from the milk, went by train to a London hotel. During the War she was a surrogate mother to five evacuees.

In September 1947, after a wait of sixteen years, I was born. The stork had finally located the row of gooseberry bushes in our top garden. My mother was thirty-eight and my father was forty-six. The winter of 1947 was also one of the coldest on record!

David's parents in 1958

21

She was only fifty-four when my father died, and from 1968 until her death in a Cornish nursing home in 1989 her life was plagued by a series of strokes.

To the end of her life her faith was rock-solid. The earthly life a preparation for the next, when she was convinced she would be "going home", where she would be reunited with her loved ones.

Communion

EACH SUMMER, ON a late hot August day, we made our pilgrimage. My mother striding through the grass beating a track with a gnarled walking stick.

"They'm come to come," she always said when blackberries on bramble bushes lay like nubs of coal upon a hearth, and flame thorns burned her naked arms.

Hooked down with a walking stick, her fingers fumbled through the foliage, finding out the choicest fruits for making into jelly, jam, pies, tarts and a cordial for the Sunday sacrament.

Suspended from an iron hook set into the back kitchen revolving beam, a muslin bag, gorged and bloated with its boiled feast, dripped juice into a white enamel bowl. In the dressing room attached to my parents' bedroom the jars on the shelf blazed with a pattern of light; a stained-glass window.

Today, I perform the ritual alone. Licking fingers blotched by the bruised fruit, I taste the blood. Floating on the breeze, echoes of laughter from far-off childhood days.

Yellow Raspberries

"HOUR UPON HOUR, and mile after mile along the country roads and lanes we went when he was very small. The time I spent taking him out," she'd recount with a smile.

The story from my childhood. Always the same. An oral photograph about our shared game of spotting haystacks from my pushchair. The details as sharp as if she was still there.

"He'd point them out, shouting loudly 'pooky' hay. During the summer we played the game each day. And once we found some yellow raspberries. How he loved his rides around the countryside."

She'd tell the tale when girlfriends came to tea. Designed to tease, words full of harmless fun, a doting mother with her grown-up son. Her eyes an album of mounted memories.

Today, when time permits I collect her from the nursing home. Inwardly cursing her second childhood I push her around, our rôles reversed, through neatly ordered grounds.

Views of suburbia with open-plan estates, the skyline of tile and Cornish slate. Once, while gazing at the distant fields I heard her say, "The raspberries were very sweet in those days."

Picnic

ONE AUGUST AFTERNOON, when mirages melted and flowed over the roads, where tar in an ooze of treacle-black bubbles seeped up through gravel, dry crusted cowpats peeled open like scabs, and the spring in Higher Orchard which provided us with water threatened to run dry, my mother and I trekked across three fields drenched in a scent of meadowsweet and honeysuckle to the river bank of the Crooked Oak. The surface pollen-flecked and silent.

At the edge of the small plantation, beneath the shade of ancient conifers, the contents of the withe basket placed upon the grass – bath towels, Lifebuoy soap and flannels. A thermos flask, pop bottle, currant buns and crisps.

Getting undressed in a flail of limbs, giggling. Apprehensive glances through the screen of trees. My first ever glimpse of her unclothed body. My face colouring. In the silence, under the cool shade of the overhanging boughs, our toes touching the surface. Small ripples echoing out. My flesh tingling with the surprise, trying to avoid looking at her soft nakedness. Blushing again as I glimpsed her reflection looking up at me. Crisps and pop forgotten.

Splashing together in the ice coldness. Back on the bank, towelling my chest and ruffling my hair. Dressed again, the picnic pop bubbles exploding up my nose. Picking a rush she slowly peeled open the stalk to reveal a slender white strand. "Rush pith. Used as a poor man's nightlight." Her fingers delicately forming it into a candlewick.

Thirty years later in the nursing home I recalled the afternoon. Her face lit up. "Your father had a lovely neck. Always beautifully scrubbed. His collar white. I'd sit behind him during church. I was seventeen, he was twenty-five, and I fell in love with him. Four years later we were married. He was a good man."

In my memory a glimpse of her soft nakedness.

This is The Disposable Age

I HAVE DISCARDED you, cast you aside, worn out. Surplus to my requirements, functions all irregular. Now I can continue with my life, leaving you sitting on the periphery of yours, staring inwards at yourself and into the centre of the lounge. Your days growing longer.

Twice weekly I rake up your memories. Your eyes light up with a twinkle, but the fire soon sputters, the embers turning dull. It's back to monosyllabic responses as you reply to your dutiful son. Is your leg still swollen? And are your fingers numb?

It's cold outside. Think it'll snow? And did you enjoy your tea? Squeezing your hand I give you a kiss before quietly leaving the home. Your days growing longer and longer.

Outside I return to my real world. Jewelled notes of the blackbird drop from the sun's gold crown. Cascades of swallows tumble down from out of an azure sky. On the wind, leaves pirouette, dancing the days away. Frenzied flurry of falling flakes, cold kiss on an upturned cheek. How quickly my year goes by.

In your world of the thermostat the seasons blur and merge. Spring is summer, autumn, winter. Your days growing longer and longer and longer. This is the disposable age.

Harvest Home

EACH NIGHT SHE read twenty verses, the pale glow from the Aladdin lamp illuminating the text of the family Bible with a mantle of golden light. Accepting each word with a childlike trust, she tended the crop sown in the spring. Her faith allowing no seeds of doubt to take root and grow into tares in her harvest field.

The withe basket heavy by her side was carried with a quiet pride.

Her contribution to the harvest scene. Home bakes, pastries, pies and cakes. Spread out on the drying grass, a cloth smothered the scent of chamomile. "Sanctify O Lord this food for our use and us to Thy service for Jesus Christ's sake. Amen."

Sanctify was a strange and haunting word. "What does it mean?" I once asked her as we folded the white linen cloth.

A pause. A smile. "It just... it just means sanctify. God's word. Now off you go and make the hay. And don't go getting into trouble."

The harvest festival was her favourite act of worship, its glut of produce swollen with ripeness. Bunch upon bunch of beetroot, carrot, parsnip and turnip spilling over the windowsills. The altar rail a cascade of chrysanthemums, dahlias and michaelmas daisies. Petals trickling over a wheatsheaf shaped out of dough by the local baker.

Cubes of freshly baked bread laid out on a white linen serviette. Home-made blackcurrant cordial in tiny thimble-shaped tumblers. Celebrating the Holy sacrament was the climax of her special day. Her eyes reflecting her acceptance with a faith total in every sense.

On her eightieth birthday I brought photographs. Scattering them like ears of wheat upon her crisp white cotton sheet, I recounted past summers. Bringing to life ageless faces in portraits, wedding groups and scenes of bygone rural days, I harvested our memories.

For two days glazed eyes gazed past the figures, as if staring over the horizon into a land beyond. Then with a rasping breath she set out on her final journey.

Across the field beneath a skim of summer swallows, the farmer's wife steps through the shimmer of a heat haze and is quickly lost from view. At the granary the farmer extends an arm beckoning her to enter and celebrate raising the harvest home.

Spread out on the trestle table, the harvest supper laid out in readiness. Figures rise and turn to greet her. As one, their voices swell the air. Welcome wife, welcome daughter. Welcome. Welcome. Welcome home.

The Parting Gift

YOUR HANDS ARE delicately lifting a day-old chick from beneath the sitting Rhode Island Red. Warm fingers in a feather-gentle touch, placing it with reverence on my outstretched tiny palm.

Your hands spreading the cloth on the hayfield, on chamomile crushed by cartwheel, hoof and boot. Scents mingling with the aroma of freshly baked buns in a melt of home-churned butter.

Your hands drying my wet hair, fingers ruffling my tousled curls and lingering over my burning cheeks. First glimpse of your body on the heat-filled day, while bathing naked in the river.

Your hands picking wild strawberries, raspberries – yellow and red – blackberries and blackcurrants for the chapel communion cordial. In the orchard, greengages and damsons, apples and plums. Juice in a trickle over my chin dabbed away by your fingers.

Hands held in mine, fingers growing colder; the memories of childhood fading. A sudden surge of summer heat passing through me. With your final breath your parting gift – your spirit passing through me. Leaving behind "the little boy I'd waited sixteen years to arrive".

An Honest Man

MY FATHER WAS born, lived all his life and died in the family farmhouse tree. During his lifetime he made only one journey over sixty miles from the village – a seaside resort for his honeymoon. On his return he never spent another night away from his own bed.

David's father on horseback in front court, 1920s

A day out was a bus trip to the local market at South Molton, a bus trip to Tiverton or a walk to the auction at East Anstey, the latter a four-mile trek driving his cattle, or in later years in a cattle lorry. Once a year, if offered a lift, he would visit an agricultural show; in October a trip to Bampton pony fair with a cousin, and in the summer the annual seaside trip on the Methodist outing coach.

Throughout the years from 1921, when he farmed Eastacott, through to 1963 all of the heavy work was done with horses. In the early years there were three horses when he farmed sixty acres with his brother on the death of their father. In the early '30s, he bought out the half share of his brother, who with his wife had moved to Braunton to run the corn merchant's business and grocery shop which she had inherited from an aunt and uncle. In the early '40s when the war effort required land to be put under the plough, he let out forty acres to a neighbouring farmer. He was a chronic migraine sufferer and the remaining twenty or so acres were as much as he could manage. From the late '40s he only had one shirehorse and in the '50s he borrowed a neighbour's. When the neighbour, an octogenarian, retired he sold the horse to my father at a much reduced rate from its true value to thank him for being such a good neighbour. He never took back the forty acres, farming just the twenty-plus acres for 365 days of the year. The herd of cows was never more than seven; there were also half a dozen bullocks which he would fatten up, and a hundred or so hens.

Electricity never came to the farm until 1963 and the farmhouse tree was never connected to mains water or mains drainage. Milking was done by hand – he never employed a farm labourer – the farm didn't run to the extra expense and he never learned to drive a tractor or car.

He always paid his feed bills as soon as he received them: "That man needs to put food on his table today, not at the end of the month. He enjoys his fried breakfast just like you."

He never raised his hand or his voice to me; the look in his eyes – a look of sadness that I had let him down – told me when I had done wrong. There were times when I wished he had been angry with me.

He found it hard killing fowls at Christmas, and the death of a cow or calf would often reduce him to tears.

At the church service on the Sunday immediately following his funeral, the vicar told the congregation that he had buried a man who hadn't got an enemy in the world, one of the most honest men he had ever met, and in all his time in the parish he had never heard anyone speak ill of him or he of them.

A Poor Farmer

SHUNNING INNOVATION AND machines, he chose the horse power of a gentle shire, preferring the stench of sweat to that of oil. Twice daily, cows were milked by hand, each one named and treated with respect. On market days he'd walk his fields when stock was driven with sticks into a truck.

Having no stomach for sticking pigs he seldom saw the gush of blood spew red-hot from an open throat. Nor could he bring himself to thrust a sharp-edged blade into the beak of a hanging fowl, allowing instead my mother to perform the task.

Each year he found the first white violets, a small bouquet pressed shyly into my mother's hand. He knew the nesting sites of robin, thrush and wren; the secret banks where strawberry and yellow raspberry grew. He enjoyed the sparkling spiderwebs, silver in the dew, the glinting kingcups golden in the rushes, the returning cuckoo's call.

The box hedges with their neatly shaped sides enclosed a tiny parcel of land. Untied each spring with a childlike glee, the wrapping paper of winter weeds was quickly torn away by his excited hands. In the summer months the rewards of his labours. Sweet peas and stocks grew by his cinder paths saturating the air. Ankle-deep around his feet, an autumn feast – potato, parsnip, carrot, bean and beetroot. The parcel contents displayed with pride.

Scraping a living from twenty-plus acres he found his profits in garden, hedgerow, pond and river. According to some in the know, my father was a poor farmer.

Stock

MY FATHER HAND-MILKED his herd of seven cows, which was made up of numerous breeds. Red Ruby, Friesian, Ayrshire, Shorthorn and latterly one Jersey to make the milk creamier. The milk was put out every morning in churns, each holding ten gallons, on the wooden milk stand by the gate where it was collected by lorry and taken to the Ambrosia Depot at Lapford.

In winter when there was a hard frost, the milk in the churn would occasionally freeze solid near the top and I would remove the lid and scoop out some home-made ice cream.

In summer if there were hot days, there was always the worry that the milk in the churns would turn sour. If a churn came back with a pink label on the top you knew that the milk had gone off and had been returned; no money for the milk in that churn.

The shippens had to be mucked out each morning and the cob walls whitewashed regularly. I never tired of watching him sitting on his milking stool, and when I mastered the age-old skill I was proud of my achievement.

Head bowed as if in prayer, forehead pressed against her flank. The warmth in the shippen stifling and moist. The scent wild and sweet, hay and sweat, permeating the cob walls. Hands cupping the roundness. The veined bag brimming over, stretched and swollen; a full moon.

Fingers stroking, coaxing, squeezing. The rhythm ancient and unhurried. Through his fingers two slender pillars, white and flowing; liquid moonbeams.

Cupped between his knees the aluminium pail froth full; a pool of moonlight.

Occasionally when a full bucket was left by the shippen door I would write my initials with my finger in the foam and while he was milking, my father would aim the teat at my mouth as I crouched down and I would have a pre-breakfast warm drink.

He also kept a small herd of half a dozen Red Ruby North Devon steers for fattening. A breed of cattle first introduced and bred by Mr Francis Quartly. They were so called because of the colour of their medium red coats. Each spring he would walk the cattle to the show at East Anstey where they were judged and then sold.

He kept his rosettes in a box together with a stick of sealing wax, a lump of chalk, odd lengths of string, pen nibs, bills, receipts, old notebooks and a pencil stub, at the back of the kitchen table drawer. In the china cupboard – tucked behind the lustreware, the tea and dinner services, the cut-glass vases and the cider jugs – the tarnished cup that he had won.

Embossed with leaf motifs, and inscribed: 'Best steer bred and fed by the exhibitor East Anstey Fat Stock Show'. Once in a while when in reflective mood, he'd tell the tale of how he drove his Rubies to the ring. The sky was blue, a golden sun, birds sang in beech hedgerows which lined his four-mile walk. No mention of grey winter months, or how his hands were chapped and calloused, red and raw. Or how each day he sliced hay from the stack, carrying it roped and bundled on his back through snow-filled fields to his herd of waiting stock.

Each spring he won for three successive years, the champion's rosette and silverware. His to keep. "The small man beat the big boys." His smile of pride, the quiet satisfaction of a job well done, how the stock had won it and not him.

Finally he'd list the wild flowers seen: red campion, stitchwort and bluebell. That final year he'd found a robin's nest complete with six warm mottled eggs. His eyes shining with delight as once again he relived his special day, saw once again that special nest, his jewelled cup.

Potatoes

A FAVOURITE TIME in summer was the harvesting of potatoes from the garden. My father was one of those rare farmers who actually enjoyed gardening. For most farmers who have a garden it is a chore which has to be completed in the evenings after a hard day's work on the farm. It was always fun in late summer following him terrierlike between the rows as he harvested the crop.

As he dug into the row he'd ask me with a laugh to guess the number of potatoes he'd unearth. Hands gripping the shaft – ash, shining and smooth. The grain polished with grease, grime, sweat and spit on the fork passed down by his father.

The forged prongs prising the summer tubers free. Lifting, shaking, counting the crop as it dropped to the soil. My guess always just one under or one over the number lying in the clump. Freshly dug, the tubers dried in the sun, irregular in size, lying like pebbles on a beach, the haulms shrivelled and brown.

Beetle-like I scurried up the drill, filling my withe basket with the smallest spoil to be stored for seed. Once, I found a fist-sized one shaped like the Methodist preacher's face. A pause. The silence broken by his laughter erupting over the garden as he pushed the barrow to the potato house.

At Sunday dinner, during grace, a downward glance. Peeping through half-open lids, each catching the other one's eye. Followed by his secret wink. Our shared smile, the meal eaten in silence.

The firkin, iron-staved, kept by the door of the potato house, became my seat when in late August, King Edward and Majestic were laid down in a clamp for winter meals. Enthroned, I watched him build the heap, checking skins for scab, disease or rot. And as he worked he intoned words both magical and strange. An ancient chant passed down by his father.

Through the next three days of harvesting I learned old measures and old ways. Gills, firkins, kilderkins, barrels, hogsheads, puncheons, pipes and butts flowed through my brain in a litany. My every response greeted with an approving nod.

For the second lesson he chose the farm, names and sizes relating to the fields, orchards and plantations. Lower Down, Higher Down, Moory Ground, Bull's Mead, West Furze Close, Higher Mead, Hither Six Acres, Outer Six Acres, Higher Orchard, Lane Field and Little Close. Fifty-nine acres three rods and twelve poles. Arable, grass, apples and soft timber wood.

Through learning his creed the farm lived and breathed. Closing the door on the darkness I entered the light. Old lore conferred, the initiate is rewarded with a beaker of milk and a slice of freshly baked fruit cake.

Hands

CHARLIE, THE SHIREHORSE, was an iron horse of a beast – a steam locomotive, snicker and snort, snicker and snort. Occasionally a piston leg struck the stones of the stable floor in a firework of sparks. He was a cider barrel of a beast, bubbles of sweat oozing in a fermentation of foam from his leather-staved belly. The scent intoxicating and strong.

Gentle hands lifting me onto the bare back. "Hold tight to the hames and don't let go."

Astride the globe surveying my realm, I was a king for fifteen minutes. Led through the newly mown hay mead in a lumber-lurch of plodding hoofs. His hands bringing me back down to earth. Sugar lumps placed on the palm of my hand with the words, "Watch out for his teeth." Gazing into the deep pools, touching the moss-soft nostrils and lips.

The stable straw was a safe place to go and hide when I'd misbehaved, from where I could see out, but not be seen. A heap glistening gold in the corner. Sunlight filtering through cobwebbed wooden window slats.

The oak manger was a safe place where the farm cat went to become thin. A kindle of wet wrinkled bodies in a squirming heap of squeaks and squeals.

A hessian corn-sack dropped on the cobblestone floor. Fingers reaching in over the manger side. Kittens removed one by one. Held by the right hip in rough hands which clench-fisted the tiny bodies lengthways. Placed in the sack, binder-twine knotted tight. No squirms, no squeals from the blackness.

The farm cat went off to get fat again. The straw tarnished, no longer a safe hiding place.

The Music of the Earth

ON AN AUTUMN morning when the sun was as bright as a newly minted coin, my father scored his autumn symphony. The newly cut sward and soil sang. The air rang with the jangle of harness, while the heavy beat of boot and hoof gave rhythm to the piece. Each new furrow forming a movement filled with harmonic resonance. On those rare occasions when he reminisced about his team of shires and how he tramped ten miles a day to plough a single acre, I heard his music of the earth and glimpsed his store of grain.

Rite of Passage

IN THE COB-WALLED stable I listened to my father's chant as he listed the items of tack hanging on the wall. Draught collar, hames, belly band, breeching, crupper strap and trace chains. Strange-sounding words filled with mystery and magic. His deft movements with fingers and thumbs as he prepared the horse. Outside in the yard his mouth-tongue clicking sounds to accompany his commands. "Whoa there. Steady boy. Back up. Move on." Standing, watching with my back pressed up against the wall.

The butt-cart crafted in the workshop across the road, blue and salmon pink, hauled steaming dung, bags of slag, wire-tied faggots, sticks and apples for the press. Iron tyres with wheels of oak, ash and elm crunched stones in a rumble of thunder. Standing watching with my back pressed up against the hedge.

The chosen morning was sunny and fine. His hands lifting me into the cart, before taking his seat on the shaft. Gripping the forehead board, clicking my tongue, giving my first command: "Move on". The lurch forward, regaining my balance. Swaying gently with the motion, I was his first mate on my maiden trip. Sailing up the road on a voyage of discovery. Hailed silently by the master of an approaching craft, my captain raised his index finger in acknowledgement. Instinctively my hand emulates his gesture. The final act in my rite of passage.

Boundary

THE LANE WAS a boundary line over which I was not allowed to cross. An ancient path between two tracts of land, our fields and a neighbour's field and copse. Under the hawthorn-banked hedge in a tangle of bracken stalks, a sunlit-slither-slumber of basking slow-worms. Woken by the heat, sliding away from the vibration of hoof on stone and the lumbering echo creak of ash, oak, elm and iron.

White violets in a secret single clump. The horse butt-cart brought to a sudden stop. Holding the reins while my father, head bent, drank in the perfume in deep gulps. His rough fingers fumbling with the short slender stems.

Back in the farmhouse tree kitchen the aroma of home bakes, potato cake and currant buns. A tiny bouquet placed on kitchen table. My father and mother in a wraparound embrace of dungarees and floral apron. My small shape thrusting against them. Flour-fleck petals floating down on my tousled head. Beneath the breeze-blown hawthorn blossom, a gentle stirring in the grass.

Legacies

EACH YEAR IN spring the farm came under siege from a marauding force. Across the fields three tribes marched unchecked. Fierce warriors, their sharp-edged blades unsheathed. By early summer their ranks had grown, their helmets feathered with purple plumes, as they laid claim to land which they considered theirs.

In mid-July the lone recruit set out with shirtsleeves rolled to halt the rout. Coiled, taut, steel-hawser veins threatened to slice through the skin of muscle-knotted arms, and beneath the metal-melding sun, hand and weapon oiled with sweat were fused as one.

From dawn 'til dusk he paced the battlefield to wage his lone assault. With measured step he swept their ranks aside. Each stroke slicing an arc through enemy platoons.

Beneath the setting sun's blood rays the weary soldier shouldered arms. His day's work done he tramped back home across the grass, its surface strewn with war's carnage. The thistles defeated for yet another year. And as my father cleaned and oiled his scythe, reinforcements for the fallen drifted in by parachute in readiness for next year's theatre of war.

The fingers which fumbled with a fountain pen, forming letters large and cumbersome in copperplate to sprawl and stumble in drunken loops across his will, would grip a billhook, and with the blade cut out his mark in beech and hazel bark the hedge-length of each field.

In a wrist-twist of fingers his hands bent branches shaping tender saplings, paring, thinning back the hedge with pride. From early in the morning the fields would ring with the singing of metal striking wood.

Across his land with an iron will, my father signed his name for all to read in strokes both light and heavy. A document laid down, a legacy of real estate to be passed down through future generations.

All Things Bright and Beautiful

ALL THINGS BRIGHT and beautiful, all creatures great and small. The bush was a jewelled fan in spring, gold pendants and tiny rubies. In autumn the real treasure to be stored in my Bluebird toffee tin for Christmas cracking around the beech- and apple-log open fire.

That summer, when the days were long and hot, a golden syrup sun melting into the next day, my probing fingers poked with relish at the boiling liquorice tar bubbles oozing up through cracks in the road, stretching it and tugging it. Sun scorched the cowpats, dried and hard, lifted scablike and peeled off the roads leaving them scarred and pockmarked.

That summer in the heat of the night, under the cover of darkness, a plague invaded the parish and the fields of the farmhouse tree. And those fields which had been burned brown by the sun's continual scorching began to echo to the sounds of creatures dying in a white-hot agony of searing pain.

That summer Sunday all the way to chapel, the tarmac aisle was lined with a congregation of twitching fur bodies. Blind, pink-eared and past redemption they rolled out of their hedgerow pews. Grey and pink balloons, stretched and taut, bounced and rolled like ball bearings in a crazy pinball table scene from hell. Overhead a choir of blowflies sang their praises of blasphemous delight as they celebrated their hideous sacrament.

My father scrambled up the hedge and quickly fashioned a cudgel with his lamb's-hoof pocket knife. The whoosh through the air. Dull thwacks. A twitch, a judder. A shake and a shudder. A soft explosion. The balloons deflating in a hiss stench of gas and pus from the swollen, stretched bodies.

The hazel stick wiped clean in the grass verge and flung high over the hedge. At the red-brick chapel steps my father, when he thought I wasn't looking, wiping his eye mumbling that he'd got something in it. The glimpse of a tear glistening.

The lay preacher whose boots always squeaked, because as my father put it they hadn't been paid for, choosing a hymn for the children. My voice starting off strongly, but quickly faltering, leaving me wondering why my aged maiden aunt's all-seeing, all-hearing God who was always watching hadn't seen the rabbits cursed with myxomatosis, and cured them.

That autumn a profusion of nuts to be secreted away by squirrel and mouse. On a shelf in my bedroom, my own treasure chest empty. The fields and hedgerow burrows empty. All things wise and wonderful, the Lord God made them all.

Back Kitchen

SITUATED AT THE rear of the farmhouse tree, back kitchen together with attic was an original branch having survived the fire of 1854 which destroyed several branches and part of the trunk.

Back kitchen with the pump, granite trough, washday copper and the mangle, where once I pressed my fingers flat. Under an old pine table on which there was a meat safe, numerous bottles, saucepans and a hand-propelled meat-mincing machine, there was a large blue tin bath, once used to bathe me in front of the kitchen fire, now filled with kindling. One afternoon each week, my aged maiden aunt went out to the 'ood 'ouse to break up branches from the wire-bound faggots stored in the 'ood ricks opposite. Each rick measured between twelve and fifteen feet in length, eight feet wide and eight feet high. These had been constructed by my father after he had laid a beech hedge. Leaning against the massive beech trees, which bordered back court, were the piles of sticks cut from the hedge and which would be sawn into logs.

Back kitchen floor was made up of ill-fitting small and large flat stones measuring up to two feet across in various shades of grey and slate blue. Embedded in soil, they were nearly always criss-crossed by the silver trails of slugs and snails which entered through an outside gulley linking into the pump trough. Once a dragon came in during the night and frightened the small four-year-old playing with toys on a blanket laid out across the stones. A sharp cry brought my mother running, and the newt was quickly picked up, carried outside and dropped into the pond.

The flat stones were nearly always damp, and in the hot summer weather they heaved up, acting like a form of primitive barometer. The cracks and crevices between the stones contained dust, dirt and creepy-crawly creatures which my probing fingers dislodged when I was playing marbles with my imaginary friends Jim and Derek. Occasionally there were red stains on the stones in the middle of the floor.

Above these stones in the ill-fitting wood-plank ceiling, which was also attic floor, a six-feet-long swivel beam with numerous slots, notches and circular holes bored into it. Carved from oak it was as brown as burned cork, and it had been designed to enable a farmer to winch up a pig's carcass with ropes where it was halved, and left suspended. No longer used in the pig-sticking ritual, my father constructed a swing for me, where I spent many happy hours swinging to and fro. It also doubled up as a countryman's gallows.

One afternoon my father scooped me up when small, and held me high in the air. A feeling of panic. My face making contact with fur which was soft and reassuring, very similar to that of my teddy bear. But the face was grey-brown, although the eyes appeared to be glassy, again similar to my teddy bear's. My tiny fingers touched the mouth. A red sticky substance. Placing my fingers in my mouth and sucking them. A strange salty substance.

From the iron hooks in the beam a public hanging of pigeon, pheasant, snipe and rabbit. The occasional drip drip onto the grey-blue flagstones.

At Christmas, hanging from the beam, the brass spring balance to ascertain the dead weight of Christmas dinner fowls.

At the back of the back-kitchen drawer where my father kept his carpentry tools, a bone-handle dagger – German. Its origins never discovered by the small boy who had his fingers into every available space which he shouldn't have been exploring.

The Swing

BACK KITCHEN FLOOR was a patchwork quilt of stone slate slabs stitched together with silver thread slug strands.

> "Swing low sweet chariot
> Comin' for to carry me home.
> Swing low sweet chariot
> Comin' for to carry me home.

He's got the finest voice I've ever heard. As deep as our back court pond. Now up you get, I'll hold the plank seat steady."

In the ceiling a revolving beam with notches carved for hempen ropes. Palms lined and rough pressing below my shoulder blades with a firm but gentle touch. His favourite song echoing in my ears.

"I looked over Jordan and what did I see
Comin' for to carry me home
A band of angels comin' after me
Comin' for to carry me home.

The pigs I've winched up on this beam. For every pound the head weighs there's a score of meat on the carcass. Hold tight and up you go again."

Flying above the familiar landmarks – the corner copper, long-case pump and mangle. Contemplating the logistical feat of my head still attached to my body being weighed on the brass dial swing balance. Stretching my legs, tucking them in. His hands pushing me ever higher.

Hands II

ELECTRICITY NOT ARRIVING in the farmhouse tree until I was sixteen meant that our evenings were spent playing cards, board games and reading. We also listened to the wireless and my mother and aged maiden aunt did a lot of knitting and darning.

On winter nights our hand tower game – my mother, father, aged maiden aunt and me. Hand on hand, palm on back of hand, eight storeys high, Stones pulled away, our edifice collapsing in a gale of laughter.

Clenched fist, two fingers extended, hand held out. Paper wraps stone, scissors cut paper, stone blunts scissors. Our second game played out around the fire.

On a summer's afternoon a hand on mine working the iron handle of the long-case pump to draw spring water up from beneath the flagstone floor. Primed, slow drips, a sudden gush. The rush of diamond bubbles cascading into the granite trough in a flood of laughter.

Today, an ornament in the garden, the painted pump gleams in the sunlight. Placing my fingers on the handle, the pressure of unseen hands; cornerstones in their constructed tower. An invisible force flowing.

Rituals

SUNDAY AND THURSDAY were special days. Days of ritual in pew and market ring. Cubes of bread and glass phials of crimson juice. Strange words in chapel, and secret gestures at the auction ring.

Water poured from the black iron kettle steamed in the white enamel blue-rimmed mug, misting the window panes. From my stool in the corner I watched the blade flish-flash over the leather strop, the badger bristle brush lathering the soap. His face uplifted, jutting towards the mirror. The pause before that first downward stroke. My own small hands clenched into tight fists, nails biting into the palms.

A gull flying across the rocky landscape in a graceful foam-flecked flight. Silver wings arcing and swooping. My fingers relaxing, mimicking his actions.

Rinsing off, drying, folding up and putting away. His cupped hand balling his chin. Running my fingers over his proffered cheek. Sharing the sensations of the special days.

Each morning the winding-up ritual. Hands grasping the chain, fingers stroking the fine metal links, before leaving the farmhouse tree to enter the shippen. Cob-walled and drenched in the breath scent of hay. Rhythmically stroked lines pitting the froth.

The weight on the end of the pulley and crook, pendulous between polished oak planks, was a bull's scrotum of heavy grey iron. Cupped in my tiny palm, sensations of fascination and fear. The enamel face spoke in sonorous tones, its resonant sound echoing down through the finely carved wooden long-case. He once told me its beat was as old as the throb of the earth's ancient pulse.

Today, the grandfather clock stands impotent in our hall. An antique by the wall, its energies spent; on the ground, its chain broken, the weight. Stroking the cold metal links, memories are awoken. In their stalls, steam haloed, the cud-chewing cows. In a bellow snort of rage and rolling eyes the bull stamps the earth with a hoofbeat of power.

Sawing Up Wood

I TRUDGE THROUGH the old grass of winter in Lower Orchard, through tussocks as thick as crows' nests. My father strides out, the Keeper of the Saws. I try to keep pace with him, attempting but failing to fit my feet into his bootprint strides. My legs a pair of dividers. Stretch out, pull up the other foot. Stretch out, pull up the other foot. We reach the apple moot, dug out the previous day. He removes a lump of lard from a brown paper bag and greases up the blades to give the teeth a better bite.

After spitting on our palms and rubbing it in, he instructs me to let the saw do all the work and to let it glide like a knife through butter. He makes a starting groove with the bow saw. Next he picks up the cross-cut. My two small hands grip one wooden handle while he grips the other with one hand.

The teeth bite into the wood. Sawdust spits back, forming a small mound as we build up a steady rhythm. My mind turns to the previous apple harvest – Tom Putt, Quarrenden, Duck's Bill and Listener. Bulging hessian sacks tipped into the wood-and-iron crusher in the pound house. Turning the iron wheel. A chopped apple mound. Perfume oozing into every cob crack and crevice. Pulp and barley straw built up on the oakpress in alternate layers. The cheese constructed. A solid block. The pressing board lowered. My excitement barely contained. Waiting for the first drips.

David and his dad sawing up logs with a cross-cut saw in 1950, somewhat earlier than this episode

The juice from the crushed apple flesh was a lion's liquid mane flowing golden into the wooden tub. My summer sun caged. Strong and potent. Kneeling on the earth floor I leaned over and sucked up its beams through a piece of barley straw.

The first drop on my lips and the apple year exploded into my head in a shower of memory sparks.

On Christmas Day the excitement after the roast chicken pulling-the-wishbone-finding-the-sixpence-in-the-pudding dinner, when the sun bursts through wrapping-paper clouds, its pale light illuminating lichen-coated branches stark against the winter sky. Portent of autumn's golden harvest.

A storm of song breaks over the trees in spring. Call of the holm-screech. A serration of notes heralding the end of winter.

In a sprinkle of confetti, spring blossoms. A pink and white petal shower as sudden as April rain saturates the lank tussocks. A May Day celebration as spring's harbinger sends his two-note call echoing over the orchard, as he flies over the farmhouse tree heralding a rich sweet crop.

In the fruit-forming months, time was suspended in my young eyes. And as I blew my seed clocks over the grass, counting the silent chiming hours drifting featherlike in the breeze, the lion's hot roar exploded across a cloudless sky.

With a final crack the moot splits in two and my mind returns to the present. We place the cross-cut on the grass, sit on the stumps and share a Mars bar, a packet of Smith's crisps and a bottle of Corona orange pop. My father tells me that if the sawing has made me sweat, the logs will keep us hot in winter.

By a quarter to one our task is completed. I look forward to the afternoon – Charlie the carthorse, the blue and salmon-pink butt-cart. Being allowed to take the reins, give commands and be a proper farmer. Being serenaded by the robin's wistful autumn song.

He picks up the bow saw and passes it to me to carry home. I become the Keeper's Assistant Keeper of the Saw. I carry it with pride, feeling a foot taller. We return to the farmhouse tree walking side by side, and I think of the hogshead in the pound house full to the brim with liquid sunshine.

Initiation Ceremony

WHEN I WAS young we went one winter's day, when the morning sky glowing and grey hung heavy and swollen above the fields, to a sale of household, personal and farm effects.

On tabletops, chintz cloths and china figurines, silver spoons, forks, brass- and copperware. A bundle of books bound with twine, a clasp with the lock of a loved one's hair. Jewellery of jet and jade. Home-made rugs of rag and cord. A sampler – 'Mine help cometh from the Lord'. Two hundred lots set out on public display. Arranged in haste, amassed with love and care.

An earlobe tugged, chins rubbed and noses scratched. A nod, a wink, an index finger raised. Each coded signal deciphered by the auctioneer. Afraid to blink, I stood with hands clenched tight, head bowed, my blushing face kept hidden from sight. "What am I bid? Are we all done?"

Outside, a book dropped on the ground. Between the tattered pages, a black-edged card used as a mark, mud-spattered. A name, two dates, an age. A text – 'The Lord gave and the Lord hath taken away'.

Placing it on the window ledge my father took my hand. His grip strong, but tender.

The echo of the gavel coming down on the final lot. "Going, going, gone." The snowflakes stinging our faces. The fields white.

Bonding

THE TERM BONDING was unheard of between father and son in my childhood. A game of snowballs in front court and a game of cricket in the mead after the final load of hay had been carried. Birds'-nesting and identifying wild flowers were our simple forms of bonding.

They grew in the summer, in a clump above the stream, beneath the box hedge and the flowering currant on the bank next to the outside lavatory. Their lemon petals gauze-flimsy in the breeze.

It was a double platform, two holes – one large, one small. Two metal buckets with their pinewood lids set into the platform. The paper, six-inch squares. *News of the World* collected each Monday morning from the blacksmith's wife across the road. Read, cut up and quartered before being hung on a loop from a nail behind the planed pine-plank door.

Sitting on the outside step my father leaned across the stream and picked a lemon flower. A blade of grass pulled from a tussock. Gripped between fingers and held to his lips it gave off an eerie squeal.

While I laughed and tried to emulate the noise he pulled the petals over the calyx, made a loop with the blade to secure them, snapped off half the stem and pushed it through to make the arms. Told me it was my one-legged flower doll called Poppy. Giving a laugh he added she was Welsh.

In the afternoon beneath the flaming sun, cutting, folding, creasing. His hands, a farmer's hands nimbly shaping an admiral's hat and a fleet of brown paper sailing ships to float in the granite pump trough. Together with a cotton-reel tractor, a trolley and a cricket bat, hand-carved, these were our shared hands-on experiences.

Conversations

As FATHER AND son we didn't speak to each other very much. Little boys were seen and not heard back then.

A sack from the stack of summer corn tumbling from the cart, falling with a slow dull thud. A few grains trickling onto the stony ground from a hessian sack tied with a twist of binder-twine. Compared to the annual yield per acre, the words in our conversation made a meagre harvest.

In the orchard bent over the cross-cut saw, hands singing in harmony, thoughts dancing to the music of the blade, the sowing of the seeds.

From a mud-lined nest, a turquoise egg speckled black, resting on his outstretched palm. Our eyes meeting. The silent flow of unspoken words; the germination of the seed.

Today in the first apple blossom, in the evening song of the thrush, echoes of his silent voice from across a distant horizon. The cornfield golden with a harvest rich beyond compare.

Boy with a Net

In THE AFTERNOON heat above the cabbage patch, a flurry of butterflies dancing in the haze in a silent shimmer of summer snowflakes. Running between the neatly spaced rows I chased my prey for bounty.

At the end of each sweep the gauze net throbbed with a frantic fluttering of flailing wings.

Gently held between finger and thumb each captive was dropped into a screw-top jar where finely chopped laurel leaves quickly extinguished life. Taken out and laid on the cider path they formed a marbled mosaic.

As he paid me a farthing for each Cabbage White butterfly my father gave me his simple philosophy – caterpillar, butterfly, life, death.

Once by mistake I killed a Brimstone. The look of sadness in his eyes.

On a good Saturday afternoon my catch earned me a shilling.

Betrayal I

IT IS BELIEVED Mark Twain said the following: "When I was a boy of fourteen my father was so ignorant I could hardly stand to have the old man around. But when I got to twenty-one I was astonished at how much the old man had learned in seven years."

Unfortunately I never had the chance to find out how clever my father had become when I was twenty-one.

On winter nights when all the cows were milked, the bullocks fed with hay sliced from the stack, the board was taken from the shelf and opened out. The playing pieces, black and white, tipped from the tin and placed on their allotted squares. Beneath the light of the Aladdin lamp we played the game he'd taught me. The game made to be handed down. A ritual between a father and his son.

In what seemed like no time at all the game was won, my one remaining man cornered by his king. Aged nine, the taste of personal defeat. Next, being told that it was just a game and that I was to set them up again.

Each night a similar routine. He'd win the first, then with a smile he'd watch me win the second, with the words that it was best to leave it at one all.

Aged twelve, away at boarding school, I learned strategic ploys, defensive moves and match-winning attacks from set positions. On my first visit home for a quarter-term weekend the board was placed upon the oilcloth as he renewed our bond.

During three campaigns each successfully accomplished, I aired my newly acquired skills. Littering the battlefield periphery, his captured men, while my crowned kings marched victorious across his land.

Replacing the pieces in the Bluebird toffee tin he quietly closed the lid and, folding up the board, placed both at the back of the sideboard drawer. Without a word he walked slowly towards the door. Turning he told me in a gentle voice that he could see they'd taught me how to win, away at school.

Our evenings were never the same again.

Betrayal II

EACH SUMMER TERM he came to the school for Open Day. Never in the morning for the service with choir-sung anthem. Cows to be milked, shippens to be cleaned.

Punctually at two o'clock he arrived at the green gates. A lift from a neighbour whose son was also at the school. Always in a sports jacket, brown check Harris Tweed, and grey Terylene trousers. Lifebuoy soap not quite masking the smell of dung.

"A good crop of hay, all safely carried and stacked away. Beans, peas and potatoes doin' really well. A bumper 'arvest, God willin'. Pays to put in a good ole 'eap o' dung."

How I despised his tongue-tied colloquial accent. His fumbling manners, juggling cup, saucer, plate and serviette. Hands for milking and cleaning out the shippens.

No kiss passed between us. This was my act of cruel betrayal. In the playground where the car was parked, turning away, pretending he wasn't really with me.

Envying the Daks suit, leather soles and scented aftershave. My thirty pieces of silver.

Cellar

WHEN INDOORS AND not sleeping, we spent most of our time in the room known as 'cellar', so called because in previous centuries, hogsheads of cider were stored here. In 1854 all the barrels were destroyed when fire swept through the house. In 1904 my grandfather sold some of the cider he had brewed around the village at 7d (3p) a gallon, less than a penny a pint even in old money.

Here we ate all our meals, relaxed and spent our evenings, cellar being made into a kitchen when Calor gas and a stove were installed.

Baking was done in cellar by my mother and aged maiden aunt sharing the work. Baking days were good fun days, and I made sure I was sitting at the table when the oilcloth was laid out to protect the surface. Next, a light brown china mixing bowl with the green line around the white interior. Baking trays, utensils and a hand whisk were taken out of the pine cupboard and the ingredients brought out from the pantry cupboard. Dried fruit always came in thick blue paper bags, the grocer an origami expert as he folded and creased the paper into shape.

It was my job to help with the weighing. Ingredients were placed on the white saucer-shaped enamelled weighing tray on the painted green iron scales and I adjusted the weights until the balance between tray and weights was steady. The small weights – half-ounce, one ounce and two ounce – were made of brass, and the four ounce, eight ounce and pound weights of iron. The ingredients were tipped into the mixing bowl and mixed with either a wooden spoon or hand whisk.

As the rock buns were being baked in the Calor gas oven I was rewarded with a small handful of currants; if really lucky a big glacé sticky red cherry was placed on my outstretched palm. To complete the baking ritual I wiped my fingers around the inside of the bowl and licked off the sticky yellow mixture. As I waited for the rock buns to bake, the scent filled my nostrils as it wafted through the room. At last the tray was taken out and the batch placed on a plate. A few minutes later a bun was placed in my hand with my mother's warning: "Hot. Don't burn your lips."

Heeding her words I took a bite, trying to make that first sensation last all day, or at least until dinner time.

Another treat at the baking table occurred on jelly-making days when the Chivers Jelly, usually strawberry or orange flavour, was taken out of the cardboard box, unwrapped and broken into chunks. My eyes puppylike, appealing for a chunk. A piece placed on my palm. "There'll be no more or it won't set and the flavour won't be so strong."

Placing it into my mouth, seeing how long I can keep it on my tongue without sucking or chewing it. Giving into temptation and sucking slowly, so very, very slowly, the taste oozing out. Thinking of the bowl of jelly and custard for afters.

Grey Calor gas cylinders to power the stove were delivered by Moors the Ironmongers from South Molton. The gas was also used to power the gas boiler on washday Monday and for the gas mantles in cellar, kitchen and front room.

In a corner, a small stove, fed with logs and installed in the early 1950s when a bathroom was put in upstairs. This heated cellar, a brown metal kettle of water kept warming on the top of the stove, and also water in the immersion tank in a small cupboard next to it which fed the hot tap in the bathroom and the tap for washing up the dishes. This was carried out in a china Belfast sink, the washing-up water made soapy by using the remains of bars of soap placed in a wire shaker which was then placed in the hot water and shaken violently to produce soap suds. My father also dried off his moleskins in the airing cupboard.

In another corner, my father's Windsor chair where he read the weekly *Western Times*, listened to the wireless on the two-feet-deep window ledge, behind it the caged budgerigar Joey. Along another wall, an old leather six-feet-long open-ended sofa, where my father would lie out when he was suffering a migraine attack which wasn't severe enough to confine him to bed.

The table in the centre of the room could be extended for ping-pong or when visitors came for dinner, by winding it open with a handle slotted into the side and inserting extra leaves into it.

On the back of the door, hanging from brass hooks, outdoor coats, jackets and aprons. These were removed and thrown onto the sofa when my father and I played darts against the plank door which resembled boards infested by woodworm. When I had a loose tooth, a length of cotton was looped over the offending tooth, the other end attached to the latch of the open door which was then slammed shut. Hey Presto, one tooth dangling to the floor to be placed under my pillow, and in the morning a shiny sixpence in its place.

In the autumn and winter nights when we weren't playing card games, ludo, tiddlywinks, draughts or snakes and ladders, my mother and aged maiden aunt spent most of their time around cellar table beneath the pale glow from the gas mantle either knitting, sewing or darning. Occasionally my services were called upon, when my outstretched hands were required to hold a skein of wool which was then wound into a ball.

For my hand-knitted mittens, gloves, balaclavas, sleeveless pull-overs, long-sleeved jumpers and stockings I could choose any colour as long as it was green, grey or navy blue. Patterns were cut out and saved from *Woman's Weekly* or *Woman's Illustrated* together with Roly Robin stories for my scrapbook.

One winter my aged maiden aunt knitted a full-length skirt with matching two-piece jumper and cardigan which was admired by fellow Women's Institute members at the Easter Day chapel service when she proudly wore the ensemble for the first time.

When not knitting, running repairs were carried out. "A stitch in time saves nine," said my aged maiden aunt as she fitted a wooden mushroom into a stocking with a hole in the heel and began darning with matching wool.

Buttons of all colours, shapes and sizes were collected and saved, together with leather bootlaces and shoelaces in a 1920s Huntley & Palmers biscuit tin, to be sewed back onto trouser flies, waistbands for braces, shirts, coats and cardigans.

As they knitted one, purled one, being careful not to drop a stitch, the voice of Wilfred Pickles attempting to 'Have a Go' with Mabel at the table, on the wireless, was drowned out by the demented clicking of the needles, as I tried to read the latest library book collected from my Sunday school teacher/great-aunts' house where the library van left two boxes of books, and my father attempted to have forty winks.

At nine thirty each night, having listened to the news on the wireless we climbed the "wooden hill to Bedfordshire" as my father called going to bed.

It... The Trailer

THE WORD 'SEX' was rarely spoken in my 1950s childhood, only in reference to the gender of a newly born baby or calf. Sex as a physical act was never mentioned. "Her've gone wrong" or "Her've gone wrong again" are words I recall, not knowing at the time what they meant.

My knowledge of sex was gleaned in shippen, field, and the boys' outside lavatory at my primary school. A very rudimentary knowledge, it has to be said. The boys' lavatory was an open-to-the-elements building with black-painted walls covered in scratch marks from the blades of penknives marking out who had peed the highest up the wall. Here a classmate, referred to by my aged maiden aunt as "that heathen boy, who is no better than he should be", would recount the rude

David with his aged maiden aunt, parents and a calf in front court, 1958

rhymes and jokes he'd gleaned from his brother for a "lick o'yer gobstopper" or a "big bite o'yer Wagon Wheel" or "three inches o'yer liquorice bootlace". A particular favourite was saying the name Tony Hancock and miming the appropriate gestures at parts of his anatomy to each syllable. "'Ere, you'll like this new one, I learned it off me brother last night."

But it all began in my aged maiden aunt's bedroom.

One afternoon, a week before Christmas, I knocked at her door to ask her advice what a nine-year-old son should buy his mother for a present.

On being ushered in I was surprised to see that her photographs, pillboxes, medicine bottles, Bible, autograph book and the tumbler for her false teeth, and her hairnet, had been removed from the lid of her oak chest and the lid was raised.

Beckoning me to sit on her bed, she leaned into the chest and removed a small bundle wrapped in a towel.

"Your grandmother gave me this dolly when I was small. Each Christmas I like to take her out and..." She paused. "If you'd been born a little girl you'd have played with her too."

She ruffled my hair and passed me the doll. "Such lovely curls you've got. You'd have made a beautiful little girl."

I eased my head away and blushed, wishing not for the first time that my hair was, as she described the hair of another boy I knew, "straight as a yard of pump water". Not that I'd ever measured pump water to see what a yard looked like.

I examined the doll. It must be really old if my auntie had played with it. The jointed limbs were made of wood, which had been crudely carved and painted, and the head felt as if it was made out of papier mâché. But it was the clothing which fascinated me. There appeared to be layers and layers of it. Intrigued, I lifted the ankle-long dress to make a closer inspection. The action was my undoing.

"I'll put her away again now," said my aged maiden aunt as she plucked the doll from my fingers.

The quick movement took me by surprise, but I had managed to glimpse tubelike pieces of material which came down below her knees, over which were two more items of clothing which I assumed were dresses. But why would a doll wear three dresses?

"You'd have had a lot of fun with her if you'd been born a little girl," she said, briefly cradling the doll into her chest, "but you weren't and instead you've got your tractor and trailer to play with."

I took a deep breath. There were still unexplained mysteries to be solved. "I could still play with her even though I'm not a girl."

Not only did I want to get a glimpse of what was hidden under all the dresses, so that I could get one over on Kenny the Gorilla Harris in the school lavatory, but I also wished to ingratiate myself having spotted an unopened bag of barley sugars on her bedside cabinet.

My aged maiden aunt laughed. "We'll see. There's always another day."

The doll was wrapped up and replaced in the oak chest.

"I thought once that I might have got married and –" she paused – "I think your mum would like a nice tray cloth and your dad could always do with a new shaving stick or a jar of Brylcreem. And help yourself to a barley sugar."

The offer of a sweet was her signal that my audience had been terminated. Plunging my hand into the bag I took a sweet and left the room, leaving my aged maiden aunt to enjoy the remainder of the afternoon in peace.

The 'another day' never arrived, my aged maiden aunt didn't see, and consequently neither did I. The doll was left sleeping cocooned in several layers of propriety and I was left wondering what it was my aged maiden aunt didn't want me to discover.

The Making of It... Strange Sensations

A COW'S UDDER was always exciting to the touch. Smoothing it with the palm of my hand I could feel the veins running just below the skin. Bulging like a balloon filled with water, it was warm and moss-soft to the touch. Each time a cow calved she became so full and distended with milk that she could barely walk in from the fields at milking time. The bag, as my father called it, felt good.

During one autumn he taught me the gentle and ancient art of milking by hand. Sitting me on the milking stool, he stood behind me and reaching over my shoulder took my hands in his and positioned them around two of the cow's four teats.

Ruby had been chosen for my initiation. She was a quiet cow, and unlikely to kick out with a hind leg and upset the milking pail wedged between my knees.

Strange sensations, which I couldn't begin to understand and which I had never experienced before, tingled through my body. The uninvited feelings made my face feel hot and prickly, and my whole body began to glow.

I began squirming on my stool, and before I could stop myself my mind began turning to the rude rhymes and jokes which Kenny the Gorilla Harris told in the boys' lavatories. A song from the previous week crept uninvited into my head, which he'd charged me two aniseed balls to hear.

"'Ere", he said. "You knows that song wot ole Uncle 'Macintosh' plays on 'Kids' Favourites' on Saturdays, called 'I Love to Go A-Wandering'? Well listen to this, me brother learned it to me –

> I love to go a wandering
> Inside my mother's vest,
> And as I go I like to climb
> The mountains on her chest."

My father's voice drowned out the unwanted thoughts. "Squeeze gently with your fingers. Stroke out the first drops. Coax her into giving it up to you. Pull down the left teat, and then do the same with the right teat and right fingers. Squeeze... Pull down... Squeeze... Pull down. Never rush it. Be gentle and get a good steady rhythm going. Now you try it on your own."

I did more or less what I was told, but nothing happened.

My father laughed. "Up you get. I'll start her off for you."

We changed places and I watched his every action, determined to get it right. A squeezing, stroking downward motion with his fingers.

"Never try too hard. You must be patient. She'll sense it if you're anxious."

As I watched, the first drips changed into a steady stream and the milk began to rattle into the pail like rain on a galvanised iron roof.

Standing up, he motioned me to take over from him. I resumed my seat and tried again, but still nothing happened.

"She's holding her milk back," he said.

Walking across to the manger he pulled out a handful of cattle-cake lumps and holding it under Ruby's mouth began speaking gently in her ear. "Come on, old girl. Give the boy a chance. Come on now, Ruby."

Patting her affectionately on her neck he turned to me. "Right. Now try her."

To my delight my first drops slipped out from her teats. I examined the tiny holes though which the milk had flowed. Again the strange sensations tingled, and raced through my body. Looking up I sought my father's approval.

He gave me a broad smile and patted my back affectionately.

"Now spit on your hands, rub it well into your palms and it'll make the milking easier."

This was fun, just like sawing up sticks. I was allowed to spit and no-one was going to tell me off. I was doing a man's job just like my father. I was growing up. Spitting on my palms I rubbed the bubbles into my flesh.

"Right. Start again and this time don't stop. Keep the rhythm going. Keep it steady. Keep it regular."

Leaning my head into Ruby's flank I breathed in the warm smell of cow and sweat, and taking hold of the teats started the gentle squeezing movements. The milk began flowing down in two streams, and I began to giggle with excitement.

Within minutes, however, my arms and hands were aching. Milking was tiring work.

My father laughed again. "Hard work, isn't it? But you've done well for a first time. Up you get, I'll take over now."

Climbing off my stool I walked to the door, the sound of milk gushing into the pail echoing across the shippen. The pail was soon full with a thick white froth-bubble honeycomb on which I could mark out my initials with my fingertip.

By the end of the following week I was able to milk Ruby and fill the pail on my own. I had mastered one of the oldest of the farming skills.

It... The Movie

BEING UNABLE TO sleep I tiptoed quietly down back stairs. Sitting on one of the wooden stair boards I listened through a knot hole in the stairs' door to a conversation between my mother, father and aged maiden aunt which they were having around the supper table.

"You're right," said my aged maiden aunt. "It's time he learnt about it. Growing up. Boarding school in September. No longer our little boy. Needs to learn about it."

"In that case," added my father, "no time like the present. Tomorrow's the day."

I crept back to bed ensuring I didn't tread on the creaking floorboard. Under the blankets I gave 'it' deep thought, excited by a mystery which would soon be solved.

The following morning I dressed quickly, gobbled down my bowl of cornflakes and cream and ran out to the shippen where my father had just finished brushing up the dung. But why was Buttercup still chained up in her stall, chewing her cud when the herd had been taken back to Long Halls field?

"You can give me a hand. I've got to take her straight to Mr Down's. Put my brush away after you've swilled it off in the stream, and join me by the gate."

A few minutes later with a hazel stick in my right hand I was marching proudly through the village, a victorious general ahead of his troops. Buttercup was special, she shared the double shippen with Ruby, and had witnessed me learning to milk her stall-mate. And this was the first time I'd been asked to take a cow with my father to Farmer Down's. Normally my mother walked in front of the cow. I was growing up and learning to be a proper farmer. This must be the 'it' they'd been talking about last night.

Halfway down the road I was confronted by Kenny the Gorilla Harris. A squeal of brakes and my nemesis of the school playground, whose bark was worse than his bite, came to a halt inches from my wellington boots.

"Wotcher, mate. Skill, eh? Where you goin' then?"

"Taking Buttercup to Mr Down's," I answered proudly.

He sniggered. "Ole man Down won't want your bag o' skin 'n' bones. He got loads of cowses. Real cowses, not like your skinny ole thing. Lucky if you gets tuppence for 'er. You won't even get a bag o' magic beans like wot Jack got. And 'e got a tractor."

"Cut along home, young Kenneth," called out my father. "We've got a man's work to do. No room for small boys."

I grew six inches. Man's work. I beamed. This was 'it', no doubt about it.

Kenny scowled, "Wait 'til Monday. Yours is an Old MacDonald's farm. Not a real big proper farm."

Before I could reply he had turned his bike and was pedalling off furiously. In a way he was right. We didn't have a tractor, only a carthorse, and Farmer Down did own a lot of animals, so why should he want one of ours.

At the farm gate I was greeted by Farmer Down who was leaning on the top bar. He gave me a broad grin and a wink.

"Take 'er up to the enclosed yard, young master. I'll follow on behind with your dad."

The two men chuckled and exchanged inaudible words. I drove Buttercup into the enclosed yard and stood back to see what would happen next.

Farmer Down's son entered the enclosed yard, walked up to the shed in the corner and opened the door. Out came...

I gasped.

Farmer Down's bull!

But why was he here and not in his field? The 'it' mystery was deepening by the second.

I stared at the bull and he stared back.

This was a locomotive of an animal. Released from its shed the train, in a bellow-snort of steam-breath, lumbered across the yard and stared at Buttercup with the same big soft eyes which had stared at me. I frowned. A beast this big shouldn't have soft eyes.

Standing on the bottom of the frame fence to get a better view, I found myself drawing back as he heaved past me, his snort of breath warm and wild against my face. I shivered; I'd never been this close to him. On the last occasion, in the snow, he'd chased me across his field. I could actually touch him. I stretched out my hand. But at the last second I drew it back as he rumbled past me.

I waited. Would he circle again? Yes, he was coming towards me.

Reaching out my arm I felt his side brush the tips of my outstretched fingers. Immediately, a thrill of excitement ran through me and into the pit of my stomach. A thrill similar to the unexplained one I'd experienced when I'd learned to milk Ruby. I breathed in deeply. I'd touched him. I'd actually touched the bull.

He was almost up to Buttercup when the sky was filled with the roar of jet engines. Squinting into the sun I was just able to make out three planes from the airbase thirty miles away. As I watched they came almost directly overhead, before breaking formation, their metallic hornet scream scorching the surrounding countryside.

Blinking the sun-dazzle from my eyes I looked back into the enclosed yard, and I was just in time to see the bull being led back into the shed by Farmer Down's son who was guiding him with a special stick which he had clicked through the brass ring in the bull's nose. Even though I hadn't touched him again, the strange sensation tingled through my body and up into my face which began to burn bright scarlet.

At the same time one of Kenny's jokes which had cost me a sherbet lemon crept into my head.

"'Ere, you knows that funny man on the wireless? Well I can point out his name on my body. Watch this."

As I stared, intrigued, he proceeded to point first at his foot and then at his knee and then his hand.

"The last one's the best. See…"

I stared again as a smirking Kenny pointed at his…

"Good, eh, mate? Tony Hancock. Geddit?"

Under my breath I swore at the jet planes. The mystery 'it', whatever 'it' was, had taken place when they'd flown overhead and I'd missed 'it'.

Farmer Down was waiting for me when I reached his yard gate. Nudging me playfully in the ribs he said, "Big idn't 'e, young master. Big."

I nodded as he winked at my father who winked back. My cheeks began to burn again and Farmer Down was laughing as he opened the gate.

"Take her home. That's her happy, and so will your dad be when he gets a fine bull calf in just over nine months. Us'll make a man of you yet, young master. And who knows, maybe even a farmer."

"When can I help again, Dad?" I asked ten minutes later when we were leaning on the five-bar gate overlooking Long Halls field where

Buttercup was standing a few feet away from us. By standing on the lower bar I could lean on the top bar and emulate my father.

He laughed. "Violet's turn to go to the bull next month. But make sure you keep your eye on what's happening on the ground. Never mind what's going on up in the clouds."

Later that evening I listened again through the back stairs' door.

"He's starting to learn about it," said my father.

"Good," replied my mother.

To which my aged maiden aunt added, "How it should be. Like we said, he's growing up."

I smiled to myself. I was growing up and that was the second time she'd said it, so it must be true. I was also learning about the mysterious 'it'. And I was also being made into a farmer. All in all, not a bad day's work. Not bad at all.

Beaming to myself I tiptoed back to bed. Walking through the village I'd been a man. That's what my father had told Kenny. Just wait until Monday. I'd done something I was sure Kenny hadn't done, and I couldn't wait to tell him.

"I saw the bull with the cow," I announced as soon as I was standing in the playground.

Kenny the Gorilla slouched towards me. "S'wot?" he sneered. "You seen a bull. I seen a bull. Us 'aves all seen bullses and cowses. So wot's new?"

I paused; this wasn't the reaction I'd been expecting. I glanced at the group which was milling around us. They were expecting a revelation. I remembered Farmer Down's words.

"He was big," I blurted out. "As big as…"

Kenny interrupted me. "Big. Course 'e's big! That's why 'e's a bull and not a cow cos 'e's big."

He sniggered. My classmates sniggered. My plan for fifteen minutes of fame in my own playtime was as usual going very badly wrong, and I didn't really know why.

I was about to tell them that I was learning about a mysterious 'it' when over their heads I saw our teacher approaching.

Kenny, however, who was facing me was unaware of her.

"'Ere, listen to this. It's a good one," he sniggered. "Not like 'is ole rubbish. Learned it off me brother last night. And cos I'm in a good mood and feelin' generous I'll tell 'e for nort."

Laughing, he cleared his throat, puffed out his chest and said, "My friend Billy got a ten foot wi…"

"KENNETH HARRIS!" Our teacher's voice drowned out the offending word, but Kenny like a river after a thunderstorm was in full flow which was unstoppable –

> "And he showed it to the girl next door.
> She thought it was a snake, and hit it with a rake,
> And now it's only five foot four."

As if anticipating what was coming next he turned, faced our teacher and held out his hand, palm upwards. He was duly rewarded with two strokes of her twelve-inch wooden ruler.

A smirking Kenny was frog-marched back to our classroom, while the group ran off laughing, in the direction of the boys' lavatories, chanting his rhyme at the top of their voices.

In defeat Kenny was victorious, and I was left standing in isolation which was far from splendid, contemplating what might have been, should have been but hadn't been.

Three weeks later I helped take Violet to the bull. There were no jets and the mystery of 'it' was solved.

"That's Violet served," said my father as we leaned on the gate. "A fine bull calf hopefully. Perhaps twins."

Violet had been served according to my father, but I hadn't seen any food. Another mystery. Monday came, but the day was a disappointment. Kenny was away with one of his colds.

It 2... The Sequel

THE FIELDS SURROUNDING the farmhouse tree were always filled with a flutter of birds. In spring and early summer their beaks split open the countryside, their songs slicing through the dawn. During each sun-filled summer day the notes dripped through the branches saturating the foliage; the flow staunched at twilight by a tourniquet of darkness.

Early each morning, during May and June, I trudged along the ditches at the base of the hedges searching out nests, my walks often taking me a couple of miles from the farmhouse tree.

It was an early May morning, and through the proscenium arch of beech trees, the countryside stage was set for the opening act of a new production. As the mist curtain rose slowly, the backdrop of hedgerows, trees and fields was revealed.

Peering through an antiquated pair of binoculars I scanned the empty stage.

Enter stage right: a couple of fields away a man was following the line of one of the hedges. I focused the glasses and watched him briefly before he disappeared from view. But why, I asked myself, was he walking along by the hedge, and why when the sky was blue without the hint of a cloud was he carrying a plastic mac over his arm? The plot thickened.

A mocking laugh from the theatre circle made me swing my binoculars upwards. My swift reflex action was rewarded with the fleeting glimpse of a green woodpecker. The thought of a high-scoring entry in my I-Spy book of *Birds* made me quickly forget the man and the mysterious mac.

The next twenty minutes resulted in a hedge sparrow's nest, a song thrush's nest and a blackbird's nest being logged in my notebook. With only one more field and four hedges to check, my thoughts were turning to a beaker of milk and a slice of home-baked fruit cake.

The final hedge was a high bank, spattered with primroses and vetch and topped with a fine beech screen, which in the autumn would be laid with a billhook and axe.

Scrambling my way to the top I raised my binoculars and scanned the distant stage. Into my line of vision, two fields away, in a corner where the grass was a little longer, appeared a pair of boots... two fully clothed legs and a fully clothed body... Lying out full-length on his stomach, his body raised up in the air by the man resting on his elbows, was Plastic Mac Man... I gave a gulp... Not just Plastic Mac Man... There were two other legs... another body... a female body... I did a double take. Plastic Mac Man had apparently fallen asleep on top of a woman.

As I continued to watch he suddenly appeared to twitch awake... Next he began to raise and lower himself up and down... up and down. Suddenly I realised his trousers and pants had slipped down and I could see his bare bum. Plastic Mac Man was a big man... He could hurt the woman.

Her face came into view in my binoculars... She appeared to be smiling... And then I noticed her summer dress was pulled up above her waist and I could see...

A tingle ran through my body. The biggest tingle ever. A tingle made up of all the tingles I'd experienced when I'd heard Kenny's rude jokes, learned to milk and when I'd touched the bull's side.

I swallowed. This was 'it'. This was the real 'it'. The 'it' my mother, father and aged maiden aunt had said I should learn about. The real 'it' wasn't just about a bull and a cow, it was also about a man and a woman. My thoughts collided, and in a frenzy of excitement I pushed my way through the beech branches. Eager to get a better view I forgot that I was standing on top of a banked hedge. One minute my feet were on terra firma, the next minute they were treading air. With a crash I landed in a sprawl of limbs and a tangle of binocular straps in the ditch of the adjoining field. Scrabbling quickly back up the hedge and eager to get another view I raised my glasses to my eyes and homed in on where 'it' had been taking place.

I was just in time to see the hero pick up his plastic mac, shake off the bits of grass, fold it up and stroll off. Exit stage left. At the same time the heroine smoothed down her dress, ruffled her hair and walked off. Exit stage right. With the show obviously at an end I clambered back down the hedge, as once again the woodpecker's yaffle rang through the auditorium.

Walking quickly back to the farmhouse tree, my mind was deep in thought. Was every man who carried a plastic mac on a dry day involved in doing 'it'?

In the evening as I sat once again on back stairs listening to the suppertime conversation. I heard my aged maiden aunt say, "They'm saying that she's gone wrong again. And he ought to know better."

I made my way slowly back to bed where I gave her words careful thought. Gone wrong and ought to know better. Having solved one mystery I'd created another. But just wait until Monday. There was no way Kenny could top what I'd seen.

But it was not to be. My fifteen minutes of playground fame had alluded me yet again. Kenny and his cronies were away with mumps. Kenny had the last laugh yet again, when I contracted mumps on the last day of term and had to stay in bed for the first couple of weeks of the summer holiday, while he had just recovered from his and was out running around again causing his own brand of Kenny havoc.

Postscript. A couple of weeks before I was due to set off for boarding school, my mother and aged maiden aunt handed me a small blue, hardcovered book with the words, "You ought to read through this, it'll come in handy one day."

They walked off as I flipped through the pages. I was confronted with line drawings of male and female figures and pages of text. I went up to my bedroom and throwing the book on the chest of drawers pulled out my latest copies of the *Beano* and *Dandy* from a drawer. The book could wait, and besides I'd seen 'it' for real in the field.

Today, there remain two unanswered questions. Was the green woodpecker mocking me because I'd missed the climax of the show or was it laughing at Plastic Mac Man's shortcomings and poor performance centre stage?

It 3

IN MY SECOND week at boarding school I joined the school choir. I joined, not because I wanted to sing, but being a member meant you were allowed to miss fifteen minutes' prep on a Monday night to attend weekly choir practice. It was also a mixed choir. The girls from the adjoining high school were allowed to enter the boys' grammar school refectory for ninety minutes' singing, and apart from that evening boys and girls were not permitted to meet or talk to one another.

In my second year we sang Benjamin Britten's *Noye's Fludde*. The best singers, together with an English master, took the lead parts with the remainder of the choir taking the parts of the birds and other animals.

I was a curlew. Not a rare stone-curlew, but a common moorland ordinary curlew. And I had a bill which measured almost twelve inches in length. I made my curlew mask during art lessons out of papier mâché moulded around a wire frame. It fitted over the top of my head covering half of my face. When I'd finished making it I cut out two eye slots and painted it a mottled brown. For the performance we had to troop down in pairs through the nave of the local church to the area between the pulpit and the altar rail, where a large outline of the ark had been constructed from hardboard, balsa and planks of wood by the woodwork teacher and a team of pupils. Over the top of it was a brilliantly painted rainbow, and in the centre of the ark was a doorway through which we walked with our partners. It led into the chancel where we sat in the choir stalls and sang the choral parts.

We didn't have to wear bird-feather costumes; instead we wore our Sunday best suit short trousers, a white shirt and black tie – our partners wore a skirt, blouse and tie – and the congregation had to use their imaginations.

'God' was positioned precariously on top of a tall pair of steps high above the congregation and hidden from view. His booming voice bellowed commands to Noah for the dress rehearsal and the two evening performances.

My curlew mate was my own age, and we fell in love with each other. As soon as we were sitting behind the ark in the choir stalls, we spent as much time as we could, when we weren't singing, looking into each other's eye slots.

During the dress rehearsal we shared our first innocent exploration of love when our bare bony knees touched briefly, and we blushed gently, half-unseen blushes behind our masks.

On the opening night I plucked up courage when the ark was storm-tossed, counted slowly to ten, as I did when I wanted to see how far away a thunderstorm was, and 'walked' my fingers over the three inches of the wooden pew which separated us.

Taking a deep breath I touched her naked leg just above her knee. Almost at once I felt her hand touch mine.

As God roared down to Noah, commanding him to release the dove for the third time, our fingers intertwined. As the white bird circled dry land, our heads never moved and we continued staring straight ahead, but the eyes in our fingertips looked long and deep into the other's.

At the end of the performance, in the general mêlée of fellow choristers running off excitedly to meet proud parents, we hung back unnoticed, or so we thought. Looking again into each other's eyes, we forgot in the heat of the moment that we were still wearing our masks. Our bills clashed, as our heads moved closer, and mine snapped leaving the end three inches hanging limply in the half-light of the dimly lit church.

It was at that moment I discovered my aged maiden aunt's all-seeing, all-hearing Methodist God did indeed watch over me at all times and that he spoke in a very loud English-sounding voice.

"Will the bird with the broken beak fly to the chemistry laboratory at nine o'clock tomorrow morning."

The following day I was told off by the all-seeing chemistry master, told to mend both my beak and my ways and not to canoodle in church again.

At the end of the final performance two curlews left the church unseen by 'God'. Beneath a new moon and a gargoyle's stony gaze, masks were removed and after a brief hesitation lips touched lips.

And in those ten seconds of my first real kiss, I discovered that mouths could be used for an activity which was more enjoyable than sucking pear drops, aniseed balls, barley sugars and even gobstoppers. This kiss was far more interesting than the slurpy wet kisses great-aunts insisted on giving me on my cheek as they pressed a coin into my hand.

Our wings which had been hanging limply by our sides flapped upwards simultaneously and became arms as we embraced in an awkward grasping of quivering bodies.

And as we hugged each other, I felt the biggest tingle ever pass through my body right down to my toes in an uncontrollable shiver. We kissed again and there were no thoughts of Kenny the Gorilla's rude verses in the boys' lavatory at primary school. Instead the words from one of the songs we'd been singing, words which I didn't understand the meaning of, briefly exploded in my head:

Kyrie eleison, Kyrie eleison.

The curlews had flown the ark. Aged thirteen I was beginning to personally experience 'it'.

Kitchen

SITUATED IN THE middle of the farmhouse tree was kitchen. As with the other branches 'the' was never used. "Us'll light the fire in kitchen tonight", or "Nort on the ole wireless to keep us in cellar. 'Tis cold so us'll sit 'round the fire in kitchen".

At harvest time and on special occasions, kitchen was used as the dining room instead of cellar. Kitchen was our sitting room, posh but not as posh as front room.

The open fireplace, where in previous decades food had been prepared, was approximately six feet long, three feet deep and six feet high. It was a cavernous mouth which devoured logs, moots and faggots. At Christmas it was lit and remained burning for the twelve festive days. By standing in the hearth I could stare up through the soot-coated throat and glimpse the blue sky. In past days, my father told me, a large gorse bush attached to a rope was pulled down through the chimney to clear the soot. A flammable liquid caused a fireball to hurtle up the chimney burning off the soot as it travelled.

The hearth was an exhibition of the blacksmith's craft – a collection of iron cooking utensils (crocks and cauldrons and kettle), chimney crooks, hooks, handy maid, a pair of firedogs and a fire basket plus tongs, poker and shovel.

To the left of the fireplace, a copper warming pan used in a previous century when it was filled with glowing embers to warm the bed. Hanging from the mantelpiece, a brass toasting fork which was used to make some of the best toast imaginable. To the right, a cloam oven. Here bread and buns had been baked, furze twigs providing an intense heat.

Dwarfing all other furniture, the giant oak table, its top measuring ten feet by three feet, was crafted from two-inch-thick planks, the grained surface polished weekly by my aged maiden aunt with either bees' wax or a purple polish scented with lavender. When not in use it was protected by a black oilcloth over which was sometimes laid an embroidered tablecloth.

In 1966 when the live and dead stock (implements and household goods) was auctioned, the table made seventy pounds (£1,000 in today's money), and the long form which ran along side of it seventeen pounds (£250). When the buyer took them away the window had to be taken out as this was the only way they could be removed.

On the special occasions the mighty Atlas never groaned in protest at the weight on his shoulders – a Willow pattern dinner service, Crown Derby tea service and silver and EPNS cutlery for fourteen people.

Three drawers ran back under the full width of the tabletop in which were stored linen tablecloths, oilcloths, cutlery, farm account books and farm notebooks dating back to the mid-eighteenth century, cows-to-the-bull sheet, stationery, fountain pens, a bottle of Quink ink, sealing wax, matches, a box of gun cartridges and at the back of one drawer the rosettes won by my father at local fat stock shows.

In a large, floor-to-ceiling glass cupboard and dresser, the dinner and tea services, jugs, mugs and vases, and my father's silver cup which he had won for three successive years for the best bullock at the local fat stock show. One wet day while playing with a Dinky toy which ran underneath the dresser my probing fingers dislodged a wallet crammed full of one-, five- and ten-pound notes. Obviously not all the money made on the farm was paid into the bank or to the taxman.

In a corner of kitchen, the grandfather clock, crafted at Crediton, its chain wound up by father at seven o'clock each morning. Another part of the morning ritual involved two taps on the banjo barometer, hanging on the wall opposite, with his knuckles. These taps were accompanied by the words to no-one in particular: "Goin' up today. Weather good for a day or so" or "Droppin' back, rain on the way". Crafted in Tiverton, this instrument governed when the three- or four-day hay harvest would take place, its predictions being given higher order than those on the wireless forecast.

Seating in kitchen was made up of two chairs which had been converted into easy chairs from two front bucket seats from an old Austin 7 car by the carpenter in his shop opposite the farmhouse tree. There was also my aged maiden aunt's rocking chair in the chimney corner. No longer a rocker, the rockers having been removed when she had almost pitched herself head first into the fire one night. On their silver wedding in the late 1950s, my mother and father treated themselves to new plush easy chairs. Luxury had arrived at the farmhouse tree, but I continued to sit on my four-legged wooden stool.

On one wall, the mahogany gun rack which housed my father's double-barrel shotgun. Beneath it, an oak bookcase with a selection of books including *Oliver Twist*, an Edgar Wallace thriller with a garish yellow cover, a treasury of mystery stories, the new illustrated gardening encyclopædia, prayer books, Methodist hymn books and *The New Illustrated Universal Reference Book*. As thick as a clenched fist, this book according to my aged maiden aunt contained "... all the knowledge one wishes to know, needs to know and more besides".

Pride of place on the top of the bookcase, next to a boxed game of solitaire and a pack of playing cards, was the black Bakelite telephone. Installed in the late 1950s it was used in an emergency, or to issue an invitation to relatives. It was seldom used to make a pleasure call, and was avoided with suspicion by my aged maiden aunt who quickly left the room when it rang.

On winter nights, when I was sitting staring into the flames, my aged maiden aunt would make up stories in the flames, each of us adding a line to build up the tale based on the characters, animals and places we could see in the fire. On other occasions when the soot was damp and there were sparks in it she would say (if there were only a few sparks), "Poor ole parson'll be miserable on Sunday. Not many going to his service to hear his ole sermon." If however there were a lot of sparks she would smile and say, "The preacher'll be happy in chapel, a full congregation."

When two-feet-high flames roared up the chimney, and kitchen was drenched in the scent of applewood smoke, my father would occasionally reminisce as he enjoyed a small tumbler of his home-brewed cider from the hogshead in the pound house. His eyes would twinkle as he told the tale of the wedding invitation.

"We received it soon after the First World War. I would have been about eighteen. My father, your grandfather who died nearly thirty years before you came along, opened it and read it out loud. At the end he paused before reading out four letters – RSVP. We was none the wiser than he was as to what they meant, but the following night when we was having our supper he announced that while he'd been walking behind his team of shires ploughing, it had come to him what the letters meant. 'They'm tellin' us what they be gwain to give us to eat after the nuptials. 'Twill be a rare feast and no mistake. Us be 'avin' Roast Sirloin and Viggy Pudding.'"

Finishing his cider he winked at me. "I wonder if Jill and Phil Archer'll 'ave viggy pudding when they tie the knot at quarter to seven tomorrow?"

Miss Methuselah

IN THE EYES of a child anyone over the age of thirty is old. Aunt Nell, fifty-four when I was born, was in my young eyes the female equivalent of Methuselah, the oldest man in the biblical story which she had once read to me. By the age of nine I had even convinced myself that she had been born an old lady because she never seemed to age facially.

Never having married she shared the indoor and outdoor farm tasks and duties quite happily with her sister-in-law for over thirty years. She lived under the ever-present fear that she was not long for this world, but despite the imagined dark cloud which loomed over her, she survived her mother and father by over forty and fifty years and her three brothers by fifteen, fourteen and eight years. As my father once said to her, "A creaking gate lasts longest, Nell."

My aged maiden aunt, who had ploughed the bulk of her savings in the Government-sponsored War Loan only to see the value of her money cut by two thirds by the time she reached her retirement. "Never trust the ole government again. Never."

My aged maiden aunt, who was my personal fairy godmother – the granter of wishes and the bringer home of small gifts whenever she went into town on the weekly market day bus. I was her little prince, the little boy she didn't want to grow up and become king. A Peter Pan in her Never Never Land of childhood. The cuckoo she never wanted to see fly the nest.

My aged maiden aunt, who as soon as the nine-o'clock news had finished on the wireless retired to her bedroom where she kneeled at the side of her bed to say her prayers to her Maker to thank Him for another day. In the morning, kneeling again to thank Him for looking after her while she slept and to guide her through the following day.

My aged maiden aunt, who together with my mother taught me at a young age the beauty of language with its cadences and rhythms as they read the stories and psalms in the family Bible to me at bedtime. Between them they unknowingly sowed in me the seeds of wanting to be a writer.

My aged maiden aunt, whose luxuries in life were simple ones – a bottle of Lucozade, two Mars bars each sliced into six pieces, a bag of barley sugars from the grocer when he called once a fortnight and the *Woman's Weekly* and *Woman's Realm* – "my little treats" whenever she went into town on the bus.

The Observer's Book of Birds' Eggs

AN ESSENTIAL INGREDIENT in my aged maiden aunt's spiritual diet were prayers in the evening and morning as I kneeled by the side of my iron-and-brass double bed, on a home-made rag rug to protect my bare feet from the cold linoleum, and grace at the meal table each day before one-o'clock dinner. "Sanctify O Lord this food to our use and us to Thy service for Jesus Christ's sake. Amen" or "For what we are about to receive may the Lord make us truly thankful. Amen".

My father would occasionally tell the tale of how, when he was a small boy at the dinner table, his father said, "For what we are about to receive, and what Herbert has already received, may the Lord make us truly thankful. Amen." Herbert, my father's brother, went bright red while my father did his best not to giggle.

There was a protocol attached to saying my prayers. "Close your eyes when you kneel by your bed. You can only speak to God with your eyes shut. If you do it with them open He won't hear you. Now you say what I say, repeat it after me. When you do it properly, when you've learned the words, there'll be no need to say them out loud because He can hear you when nobody else can, and when you can't even hear them yourself except in your head. And put your hands together. Fingers pointing up to heaven like a church spire."

I imitated her hand movements and repeated the words after her –

"Heavenly Father, hear my prayer,
Day and night I'm in Thy care.
Look upon me from above,
Bless the home I dearly love.
Bless all those with whom I play,
Make us better every day.
God Bless Mum, Dad and Auntie. Amen."

After a few mornings and evenings repeating it under her guidance I knew every word of her special prayer. At the end of the final line I was allowed to add the names of the two farm cats – Mick the Manx and Grey Puss – and Joey the budgie. Over the years I was allowed to add Scamper the grey squirrel, the lizard and my mother's own pet cat Bimbo. "God likes birds and animals, but in their proper place," said my aged maiden aunt when I told her of my additions. She drew the line however at me adding the slow-worm I had adopted for a couple of days. "Nasty ole snakes. God doesn't like them. Nasty slithery things. Remember the Garden of Eden." I didn't tell her that slow-worms were legless lizards.

Next came the big prayer. The grown ups' prayer. The Lord's Prayer. The day finally arrived when I could say the long list of words without any prompting and I was paraded in front of my parents at the supper table. As my father tucked into his bread and cheese I parrot-fashioned the words and was duly applauded for my efforts.

By her bedside on the chest, my aged maiden aunt's copy of the family Bible, carried up each night so that she could read a portion of scripture before going to sleep. By day it was kept on the mahogany bookcase next to the black Bakelite telephone where it was guarded by my father's double-barrel shotgun in the gun rack attached to the wall above it.

My Bible was *The Observer's Book of Birds' Eggs*. My classmate owned a copy and I coveted it. All the eggs you could ever wish to see or dream of seeing. All the eggs you wished you had in your wooden box full of sawdust, laid out with a picture and a page of information on each one. I didn't covet my classmate's house and he didn't own an ox or an ass, but I desperately wanted my own copy of that book.

On market day I jumped off the Western National bus under the clock tower in the square followed by my aged maiden aunt. Thursday, the day I'd been waiting for, reward day. Quickly, I led the way to the newsagents where I was going to be allowed to choose my reward.

"Up to five shillings –" (25p) – "Not a penny more, now. Off you go. Five shillings, mind. Auntie isn't made of money."

I didn't have to look for long. The previous Thursday, knowing I would earn a reward, I had hidden the small book I wanted behind a larger volume at the back of the shelf. Carefully I eased out the big book and my fingers clutched *my* book. Five shillings exactly. Not a penny more, not a penny less. I waved it in front of her. "You'm sure that's the one you want? There's a nice little book here full of Enid Blyton stories. Only three and six." (17½p.)

Enid Blyton was considered a nutritious part of my diet. "Nice little stories. Good stories." I stood my ground. Learning the Lord's prayer had involved a lot of hard work. Certainly five bob's worth. I held out my chosen prize; two half-crown pieces were slowly handed over with the words, "Well, if you'm sure. And you have been a good boy."

Walking out of the shop, turning the pages over as I went, I gave prayers careful thought as I drank in the illustrations. My aged maiden aunt's all-seeing, all-hearing God certainly did possess good aural powers. Only the previous month I had told Him about the book I wanted without moving my lips or making any sound at all, and I didn't have enough saved up in my money box, and perhaps He could see His way clear to do a bit of magic, or as Auntie termed His work – "a miracle when He moves in mysterious ways".

But what would Auntie have said if she had known that I had asked Him with my eyes open? He'd certainly moved in a mysterious way, His wonders to perform, and I marched through the square proudly clutching my reward, glad that I would no longer have to break the tenth commandment. Now I could put my new book next to the Observer's Books of Birds, Flowers and Butterflies.

A few weeks later Kenny the Gorilla Harris, a classmate so named because he always slouched along, shoulders hunched, his hands hanging below his knees, a heathen boy according to my aged maiden aunt, rolled up on his occasional visit to Sunday school. Normally he only put in an appearance when he wanted to book a place on the Sunday school summer outing coach to the seaside, book his place for the Sunday school Christmas party or when he was planning trouble. The summer outing trip was over and it was months before the Christmas party. So it had to be trouble.

"Please Miss can I say the Lord's prayer today Miss? Please Miss. Can I Miss?"

Kenny meant business. He's said please twice, a word virtually unknown in his vocabulary. The two ladies were so amazed by his persistent pleas that they completely forgot about his previous misdeeds, and consented. I was amazed by his request, because there was no way Kenny knew the Lord's prayer off by heart. At school he couldn't even learn ten words for a spelling test or the first line of a poem, let alone all six verses.

Grinning broadly, he stood up, wiped the sleeve of his jacket across his nose, sniffed, coughed, winked at us and said, "Our Father which fart in Heaven, Alfred be Thy name." He skipped the rest of the prayer before adding as an afterthought "Amen".

The word was barely out of his mouth and Kenny was making a speedy exit, banging the door with a thunder crash behind him, leaving us sniggering behind our hands and my great-aunts looking at each other forlornly and tut-tut-tutting.

A rich spiritual meal indeed, but not one my aged maiden aunt wanted on the menu when I attempted to tell her what he had said over the table. "Drat the boy. He'll come to a sticky end. You mark my words."

When sugar rationing ended in 1953, Easter Sunday became a really good day. I was given tons of chocolate eggs and the rule relating to not eating chocolate and sweets on the Sabbath was relaxed for the day. One Easter, my aged maiden aunt gave me an egg which made me gasp with amazement – a sugar egg. This was an egg I would never find in my *Observer's Book of Birds' Eggs*. But I didn't eat it; I saved it for the first day of the summer term.

"Wotcher got there, mate?" The dulcet tones of Kenny the Gorilla Harris echoing above the voices of my mates who had gathered around me. He stared in disbelief. "Cor beaut. Us'll eat'e boys. Bags first bite."

This wasn't what I had intended. It was only for show in school, certainly not for the gorilla's gob to bite into. He pressed his nose against the box then hastily withdrew it. "Don't want none."

I gave a double take. Kenny always wanted your sweets. A playground Guinness Book of Records entry.

"That's a girl's egg. Got pink icing. Us mens 'aves blue, not pink, not sissy-girl pink." And with that he slouched off followed by his cronies. I thanked my aged maiden aunt's all-seeing God for watching over me, and for pink icing, and I was glad that Kenny was as daft as he looked.

The March of Progress

IN 1963 A new god entered the farmhouse tree and our lives were changed for ever. In the flick of a switch we did away with Aladdin lamps and candles upstairs, and downstairs the gas mantles were taken out. The Calor gas cylinders were kept for cooking and the boiler for washday Monday. It wasn't connected to shippens and outdoor buildings where paraffin lamps were still used.

The cost of all materials including bulbs, shades, plugs, switches and cable came to under £27, and when labour was added the total bill was well under £100.

In those good old days the more electricity you used the cheaper it became. The first 70 units were 7*d* (3p) per unit, the next 70 at

2¾*d* (just over 1p) and all other units were 1¾*d* (well under 1p per unit).

The first quarterly bill was three pounds, ten shillings (£3·50).

On the first night, to celebrate, my mother, father and aged maiden aunt assembled in front court while I was dispatched to run like a nursery-rhyme character upstairs and downstairs and in my aged maiden aunt's bedchamber where I was rarely permitted entry, to switch on every light.

Outside and out of breath I joined the admiring throng as we stared open-mouthed at the illuminated farmhouse tree, every branch bathed in light. After only a few seconds I was sent back in to turn them off as according to my mother and father we didn't have money to burn and we didn't want neighbours thinking otherwise.

"Lit up like a gin palace," said my aged maiden aunt. I didn't know what that was but it sounded very exotic and oriental. She then showed her charitable Methodist nature by adding, "Best to turn it all off, otherwise the juice'll run out before it gets to the bottom of the village and they won't have any lights at all. Mustn't be greedy."

A black-and-white television set was rented from Rentaset for ten and sixpence (52½p) a week. My aged maiden aunt loved it, especially the quiz games *Take Your Pick* with Michael Miles and *Double Your Money* with Hughie Green. The laws of the Sabbath still applied for a while but were gradually relaxed. I sometimes think this was due more to economics than religious beliefs because if we'd rented the set for seven days and were only using it for six we were wasting one shilling and sixpence (7½p).

Sitting down one Sunday morning the set was quickly turned off when it was discovered that the service was Roman Catholic. "They gets everywhere," announced my aged maiden aunt, "even inside the ole television set." Pausing, she chuckled, "Mind you, 'twill be some spectacle when the ole pope passes on and they show his funeral. Just think of all the flowers there'll be. And us'll be able to see it all. Pity 'twill only be in black-and-white though."

With the advent of electricity, and more especially the television set, our lives changed for ever. Conversations in the evenings became less, as did card games, draughts and tiddlywinks. Like other families in towns and cities our evenings were focused on the box in the corner of the room.

Chapel – Travel Arrangements

THE METHODIST CHAPEL, or our "Sunday spiritual home", as my aged maiden aunt termed the red-brick building, was opened in 1927, and replaced a wooden hut a quarter of a mile away. Built largely through the generosity of the Nonconformist parishioners and donations from Methodists in a neighbouring parish, several of the bricks at ground level were inscribed with the names of some the families who had been benefactors. "A seat at God's right hand and sharing and participating in His heavenly delights will be theirs at the end of their final journey," announced my aged maiden aunt one Sunday afternoon as we stood on the chapel steps in the biting wind and the weekly gossip was shared out between fellow members of the congregation.

Too busy thinking of the earthly delights to be found at the end of a Saturday journey to the village shop, such as sherbet lemons, gobstoppers, aniseed balls and sweet cigarettes with free cards, which could have been purchased with their donations, I gave the bricks barely a second glance. I frowned; I'd only just placed a thrupenny bit (just over 1p) in the collection box. Twelve blackjacks, three liquorice bootlaces or a box of sweet cigarettes and a gobstopper had just been donated to the feast for those lucky souls who had recently completed their final journey. As to what means of transport they would use, I was not sure. Few members of the village possessed cars, the market day bus only ran on Thursdays and our only means was a carthorse borrowed from our octogenarian next-door neighbour – my farming hero. The horse was so slow that the heavenly delights would in all probability run out by the time our final journey ended.

As if reading my thoughts about donations my aged maiden aunt announced, "Children weren't expected to donate towards a brick. One or two of those names were probably distant relatives."

This was said in a reflective tone, as if indicating the hope that our Heavenly Father would extend His bounteous delights in her direction at the end of her allotted biblical span of three-score years and ten. As I stood hopping from one foot to the other, waiting for the tasty morsels of gossip to be shared out and eaten, I gave the journey even more thought. Would the journey be bareback on the shirehorse or in the butt-cart? Neither appealing if it was a long journey. Perhaps it would be by Royal Blue or Black and White coach, or perhaps God might even dispatch a special taxi. The conversations broke up and we headed home with me none the wiser as to the final journey travel arrangements.

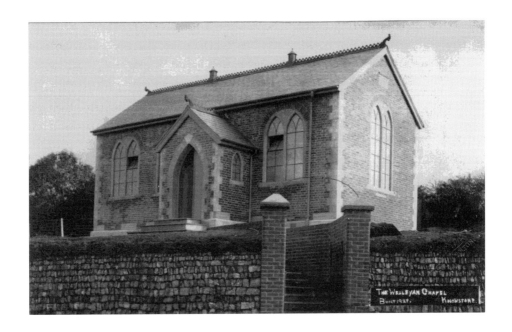

What's in a Name?

IT WAS A wet afternoon, and I was fed up with being confined to the farmhouse tree. Not even a new Dinky toy could make up for the fact that it had been raining since well before I had got up. My aged maiden aunt's maxim that rain before seven cleared up before eleven was certainly not true this time.

As I was deciding what to do next, my aged maiden aunt entered the room where I was sitting, staring at the window, wondering which raindrop would reach the bottom of a glass pane first.

"The devil makes work for idle hands," she stated.

I looked at my fingers, feeling my face turning red, wondering what it was he was going to find for me to do.

"He gets you into trouble," she continued. "Makes you do things you wouldn't normally even think of doing." As she spoke she removed the kettle from the top of the stove, made herself a cup of tea and sat down.

"Auntie," I said, "what does Michaelmas mean?" It had been my birthday the previous week, 29th September, and I was intrigued by it being called Michaelmas Day.

"It's a quarter day in the farming calendar. A farmer's day when farms change hands or rents are paid."

I wanted more information. "Yes, but what does Michaelmas mean? Was Michaelmas a person?"

She smiled. "Named after Michael. Saint Michael, the slayer of the evil dragon. The Book of Revelations."

I gave this careful thought before asking my next question. "If I was born on St Michael's Day how come I'm called David and not Michael?"

She gave me one of her looks which indicated after this answer there would be no further questions. "Questions, questions, questions. That's all you ever ask." Picking up her cup of tea she walked to the door where she turned, and gave me her parting words. "Did Michael kill Goliath and become king of Israel?"

Yet again her logic had defeated me. Many years after, my mother told me that I had been called David because it meant 'one who is much loved' – "and you certainly were, after the long wait you put us through."

Sunday Ritual

EVERY SUNDAY FROM a very young age I made the weekly chapel pilgrimage, if the weather was sunny and fine. "And cross the road when you reach the Masons Arms. No need to be on the same side as that heathen house. Just keep looking straight ahead," said my aged maiden aunt as she opened the back door for me.

One short mile and forty-two paces exactly, measured out by Jim and Derek my imaginary friends and me, all aged nine years and ten months exactly. Every Sunday unless it was raining. At the end of my prayers on a Saturday night I added, "And please make it rain tomorrow, God. Please, God, please. And I promise I'll be good. Amen."

My all-seeing God might have been always watching me but He didn't always hear my heartfelt pleas. If He did, He ignored me with a sense of humour wry and dry. In the morning how it rained and rained and rained and rained.

"Rain before seven, clear up before eleven," announced my aged maiden aunt with a knowing smile. Her prognostication sealed my fate, and although not spoken in a silent voice, God heard her every word. Before the grandfather clock had finished striking eleven, a patch of blue came into view. "Enough to make a sailor's suit," she chuckled.

"God's in His heaven smiling down. You'll be able to go to Sunday school."

At one o'clock, the Sunday roast. "Sanctify O Lord this food to our use and us to Thy service for Jesus Christ's sake. Amen." Around the joint of best topside, a rippling lake all red and greasy. "Best beef blood to make you strong and healthy. Drink it up." Next the hot rice pudding before those dreaded words, "Now off to Sunday school you go."

"Do I have to?"

"Yes, you do."

Dressed in my Sunday best blazer and grey flannel shorts

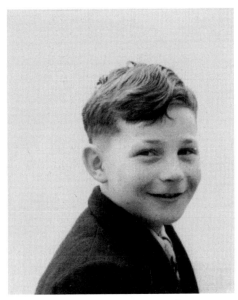

School photograph of
David, aged nine

which revealed pink scrubbed knees I set off, scuffing my Cheery Blossom black polished shoes along the road. I played hopscotch with Jim and Derek. Threw stones at birds and rabbits. Spotted flowers with the strangest names. I-Spy Ramsons, Devil's-bit, Shepherd's-purse and Yellow Rattle. I walked through all the deepest puddles, paying not the slightest heed to leaking shoes and soaking socks. Then making sure no-one was looking, shouted "WHY DID YOU MAKE THE SUN SHINE, GOD?"

As if in answer black clouds came storming in from near and far. His emissaries unloosed their weapons, soaking me from head to toe. "I HATE YOU, GOD, I REALLY DO."

Duly drenched at two fifteen, I sat with others scrubbed and clean. "There's a friend for little children above the deep blue sky. A friend who never changes, whose love can never die." The little lad next to me, half-starved, bony knees scarred, grubby hands and hand-me-down clothes. "In our dear Lord's garden, planted here below; Many tiny flowerets in sweet profusion grow." At the back, a rare visit by Kenny the Gorilla Harris booking his seat for the Sunday school summer outing coach trip to the seaside. At the same time planning and scheming tricks to annoy my Sunday school teacher great-aunts. "Jesus wants me for a sunbeam, to shine for Him each day. In every way to please him, at home, at school, at play."

Next, the moral tale of the naughty boy who said he hadn't when he had. Did things he shouldn't have done and every day was very bad. Said sorry and was forgiven by the all-seeing, partially hearing God. Finally prayers that we should be made good, and Kenny's voice roaring out his favourite line, "Our Father which fart in Heaven, Alfred be Thy name."

After Sunday school, the service proper. While the lucky children who didn't have to attend chapel played outside, whooping and catcalling, I sat upright on my brown pine bench pew anticipating the event with my father, mother and aged maiden aunt. In came the old Methodist man in his gert big hobnail boots. With a crash he slammed the chapel door, allowing no-one to escape. His leather boots squeaking. "They're not paid for," whispered Dad. And I thought to myself that they'd squash the innards from twenty snails, and the pain if he trod on your toes.

The chapel became silent. The breaker of bread and his baker's dozen congregation. The man who took the collection. "Where does he take it?" I once asked my aged maiden aunt. A withering look. "He doesn't take it anywhere."

Daring myself to make a lucky dip. Put in my thrupenny bit and pull out a shiny shilling. Another withering look as if she'd read my mind.

The man with the bump at the back of his head. "A magic eye," said Dad when I asked him about it. "He can see around corners with it."

Perhaps God has an all-seeing magic eye at the back of His head. Perhaps God is in league with the man with the bump.

The lady with the goiterous lump which wobbled when she hit the high notes. "Swallowed a pip," said Dad. "Got stuck and grew into an apple."

Occasionally the sacrament was celebrated, prolonging the service by eighteen minutes and twenty seconds, exactly measured and timed by David John Hill aged ten years and one week exactly, on my brand new Tick-a-tick-a-Timex birthday present watch. Fitted with a shiny stainless steel strap.

"This is my blood which is shed for you. Drink this in remembrance of me."

One afternoon I hung back, and when no-one was around I lifted up the glass decanter chalice and without a sound drank the dregs of my all-seeing God's most holy blood.

Blackcurrant. And all the way home I wondered how it could be that the all-seeing-magic-eye-at-the-back-of-his-head, all-hearing God had Ribena juice coursing through His heavenly veins in a body made of crustless bread.

After hymns, prayers, Bible readings old and new, the long-awaited sermon, if lucky from the last-of-the-diehard-fire-and-brimstone Methody man.

"John Wesley was a great man, who through sun and wind and rain rode forth each day to preach and say – God is your father and your friend. Across the countryside he'd ride, and they do say that in a single day on horseback seventy miles he'd roam, to preach to people in their homes. And when his life came to an end, twenty-five thousand miles he'd ridden, and forty-five thousand sermons preached. Just fancy that."

Bet he had a sore bum, I thought to myself. Should have sold his horse and bought a car. And as he continued with his theme I sat there hoping he wouldn't notice me but...

"And, my small friend, he thought of you, being especially fond of children too. He was the first to hold a Sunday school!"

Immediately I hated him as the Methody man continued, "And do you know what he said about you?"

"N... n... n... no, sir," I stammered.

"He said this: Remember God your Heavenly Father is always watching you. Do you understand?"

My mind was in a whirl. I'd never met John Wesley so how could he talk about me? I nodded and thought of the great big magic eye floating in the sky.

"And now, brothers and sister gathered here today, to you I only have this to say: beware the demon drink. The water of the devil." While the Methody man brandished sharp-edged words I ducked the cut and thrust of his sword and stared at the walls, the ceiling and the floor. Counted the panes in the leaded diamond windows, added up the numbers on the hymn number board, computing vertically, horizontally and diagonally.

"AND SO I SAY TO YOU GATHERED HERE TODAY, THE EVILS OF STRONG DRINK ARE MANY. IT IS THE DEVIL'S WATER."

His fist thumped down to emphasise his words and finally he said, "If only we could empty every barrel, bottle and mug into the river. What a wonderful day that would be."

A nod of heads and murmurs of approval.

"And to close our joyous service a hymn I know you all enjoy."

Stiff limbs jolted into action as we became upstanding men and women sending voices flat and tuneless echoing to the rafters high. The organ wheezed a mournful dirge, the goitre wobbled up and down as we all praised our all-seeing God for His never-ending mercies, each abstemious one and all. "Strictly medicinal, you understand. Mind you, I must say, warms where goes."

With gusto we sang our song of praise, led by the Methody man –

> "Shall we gather by the river
> The beautiful, the beautiful river.
> Saints all gather at the river
> Which flows through the land of God."

The Flood

RESTING ON HER knees, the treasure chest contained a trove of precious stones. Each night opening the lid, reaching in, removing a hidden gem.

Bedtime stories read with additions of her own. "The length of the ark shall be three hundred cubits, the breadth of it fifty cubits, and the height of it thirty cubits. Higher and longer than the barn. And of every living creature of all flesh two of every sort shalt thou bring into the ark. Pigs, cows, sheep, horses, hens. In they went. All your favourite birds and animals. Robins, blackbirds, wrens. Even the old fox, then the rain came. Poured and poured. And the flood was forty days upon the earth. Just think of it. Well over a month. Non-stop rain. Fifteen cubits upwards did the waters prevail; and the mountains were covered."

Half-listening to her story. My head awash. How long was a cubit? How could it rain for forty days? What did he do with all the dung? And how could he be over six hundred years old? The terrifying thought of water deep enough to cover the farmhouse tree. Deep enough to cover my world of the court and all the fields.

Higher Orchard, where beneath the stormcock's dive-bomber flight, natural springs bubbled to the surface. A letter from Tiverton. Lowman Ironworks, dated 11th August, 1904. Two hundred and thirty yards of lead pipe at sixteen pounds, seventeen shillings and sixpence. Best quality high-pressure taps – brass at five shillings and ninepence each, plus our charge for fixing same, terms to be discussed and determined. We hope to be favoured with your order which shall receive our every attention. Yours very obediently, Stenner and Gunn.

Priming the pump with a jug of water, working the long-case handle to suck up the spring. In a rush-gush of liquid diamonds, a laughter of bubbles erupts into the granite trough. Cupped hands dipped. Raised to my lips. An explosion of ice-cold sweetness.

In winter the farmhouse tree froze, ice ferns flourishing on window panes, muslin-bag breath ballooning the ceiling, the cold oozing out of the cob walls. Dagger-blade icicles hanging from gutters, snapped off and sucked like lollypops. And the water solid in lead pipes refusing to run through the pump or shining brass taps.

Throughout the summer, excess water from the springs ran through a channel in the court where swallows and martins skimmed for mud at nesting time in May. On a hot summer day two hessian sacks crammed full with golden barley straw created a dam beneath the flagstone stepping-stone bridge.

For an afternoon the yard is an ocean, my father fashioning brown paper boats and hats from the weekly *Western Times*. Promoting me to Admiral of the Eastacott Fleet. At five o'clock the plug is pulled. In a surge, my mythical sea is sucked under the outside lavatory, down through the ditches in Bull's Mead, Furze Close and Moory Ground and into the Crooked Oak river.

During autumn and winter the water is diverted over the grass in Bull's Mead. Lavatory buckets tipped into the stream enriching the ground for springtime grass to fatten steers and bullocks. On ice-filled days, pewits and snipe billing the earth for worms and grubs. In summer the river was thin, a meandering stillness, pollen-flecked where my mother and I came to bathe one August when the springs piped into the farmhouse tree threatened to run dry.

Once a dead sheep haloed in flies floated slowly by as we picnicked on the bank. In the autumn the river was swollen and gorged with fish which my father and a great-uncle gaffed with iron hooks fixed to hazel poles.

One late-summer day the black sky, split by lightning flashes, poured down rain. The stream through front court became a torrent, flooding under the pine front door, through the hall into the dairy and out through a drainage pipe. Furniture in front room hurriedly piled up in a Leaning Tower of Pisa.

My aged maiden aunt's voice interrupting my thoughts. "I do set my bow in the cloud, and it shall be a token of a covenant between me and the earth. Richard of York gave battle in vain. All your colours in a single sentence. And the waters shall no more become a flood to destroy all flesh. Your birds and animals safe for ever. Even fleas. Beast and man. No more drowning. And all the days of Noah were nine hundred and fifty years and he died." Her gentle laugh. "Even older than your auntie."

Closing the chest lid. A brown paper bag taken out from her dressing room. A package produced. "For you." In my hands a kaleidoscope of shimmering coloured shapes shaking into a pattern.

Today, with each twist of the tinplate container, childhood rainbows form, split and shatter. A flood of memories. Drowning.

The Transmutation

THE OLD LADY was an alchemist who had perfected the ancient art of making gold. Once a year between chutney-making and Christmas Day, she decided that the omens were right for the transmutation to take place.

In a flap of apron strings, a gathering of blue paper bags and jars of secret ingredients, she whirled dervishlike around her laboratory. Gold-making always took place on a wet afternoon, and on the chosen day, instead of taking her daily two-hour siesta, she darted around her work bench stirring, beating and mixing her philosopher's stone with the base metals in the iron cauldron.

I was allowed to watch the spellbinding process providing I sat, the passive apprentice to the sorceress, on my wooden stool in the corner. If I so much as dared to twitch or glance in the direction of the door she tapped her wand on the bench and said, "I need to concentrate. I can't work properly if there's a little mommick forever jigging about under my nose."

Chastised, I watched in silence as she continued stirring her raw materials. Suddenly from the cauldron came the sound I had patiently been waiting to hear – the hubble-bubble of boiling molten gold.

Frothing up the sides of the cauldron, the liquid heaved its way to the top in a gauze of tiny bubbles. After testing its consistency by dropping a blob into a dish of cold water, she carefully lifted the cauldron from the flames and poured the liquid into a flat metal tray.

The wait for the gold to solidify seemed endless. At last the process was completed to her satisfaction, and the alchemist scored lines over and across the surface of the hardening metal. As soon as the block was solid, the tray was turned upside down and given a sharp tap with a miniature silver hammer. The gold block was tap-tapped and a hundred ingots, each about an inch square, glittered on the work surface. Finally they were dusted with a fine white powder and dropped into four treasure chests.

"You help Auntie and we'll see what little reward we can find," smiled the little old lady, her voice breaking my magic spell.

In the twinkling of her eye, the china bowls, wooden spoons, saucepans, enamel weighing pan and plates were washed, dried and put away.

"And this one's for you."

Hurrying up back stairs at bedtime, my reward clutched tightly in my hands, I ran into my bedroom. Sitting on my iron-and-brass double bed I slowly opened the tin.

Pausing to savour the sensation, I gazed at my treasure trove, my mouth becoming moist as I anticipated the flavour. Slowly, wanting to make the moment last for ever, I took my first gold ingot from the tin and placing it in my mouth began to suck.

Meanwhile, my aged maiden aunt, her energies spent, retired early, taking her secret recipe book with her. Beneath the flickering candle flame she kneeled at the side of her bed and attempted a spiritual transmutation.

Here, my aged maiden aunt's personal transmutation took place, her state of leaden earthly impurity changing into a state of golden perfection.

Sucking hard on my third piece of icing-sugar-coated butterscotch, I snuggled down under the sheets and closed my eyes.

The golden end to a golden day.

My mother's voice from the bottom of back stairs: "And make sure you brush your teeth."

Auntie's Little Mishap

IN THE EVENING when it was my aged maiden aunt's turn to tuck me up in bed with a story, she would sit on my iron-and-brass double bed and read me either an Enid Blyton story or one from the family Bible. It was winter and instead of the last rays of the setting summer sun illuminating my room, the ritual was bathed under the flickering candlelight. "His story," she said as she read me the parable of the sower and the seed. "True stories. Earthly tales with heavenly meanings."

The Bible, over a century old, was heavy and it was as much as she could do to balance the three-inch-thick tome on her knees. Suddenly, a crash and it tumbled to the linoleum-covered floor. Uttering a small cry she got down on her knees on the rag rug, retrieved the Bible and asked the Lord's forgiveness.

"No need to mention Auntie's little mishap to your mother and father," she said, placing it on my chest of drawers.

I nodded as she left the room, only for her to return a couple of minutes later with a slice of Mars bar. Each Monday she sliced a Mars bar into six pieces, one for each weekday – her "little treats".

"You shouldn't be eating it in bed, but I won't tell if you don't. Brush your teeth later and no chocolate on the sheets. That's the slice I'd have eaten tomorrow. I'll be back in five minutes to blow out the candle."

Giving me a kiss on my forehead she left the room, and I lay back in bed enjoying my piece of Mars bar. The Bible hadn't fallen on stony ground. Perhaps she'd drop it again. But she never did, and blackmail wasn't a word in my young vocabulary.

A Place of Sanctuary

MY AGED MAIDEN aunt's bedroom with the adjoining dressing room, the only place I never set foot in as a child, was her sanctuary, the one branch in the farmhouse tree where she could find peace and privacy. It was here where she retired each afternoon for two hours to either have a nap, read or knit.

She believed she was frail and delicate, having suffered attacks of shingles and quinsy, and always feared she was on the verge of illness.

Her room always seemed to be in a permanent state of semi-darkness, because the curtains which were made from a thick coarse material and which touched the linoleum were usually kept closed.

Even in midsummer only a trickle of sunlight was permitted entry when, as a concession to the intense heat, the window was opened slightly and the gap between the curtains increased from six to twelve inches.

Because of the walk-in dressing room there was no wardrobe, and the largest piece of furniture was an oak blanket chest.

"Made when they built the farmhouse, so I been told. To be passed down through the generations. Been dated about 1690," she said when I asked her about it.

Carved from planks which were held together by home-made iron nails, the front panels were patterned with diamond and twisting carved shapes and the wood was as dark as the room.

On the top of the chest, her collection of treasures, medicines and luxuries. Her treasures were family photographs, an autograph book and a recipe book. The photographs included one of me in my Sunday best clothes, one of her parents on their wedding day and two of her brothers on their wedding days.

Dated 3rd April, 1907, when she was thirteen, the autograph book had been presented to every relative, close family friend or acquaintance who visited the farmhouse tree over the next thirty-plus years. They were expected either to inscribe an entry or, if artistic, to paint or draw a picture if they came to stay for a few days. It contained a rich variety of entries beginning with an acrostic based on her name on the title page –

No excuses to contribute, can I take at any time
Each one asked will be expected to give poetry, prose or rhyme;
Lessons that the wise recorded in their ages past and gone
Lines with jokes and humour mingled, also any hymn or song.
Incidents worth recording, anything you learn or teach.
Enter thoughts on any subject that you find within your reach.

Healthy maxims, charms or physic, parables and proverbs blend,
In it you may show your talents with the use of brush or pen.
Leaves are here provided for you, and no more I need explain
Lose no time but do it quickly for I must not ask again.

Verses were seldom attributed to the famous writers who had first penned them, and it was only when I was older that I realised a great-uncle hadn't thought up the line "There are more things in heaven and earth, Horatio, than are dreamt of in your philosophy", assuming Horatio to be a third cousin I'd never met.

In the pages were a variety of poems, quotations, witty couplets and verses –

> The happiest days in my life
> Were spent in the arms of another man's wife –
> My mother.

> Where is the man who hath the power and skill
> To stem the torrents of a woman's will?
> For if she will, she will, you may depend on't,
> And if she won't, she won't, and there's an end on't.

> Man wants but little here below
> And is not hard to please.
> But every woman that I know
> Wants everything she sees.

> It's not the one that knows the most
> That has the most to say.
> It's not the one that has the most
> Who gives the most away.

> Definition of a kiss

> Something rather dangerous,
> Something rather nice.
> Something rather naughty
> Though it can't be called a vice.
> Some think it wrong.
> All agree its jolly
> Though it don't last long.

My grandfather wrote the following –

A little house well filled
A little farm well tilled
A little wife well willed,
Three great blessings.

The following month his nephew called and wrote –

A bigger house well filled,
A bigger farm well tilled,
A bigger wife well willed,
Three bigger blessings.

Human nature it would seem has always been the same!

You ask me to write in your album
To put something original in,
But there's nothing original in me
Excepting original sin.

The final entry dated 9/12/40 read –

Find tongues in trees
Books in the running brooks.
Sermons in stones
And good in everything.

It was only when I went to college that I realised this came from *As You Like It* and not a local farmer's wife.

Within the pages is the following riddle which I've never been able to crack.

Twice three of us are six of us
And six of us are three
Three of us are five of us
How many can we be?
If this is not sufficient
And you think you'd like some more
Seven of us are five of us
And five of us are four.

E.F. Aug 1914

My aged maiden aunt's recipe book contained a variety of recipes, some of which she tried and found to be successful. Tips gleaned from magazines and handy hints were added to pages containing recipes, handed down through the generations.

Apart from recipes for every type of chutney, pickle, jam, jelly, cake, sponge, pudding, soup and meat dish known to man there were the more exotic, for curing common illnesses and for improving the house –

Cough Mixture

1oz horehound, 1oz coltsfoot, ½oz hyssop, ⅓oz ginger, ½oz liquorice root

Simmer in 2 quarts of water down to 1 quart. Strain and add ½lb of honey, 4oz of rum (medicinal)

Take a wine glass full three times a day or when cough is troublesome. Half quantity for children

Worm Soup

Will remove any kind of worms in children
½oz male fernroot ¼oz of mandrake ½oz wormseed ¼oz tansy ¼oz kousso. All in powder
Add 3 gills of water, boil to 2 gills. Strain and press and then add while hot ½oz tincture of myrrh, ½lb of sugar
A wine glass full in the morning early.

Diarrhoea mixture (never fails)

2 drachma of tincture of catechu. 3ozs of chalk. 1oz aromatic confection
Mix and take one tablespoon as often as required

Carpets are brightened by cornmeal and salt.
Lavender oil will keep off fleas.
Paint on glass is removed by strong hot vinegar.
Lemon juice will improve flavour of scrambled eggs
A dish of charcoal in the larder will keep meat sweet.
Salt will improve flavour of apple sauce
Water and milk will remove flyspots from varnish.

To which I can only add – Attempt any of the above at your risk!

When medicinal recipes had been tried and tested, the concoctions were decanted into glass bottles, and placed next to the pills and tablets prescribed by her doctor.

On a winter's night when her candle was lit, the surface of the oak chest was illuminated and it became a small town of twinkling lights as the flickering flame ricocheted off the glass surfaces. Clear, purple, brown, blue and green glass bottle houses made up the lit streets, while the unlit houses were the white cardboard boxes of various shapes and sizes. Over the town hung a fume-filled fog of candle smoke and the odour of camphor, liniment, Vicks, eardrops and mothballs.

David's aged maiden aunt as a young maiden

Every fortnight a grocer from ten miles away called, took an order over a cup of tea or a glass of cider and delivered it a few days later.

"And don't forget to let him have the old Lucozade bottle back. There's thrupence on each one returned," called out my aged maiden aunt each time he was due.

Every Monday morning a Mars bar was taken out of a brown paper bag and cut into six equal pieces – one for each weekday. Sunday was excluded from the calculation; we all abstained from chocolate on the Sabbath. The slice of Mars bar was usually eaten before her daily afternoon nap.

Lucozade, as well as being a luxury, was considered as nourishing and health-giving – half a tumbler being consumed each afternoon after her nap.

"But I do wish they'd get rid o' they ole bubbles. They blaws me up and give me wind something terrible at times."

Honey was also considered as life-enhancing, as it was "made by God's busiest little workers making God's medicine for us".

She also enjoyed Polo mints. "They without the hole in be much too strong for me. Burns me mouth up. These be just right."

Zubes, Imps, blackcurrant pastilles, Horlicks tablets and barley sugars were also considered medicinal; the latter was considered essential for any journey by car, coach or bus over two miles.

For the everyday common cold, warm blackcurrant juice, diluted with honey and a slice of lemon added, was drunk.

Two other items were also kept on the blanket chest – a hairnet and a tumbler half-filled with water in which her false teeth were stored overnight.

"Wouldn't want to swallow them when I'm asleep," she announced one evening while replenishing her glass at the sink.

"Don't expect you'd want to swallow them when you was awake either," laughed my father.

A withering look blasted the oak tree, and he continued reading the local newspaper without another word.

On the rare occasions when I was granted an audience in the inner sanctum I would step in, after being told to enter, and peer through the gloom. Occasionally she would be knitting, and guided by the demented click, click, clicking of her knitting needles I would make my way towards the seated figure, a blanket over her knees and a shawl over her shoulders.

"Sit down on the side of the bed and tell me what it is that brings you up here."

When she decided that my audience was at an end she would say, "Help yourself to a barley sugar on the way out from the bag on my chest and close the door quietly behind you. Children should be seen if they must, but only occasionally heard."

When my father died suddenly, she was in her bedroom taking her afternoon nap. My mother and I broke the news to her. Putting her head down in her hands she sobbed and sobbed. When her tears had subsided she said, "John was right. He always said that whenever Nell was needed she was forever in her room. And that's where I was when he needed me the most. Whatever'll become of us now?"

The Telephone

THE TELEPHONE HAD recently been installed. Majestic and black, the Bakelite instrument took pride of place on the top of the bookcase next to the family Bible beneath my father's double-barrel shotgun.

One afternoon my aged maiden aunt was walking through kitchen when the phone began ringing. She jumped and hurriedly left the room. Someone else could answer it. My aged maiden aunt was having nothing to do with the new-fangled gadget.

It stopped ringing and she reappeared. "When are you going to use it?" I asked.

She gave me one of her looks I knew so well. "All in good time, my lad. All in good time."

"You could use it to phone God," I said mischievously.

"God doesn't need a telephone, as you well know. We speak to Him in a silent voice. I can't see Him and I can't hear Him. But He sees and hears me. Telephoning God indeed. Whatever will you come out with next?"

I was pondering what she had said when she interrupted my thoughts. "And just you remember what I've told you before. He's always watching you. You can't see Him but He can see you. Whatever you do, wherever you go, He knows all about it."

I recalled what my father had said about the male member of the chapel congregation with the bump at the back of his head which he said was a magic eye. I'd searched for God before, but had had to admit defeat, acknowledging the fact that He was indeed invisible as my aged maiden aunt had said He was.

She interrupted my thoughts again. "The telephone is for an emergency – the doctor or the vet. Occasionally at Christmas to issue an invitation. Anybody in the village, we use our legs and walk. Tuppence to make a telephone call is a lot of money, even though we do save by having a party line."

Logic and the Obvious

MY AGED MAIDEN aunt's bedroom was situated at the top of the front stairs. These were the posh stairs, and were only used by my mother and father, aged maiden aunt, migrating relatives who came south in late summer to stay for a week, and the two hundred tortoiseshell butterflies which hibernated along the stairway walls in a shimmering silk screen during the winter. The front stairs were strictly out of bounds to me, as was my aged maiden aunt's bedroom. Occasionally I could gain an audience with the venerable old lady, if I was on an errand, and to speed my journey I was allowed to run up the front stairs and on reaching her bedroom I had to knock quietly on her door. On those very rare occasions when I was the only one in the farmhouse tree I would grab a tray and slide down the stairs from top to bottom pretending it was winter and I was sliding down one of the fields.

Each afternoon she went up to her room for a couple of hours and this was where my problem lay. I never knew if, when I knocked and when there was no response, my aged maiden aunt was asleep, or whether she was wide awake and had chosen to ignore me, or hadn't heard my knock.

On one occasion when my first gentle tap was ignored I plucked up courage and clenching my hand into a white-knuckle fist gave the comb-varnished door two loud thunder-crack thumps. The response was immediate and the storm broke as her door was wrenched open and she erupted in front of me.

"Well, what are you doing? Is the house on fire? Is it? Is it on fire?"

"N... n... no," I stammered. The logic behind her question totally defeating my young mind, and making me forget the message my mother had asked me to deliver. "I'm doing nothing... I'm doing nothing," I blurted out.

"Seems to me you do a lot of doing nothing. Go outside and do it where you won't disturb me. And don't come up again until there is a fire."

The door was closed and my audience abruptly terminated, leaving me to ponder the hypothetical question that if ever there was a fire, how would I be able to get her attention if I had to knock quietly? And besides, what would be the point of me putting my young life at risk if there was every possibility she wouldn't open the door? Best to wait until she smelled the smoke creeping under her door and she could make a run for it and take a chance.

The image of my aged maiden aunt lifting up her skirt and petticoat and attempting to run down the stairs made me giggle as I walked slowly down the stairs.

"Did you give her my message?" asked my mother when I met her an hour later. I shook my head and told a little white lie, which in the circumstances I considered would be understood by my all-seeing, all-hearing God.

"She was asleep and I didn't want to disturb her."

My mother smiled her knowing smile. "That's all right. I'll go ahead and order a box of matches for her candle anyway. Where would we be without fire?"

I gave her a sheepish smile. Obviously my mother was all-seeing and all-hearing as well.

Money and Even More Logic

MY AGED MAIDEN aunt was busy sewing name tapes on every article of new clothing in readiness for my first term at boarding school at Crediton. "Good job you passed the eleven-plus; at least your mother and father won't have to pay for your learning and your board and keep. You'll miss cream on your cornflakes and fat bacon and mushrooms for breakfast though. And all these clothes cost them an arm and a leg."

At once a picture in my head of my mother and father minus the various limbs attempting to carry out the various farm chores. My father milking the cows with one hand and my mother attempting to roll a pat of butter with only one hand. Next I visualised them hopping around the fields in a vain attempt to catch a hen or round up the herd of cows.

My aged maiden aunt's voice interrupted my thoughts. "Look at all these pairs of trousers. More than is needed." I smiled to myself. If ever I said I wanted anything she would always go "Tut, tut, tut. Need, yes. Want, no". If, when I was with her in a bookshop on market day and I spotted a book I would like and I mentioned it to her, she would say, "Need, yes. Want, no. Plenty of books at home." The same philosophy applied to pocket money. If I dared suggest that thrupence a week was not enough she would tut, tut, tut and say, "There's plenty of things your auntie would like but nobody gives her any pocket money, come to that, let alone a little bit extra."

Her voice disturbed my thoughts. "Two grey flannel suits, a blazer and trousers. More here than your father has had in his lifetime. How can you wear two suits? They must think money grows on trees."

I clenched my right fist in delight. She'd said it. She'd said my favourite saying of hers. In my mind's eye, I conjured up my aged maiden aunt's magic tree which took root and blossomed in my imagination. Growing up into the highest clouds it resembled Jack's beanstalk which we'd seen back in the winter at Barnstaple in the pantomime. And on it fluttered pairs of trousers, books and suits. But the richest crops were the silver coins which jangled in the breeze and the ten-shilling, pound and five-pound notes which cascaded to the grass every time the wind blew. The magic tree sprouted majestically in Lower Orchard and we all harvested the crops, including my aged maiden aunt, and became millionaires and lived happily ever after like Jack, in a huge castle (with a moat) which my father bought. And I bought everything I wanted.

To my delight she then said another of her favourite sayings: "Your auntie isn't made of money either."

A little old lady made entirely of copper and silver coins dressed in clothes made out of five-pound notes left my mind and jingle-jangled her way across front court, the occasional half-crown falling from her and rolling straight into my outstretched open hand.

"We haven't got money to burn even if they have, so you look after these clothes. You won't have Auntie or Mum to put in a little darn if you rip them."

I gasped. Who did she know that burned money? But before I could get my head around it out came another of her monetary maxims: "The love of money is the root of all evil. Not money, we all need money, but the love of it."

The root must be the one belonging to her magic tree. Things were beginning to get difficult to understand. Was this root stretching down to hell because she'd said it was evil, but her voice once again interrupted my thoughts. "And no wasting your pocket money they give you on comics and bubblegum at your posh school, because it'll be your mother and father who'll provide it, for they to give it to you. Just remember a fool and his money are soon parted."

Frowning, I left the room. She'd often referred to me as a little mommick, whatever that was, but never a fool. Besides, how could I be a fool when I'd passed my eleven-plus? Once again her logic had defeated me.

The Epic

Subtitled: Q When is a cinema not a cinema?
 A When it is a brassica.

A VISIT TO the cinema was a rare once-a-year treat if I was lucky.

"We'll have to go," announced my aged maiden aunt excitedly as she sat reading the weekly *Western Times* recently delivered by the baker with our two crusty loaves, a currant loaf and the *Radio Times*. "*The Ten Commandments* is coming to Barnstaple. On at the Regal."

I gave an audible gasp. The Regal was a fantastic cinema with plush velvet seats. Hundreds and hundreds of seats. There was also a gauze curtain which covered the mega-big screen and shimmered in various shades of orange, green or gold as it fell in folds from the ceiling to the floor in the manner of a gigantic multicoloured waterfall. *The Ten Commandments* was a super-duper film, a long one as well.

"Marvellous. Marvellous," she continued. "A wonderful story. One of my favourite parts of the Old Testament. I wonder if they'll show the burning bush, and goodness only knows how they'll get the sea to open back. We'll have to go."

While my aged maiden aunt continued recounting the epic journey out of Egypt in the manner of someone describing a close friend's hiking holiday around the coast of Devon, I gave the forthcoming film careful thought. For us to get to see the epic would be the modern-day equivalent of the exodus from Egypt.

Barnstaple was a good twenty miles away. We didn't possess a car, and it would be impossible to make the bus connection on market day Thursday, the one day of the week when our village was linked to the outside world of South Molton. Even if everything went according to bus-timetable plan, we would probably arrive at the cinema having missed the plague of bursting boils, or the locusts flying in, or the river running with blood, and at worst we would have to leave long before Moses had been given the tablets on the mountain. At least I might see the staff turning into a snake.

But I needn't have worried; my aged maiden aunt had the campaign planned out with precision, right down to the last detail, in the manner of a great general planning a wartime military manoeuvre.

"A bit of luck your auntie and uncle coming to stay next week. They'll be able to take us. A little treat. A run out in their car for all of us. They'll want to go when I tell them all about it."

Auntie and Uncle weren't real relatives; they were the parents of two evacuee sons who had been evacuated to a nearby cottage during the war. My mother had made friends with them, which had remained strong long after the war had ended, and at the end of each summer they drove down from Southend-on-Sea to stay with us for a week. And they brought a big box of sweet juicy eating Conference pears which lasted us for days after they'd gone home again.

The chosen day duly arrived, and after an early cold dinner we set out in our Sunday best, my father having to stay behind because there wasn't room in the car. To see us you'd think we were all going to chapel because my mother, aged maiden aunt and the aunt who wasn't my aunt each wore their chapel hats and gloves.

"I'll pay for all five of us. My treat," my aged maiden aunt said smiling as we entered the foyer.

A tingle of excitement went through me. This was almost as good as my birthday and Christmas Day rolled into one. A pound note was taken from her leather purse, made by a second cousin, and pressed into my hand with the instructions. "You can be grown up and get the tickets. Best seats. And get a small box of chocolates. But remember –" would she say it? Yes – "Auntie isn't made of money and she'd like just a little change."

Tickets and chocolates were purchased and we followed the usherette, who guided us to our seats, her torch illuminating our pathway past those already seated, and we waited for the biblical epic to begin.

The matinée performance was a total success. From the moment we entered the plush interiors, my aged maiden aunt gasped and marvelled at everything that caught her eye. Each new sight being greeted with a gentle smile and a muttered "Well who'd have thought it? Well I never did".

How she enjoyed the soothing wash of violin strings which swept in waves over the auditorium, and I think she would even have forgiven the Pharaoh if he had managed to prevent Moses from reaching the Promised Land, so engrossed was she in the action on the screen and her selection of soft centres.

During the intermission I was dispatched to the area beneath the screen to buy choc ices, dairy cup ripples and a Kia-ora orange drink from the uniformed ice-cream lady with her illuminated tray of goodies.

On the journey home my aged maiden aunt sat in total silence as she relived the afternoon in her mind, and it wasn't until the car pulled up in front court, where we were greeted by my father, that she spoke. "You never saw anything like it. To think I've seen how it all happened – the plagues, the journey, everything. Now I know what Moses looked like and didn't the ole bush burn. Flames up to the ceiling and then the sea split asunder. She chuckled before adding, "Waves went up as high as our chimney. Then wallop. Down they crashed and drowned they ole Egyptians and their carts. Served 'em right."

Shaking her head as if unable to believe all that she had seen, she smiled and continued, "There'll never be another like it. Mind you, I would dearly 'ave loved a cup of tea in the middle when we had that break and you got the ice creams. Must've been all the heat from the desert, I was some dry. 'Tis a marvellous cinema though, and no mistake. No wonder they calls it the Regal. A palace. A real palace."

There was a slight pause before she delivered her final line on the proceedings. "But why is that ole cinema in South Molton, the Savoy, called after a cabbage? Right, I'll go in and boil the kettle."

My aged maiden aunt was a well-contented lady. She had journeyed to the Promised Land and even got change from a pound.

Dairy

THE FARMHOUSE TREE'S L-shaped dairy was a North Pole of a room, its whitewashed walls as bright as January snow glistening in the early-morning sunlight. Here, in winter months my exhaled breath billowed out, rising like a balloon to the ceiling where it hung like the muslin bag used in autumn jelly-making.

The floor was made up of gigantic blue slate flags and in the far corner was a drainage hole where water ran out when the floor was brushed down. Nearby, a mousetrap to catch an unwary night visitor.

Above the comb-varnished door, square panes of coloured glass – blue, red and yellow – which were lit up by sunlight, streaming in through the plain glass square panes above the front door opposite.

Along one long wall, slate shelves on which were placed late-summer fruits – greengages, plums and damsons to be eaten raw or to be transformed into jelly and jam. Later the stored fruits for winter, apples – eaters and cookers for delicious pies, tarts and dumplings. Occasionally a two-legged mouse would sneak in, grab an eating apple and run out again.

There were also stored tins of exotic fruits from sun-filled Commonwealth and foreign climes, apricots, peaches, pears and pineapples, and an assorted cocktail with cherries in. Tins of ham and tongue for an emergency, and Christmas fare. Pride of place was given to a meat safe, its gauze-wire front a barrier against the most devious fly.

In a corner, the butter churn, butter bats and Scotch hands. As my mother churned and made the butter pats she would recite, "Come butter come. David stands by the farmyard gate, waiting for a buttered cake. Come butter come." At the farm sale of 1966 all the butter lots were sold for three shillings (15p).

In another corner opposite the door, my favourite indoor

mechanical appliance, the separator, because it created my favourite food – cream, beautiful cream. But not just ordinary cream. Separated cream. There were certain times of the year when there was a glut of milk and on those days I had cream with every meal. At breakfast a big dollop on my big bowl of cornflakes. For dinner an even bigger dollop on my afters, on whichever fruit pie – gooseberry, plum, blackberry or apple – was the flavour of the day. At teatime, a doorstep slice of crusty bread, delivered weekly by the baker from Bishops Nympton together with a currant loaf and copies of the *Western Times* and the *Radio Times*, smothered with half an inch of cream and golden syrup – thunder and lightning. If I was lucky this would be followed by a big wedge of my mother's freshly baked sponge, opening back the slice to smother the home-made jam filling with a layer of cream.

In June the favourite meal with cream – strawberries. Each half of a strawberry placed in the mouth, slowly sucked letting the cream-and-fruit taste permeate all through. Giving in and biting into the berry.

Our cream was produced in a hand-powered separator mounted on the floor – a Lister cream separator which separated the cream from the milk. Gallons of milk were carefully poured into a large tank on the top of the machine, and a handle was turned on the side of the machine to build up a steady rhythm and momentum. With each turn a bell would ring and when the ringing ceased, the correct speed had been reached for the machine to separate the cream from the milk. This speed had to be maintained as a tap was turned on, to allow the milk to pass through the intricate parts of the separator and for the cream to be separated out. The milk flowed through a series of cones, the cream dripped from a short spout into an enamel basin, and the separated milk through a longer spout into a pail. The drips turned into a steady flow until the tank was empty.

The separated milk was either used as animal feed or was tipped into the stream which flowed through front and back court. My mother and aged maiden aunt were left to disassemble the machine and wash the numerous parts in hot water – an onerous task.

During the separating process I helped my father turn the handle, his hands on mine as we built up the momentum. I was proud to be doing a man's work, but my arms tired long before the bell stopped ringing. I then stood to one side waiting for the first cream dribble and thinking of my next breakfast bowl of cornflakes.

At the farm sale the separator made five shillings (25p), less than an ounce of clotted cream today.

Evolution

IN 1959, HAVING passed the eleven-plus exam, and living over twenty miles away from the nearest day grammar school, the local authority paid for me to attend a boarding school. Although sad to see their little bird fly the nest, my parents and aged maiden aunt were proud of my achievement.

"If you've got brains," said my father, "use 'em and get an easier job than farming for 365 days of every year."

My aged maiden aunt echoed his sentiments. "One with a good pension at the end. Teaching, now that's a good job. Good holidays too. Always want teachers. Mark my words."

Every time I returned for a holiday, or a quarter- or three-quarter-weekend break, she would be waiting, eager to hear of my new experiences at "your posh school", as she termed it.

And I was only too eager to oblige. "At school last week I read a library book about a man called Charles Darwin, Auntie."

Her face broke into a smile. "I've got a book of his. On the middle shelf next to Edgar Wallace. A grand tale with a happy ending. The story of an orphan boy. An imp of a lad. Just like that Jimmy Clitheroe on the wireless. Always getting into scrapes in London. A real scamp."

"He was a naturalist. A botanist," I explained, keen to air my newly acquired knowledge, but mystified by her revelation about the book on the middle shelf.

"You always did like your wild flowers," she continued. "You'd write their names down in a book. Kept them in a jam jar when you was younger. And does your Mr Darwin like wild flowers?"

Nodding, I charged on in all innocence. "He went on a long voyage and wrote books on how the world was made. He says that we all come from apes."

At the mention of prehensile beasts her face became grim.

"Not your auntie!" She exploded from her chair and stormed to kitchen table where she banged her clenched fist on the polished surface. "Stop where you are. How dare you tell fables. Fetch me down the Holy Bible."

Removing the book from the top of the bookcase I placed it in front of her, and found myself transfixed by the withering look I knew so well.

Beneath the glow from the gas mantle she opened the worn cover and, turning to a page *she* knew so well, began to read and read until the words whirled in my head. For several minutes I stood watching the flames dance as she continued reading from the Book of Genesis. At last the Holy Book was closed, and looking me straight in the eye she said, in a voice which defied anyone to contradict her, especially a callow-faced youth, "That's the creation story as written down by God in His good book." She emphasised the words 'good book', paused and then continued, "Not by your so-called Mr Darwin in a tuppenny comic. Now you listen here. God made man. God made woman. God made you and your auntie and your mother and father. Does our Holy Father mention monkeys?"

"No, Auntie," I replied in a sombre tone. "Our Holy Father never mentioned monkeys, apes, baboons or chimpanzees."

Metamorphosising me with another look, she gave full vent, once in her stride, to the pent-up anger deep inside. "How dare you mock the Holy Book. How dare you say that your Aunt Nell comes from a pair of jungle apes. Filthy beasts, monkeys. Dirty habits. Why, you'll be telling me when you come home next that Noah never built the ark, that David never fought Goliath. If that's what they'm teaching you at your so-called posh school then 'tis a pity you ever went there in the first place. Heathen talk. Whatever next? Well, what have you got to say for yourself, my lad?"

Before I had time to reply, she continued in a softer tone. "We'll say no more about it. And I suggest tonight when you say your prayers you ask God's forgiveness. I won't mention it to your mother and father. Enough to drive him to drink."

Shuffling my feet I answered, "Yes, Auntie." The thought that a monkey could drive my father, a Methodist man, through the door of the Masons Arms had a sobering effect on me.

Her voice interrupted my thoughts. "Now off you run. I'll overlook it just this once. Apes and monkeys indeed. Whatever next? Do I look like a monkey? Well do I?"

"No, Auntie," I mumbled.

"What do you say to your auntie then?"

I bowed my head in contrition. "Sorry, Auntie."

Having spluttered my scant apology, I kissed her on her proffered cheek and, feeling suitably chastised, watched as she resumed her seat in the fireside chair muttering inaudible words to herself. A little old lady with a bark far sharper than her pearl-white dentured bite.

The following morning when I walked past the bookcase beneath the gun rack, I noticed an empty space in the middle row of books.

Young Oliver Twist, the imp of a lad, was once again roaming the streets of London. And never again was the author's name mentioned by my aged maiden aunt.

In those few minutes, the nephew had boarded the *Beagle* sailing to new climes and foreign shores, and our relationship altered for ever.

Summer Tar

WHEN THE SUN was a symphony of golden notes which ricocheted off the galvanised iron cart-shed roof, the village was invaded by an alien army.

As I was standing by the front court gate talking to my aged maiden aunt who had just returned from collecting her copy of the *News of the World* from a neighbour, a familiar figure came whizzing down the road towards us on his bike.

After being rude to my aged maiden aunt, who informed him that he would come to a sticky end for being so cheeky, he zoomed off.

Fifteen minutes later, a low grumbling rumble which grew louder and louder. Into sight came a troop of dungaree-uniformed men and their war machines. Suntanned brush- and spade-carrying men to clean the road surface. A huge lorry with roller brushes assisted them. The driver gave me a friendly wave as I stood watching behind the front court gate, and I recognised him as living in the next village.

Next the tarmac tanker sprayed a sheet of hot black steaming liquid across the road, fossilising insects in jet-black tar amber. With a whoosh, a reversing lorry machine-gunned gravel bullets over the boiling tar. Finally the climax. In seismic vibrations which shook up through my summer sandals, the mighty green steamroller. With a toot and a wave from another man who lived nearby, the gigantic machine rolled by, then back, then by again, and then it was gone.

The village road had been conquered, and the army wouldn't return in my childhood. Stepping right up to the gate I breathed in that never to be forgotten summer smell of the tar battle and dipped the toe of my sandal into the tar pool. At that moment I was re-joined by my aged maiden aunt. "You haven't been outside the gate, have you? Only we don't want that sticky mess brought inside."

I answered quite truthfully that I hadn't, and then once again Kenny the Gorilla Harris came cycling into view.

"See that puddle by the wall. Watch this. I'll ride right through it. I bain't afraid of ole tar."

A big smile lit up my aged maiden aunt's face as she whispered, "There'll be trouble now. Mark my words."

With a ring of his bell, and a revving up sound with his lips, Kenny rode his bike into the tar puddle. And there he stayed as his front tyre became stuck in an ooze of black chewing-gum tar.

My aged maiden aunt laughed. "There, Kenny Harris, I've been saying for months that you'd come to a sticky end and I've been proved right."

Kenny gave a gorilla scowl and jumping off his bike yanked at the wheel to free it. As he attempted to do this his sandals became stuck, and it was only with frantic tugs that he managed to free his feet and his wheel.

"Wouldn't stick round if I were you, Kenny," I called through the safety of the bars in the gate.

"You might became a fixture," added my aged maiden aunt.

Kenny remounted and slowly rode off, the black chewing-gum tar strands hanging from his wheel.

From the distance came the final shrill whistle of the steamroller and a blue smoke flag of victory unfurled above the village. Our road had been resurfaced and the fun was over. Summer was coming to an end.

Prayers

ALL HER LIFE she lived for her God, kneeling morning and evening crouched over her patchwork quilt. Bowed head resting on bony hands, her fingers interlocked, her lips silently intoning words at the side of her bed. Her face was the finest vellum, my lips touching the softness. Her eyes a twinkletime of stories which I read as I bounced on her knee.

In old age, the onset of illness. Unable to kneel by her hospital bed, she lay between the crisp white sheets, afraid that her God would desert her. Her fingers trembling, her dry lips quivering as she silently begged His forgiveness. The parchment was yellow and cracked, my lips hesitating, drawing back. Her stories haunting and strange, which I found myself unable to read.

In kitchen, a bowl of fruit cake mix. Her right hand resting on the rim, my right index finger swallow-skimming the surface, her left hand touch-tapping my knuckles. The ice in her eyes quickly thawing, to be replaced by a dance of sunlight. "Go on then. But only one fingerful."

In her rocking chair in the chimney corner, flickering flamelight on the spiralling skin from an apple deftly peeled in a single strip dangling down through the air in a ribbon, silently landing on the red-leaded hearth. Her hand squeezing mine as I joined in her game. "It's the first initial of your girlfriend's name."

In front court the benefactor with her purse, a florin pressed into my outstretched palm for ice creams on the seaside outing. A rejoinder of how I wasn't to spend it all at once. The sprig of leaves on Oakapple Day, her fingers fumbling it into my buttonhole. "Remember to remove it on the stroke of midday."

In my bedroom kneeling on the rag-rug floor. Her hands taking hold of mine, placing them in front of my face, pressing the palms tightly together. Peeping through half-closed eyes I parrot-fashioned rudiments of prayer. "Eyes closed. We're building our tower to God."

Lost moments of childhood glimpsed as I grasped her wrinkled hand, our bond renewed through that simple act of touch. Never before had we been so close as in those fleeting moments. Her voice interrupting my thoughts. "I know you're a man, but you're my little boy. Say a prayer for your auntie tonight."

Her eyes filled with a happy ending, safe in the knowledge that her tower was built on a foundation of rock.

Front Room Branch

LEADING OFF FROM the front hall were the front stairs. Wide enough to slide down on a tray, the high walls were decorated each autumn with a silk screen of over two hundred hibernating tortoiseshell butterflies, small and large. The shimmer-sheet of four hundred gossamer wings tightly closed against the approaching winter. In late spring, when the downstairs windows were thrown open to let in the warmth, the butterflies flew up and left the farmhouse tree for the beech hedgerows and fields.

At the foot of the stairs, to the left of the dairy, was front room with a door which looked almost good enough to eat. Varnished and comb-grained at the turn of the twentieth century, the initials of the craftsman and a date were just visible beneath the top right-hand panel – AH 1906 – his handiwork having remained untouched for over half a century, resulting in the varnish becoming a richer golden brown with each passing decade until it resembled a gigantic slab of my aged maiden aunt's butterscotch.

Front room, the best room reserved for Christmas, Easter, occasionally in summer after the chapel evening service, and for a week in September when two migrating relatives, who weren't really relatives, but the parents of two evacuees in the Second World War and had become friends of my mother and father, came to stay. Uncle Ray and Auntie Lily arrived just as the migrating house martins and swallows were gathering on the telegraph wires, bringing with them bags of home-grown Conference pears and other goodies.

During the summer months thick curtains which brushed the lino floor were pulled tightly across the window alcove, blotting out the summer sunlight which threatened to fade the recently purchased three-piece suite. In winter, dull daylight was allowed to invade, revealing strange damp continents which expanded their boundaries across the wallpaper world during the wet season.

On each side of the early 1950s tiled fireplace, built-in cupboards, the lower sections too damp for keeping china in, were stacked with beech and apple logs. Beech for heat and apple for heat and perfume. In the top cupboards behind glass panel doors, the family collection of china, glass and porcelain. Handed-down heirlooms and wedding gifts.

Pressing my nose into the glass I could glimpse a vast array of china dogs, figurines, tea and dinner services, a mug with the face of William Gladstone on it, a plate celebrating Queen Victoria and the Empire, a moustache cup and saucer, crested Gossware, clear glass, cut glass, green and red glass items.

Too delicate to be used, many of the pieces were inherited. China from past generations, taken out annually on a wet December afternoon and carefully wiped over by my aged maiden aunt.

Unnumbered and uncatalogued, the museum exhibits, each with its own piece of family history, were kept to be taken down, dusted down and handed down through the generations.

In a small wooden box, tucked away from prying eyes in the top corner of the right-hand cabinet, a treasure trove of initialled silver teaspoons, dessertspoons, serving spoons, sugar tongs and napkin rings. Dating from 1757, initials and dates relating to marriages and christenings were inscribed on the handles with hallmarks from Exeter and London. From these artefacts I delved into my family roots and climbed the family tree. Too precious to be tarnished through everyday use these were also taken out annually and unwrapped from their tissue-paper shrouds by the museum curator.

Laid out by the curator on the black oilcloth on kitchen table, initials became names which in turn became relatives as she cleaned, polished and inspected them. Her fingers gently caressing them as she relived past days. A silver collection kept but not displayed, a part of my grandmother's dowry (another item, my great-grandfather's christening spoon), also used at Christmas for the festive chicken dinner and the pudding afters.

Against one wall, a mirrored mahogany sideboard. In one cupboard compartment: glasses, tumblers and my aged maiden aunt's silver tea service. A bottle of Stone's green ginger wine for the Christmas after-dinner toast and for toasts on other festive days. "For they that drop in unexpected, during the twelve days." A bottle of brandy. "Strictly medicinal you understand. Mind you, warms where goes."

In the drawers, linen tablecloths embroidered by my aged maiden aunt and her mother. Matching napkins, crocheted place mats, Christmas tree baubles, tiny coloured wax candles in metal holders, thirty-year-old crêpe paper decorations. Two brown paper bags. One containing a Christening robe, the other a funeral shroud. And right at the bottom of the drawer, packs of photographs and black-edged funeral cards – past guardians of the farmhouse tree and their assembled kith and kin.

Each Christmas a deck of photographs was taken out, shuffled and dealt – the lives of the characters relived around the blazing fire under the pale glow of gaslight and candles. The joker in the pack, the mad-eyed staring uncle whose exploits and life were never discussed, whose life was never relived and whose name was mentioned only in hushed tones, accompanied by a sideways glance in my direction.

Next, the black-ribbon-bound pack of funeral cards, each illustrated with a flower and/or a cross. Exhumed, the names, dates and accompanying verses were read out loud, the cards in many instances being matched with the photographs in bizarre, macabre games of snap and happy families:

"Photographed by C.H. Braund's Studio, Bampton Street, Tiverton. Copies may be had by sending a name and address. The negative for who this print is produced may be enlarged to any size and finished by the new permanent process in oil or water colours."

In my mind's eye, a fleeting image of a sixty-feet-tall giantess towering over the farmhouse tree, as my aged maiden aunt turned the card over to reveal her trump picture card. Her trick-winning card. Her trick-winning queen. A sepia old lady in a long black ground-brushing dress, sitting outside of her castle. A past matriarch, the old maid of the pack in the game of happy families.

"A great-great-aunt, spinster of the parish. Farmed here with two bailiffs and her niece (your great-grandmother) for well over forty years. Died in 1897."

A shuffle through the second pack and an envelope was dealt. I was invited to open it and remove the card. Snap.

"Go on then," said my aged maiden aunt. "Read the verse."

Below black-and-white etched lilies the words –

> Gone from pain and sorrow,
> Gone from toil and care.
> Gone to be with Jesus
> And we hope to meet her there.

A pause. A brief reflection. "Lovely words. Beautiful verse. Real poetry. Eighty-six," she continued as she dabbed her eyes with a handkerchief sporting a hand-embroidered violet in the corner. "Good age, mind you. Well past her allotted span of three-score years and ten."

I waited for the final sentence. Her annual command. "Now if she was alive today she'd be... You tell us."

The mental calculation. My chance to shine. Impress and play my winning ace. "One hundred and forty-five!" I exclaim. The fleeting image of a wrinkle-faced giantess shrivelling up and collapsing into the roof of the farmhouse tree.

A smile from my aged maiden aunt exchanged with my mother and father. "He's some sharp. He'll cut himself one day if he isn't careful. Time for a Chinese fig, a piece of Turkish Delight or a piece of my home-made butterscotch. Christmas is a time for little treats. And then we'll sing some more carols around the piano. I dearly love snaps and reading the verses. Brings 'em all back."

Spread out on the tea trolley, photos and funeral cards relating to the silverware in the treasure chest. My eyes straying to the bags of nuts, the silver-armoured, tissue-wrapped tangerines, the sugared almonds and the other boxes and bags of the once-a-year edible treats.

Tints on Glass, Sepia and Monochrome Prints

IN THE MAHOGANY sideboard drawer, buried deep beneath shrouds of lace cloths and linen serviettes, figures from four generations shared a communal grave. Annually and on special occasions the tomb was opened, the contents exhumed and strewn on the tabletop where fumbling fingers rummaged through the pile.

Tongues resurrected lives. Some stretched a biblical span of three-score years and ten, while others were all too brief. Passed from hand to hand, past lives in the passing are brought to life once again as a loved one lives and breathes. A life re-enacted in a kaleidoscope of memories.

On a thick pile rug a chubby baby gurgles. In life, film developed, but no print from the negative. Teenage sweetheart cuts dashing pose in double-breasted Sunday suit and trilby. In life, tints faded soon after the print was displayed.

A farmer, with sleeves rolled up, pitches summer sheaves into a horse-drawn cart. In life, print soon mounted in a stiff cover album. Here are those destroyed by war's harsh bullet. Kept upright by their loved ones' memories, they stand rigidly to attention in faded khaki, their faces frozen in celluloid smiles. Click of the shutter, click of the safety catch. Two shots, one prolonging, the other ending life.

Framed in the fish-eyed lens of a tear-stained eye they hold their poses and will not age. Snapped when time stood still – a collection of tints on glass, sepia and monochrome prints. Homage paid, the drawer is closed as they are laid to rest once more.

Visiting Gran

WHEN I WAS young there were visits to stay in the terraced town house. The front step regularly scrubbed, the brass strip polished until it shone corn-yellow in the morning sunlight. She was always bustling around, cooking, cleaning, washing, ironing and baking. The retired farmer's wife.

Once, and only once, I asked her age. Frowning she told me it was rude to ask a lady such a question, then, in the same breath informed me that ladies glow, men and boys perspire and only horses sweat. Smiling, she pressed a coin into my hand.

In a cabinet, a fourteen-inch black-and-white TV, the picture flickering because of traffic passing by the door. Sitting side by side on the living-room settee, we watched exotic birds, enjoyed their songs in what she called her cage of sweet delights. She'd tell the tale of how my mother and my grandfather, while he shaved, watched a cuckoo in a hedge sparrow's nest through the farmhouse kitchen window.

One day the birds pecked through the bars, wings flapping furiously, to fly around her neatly ordered house. Their plumage taking on horrific garish hues, their liquid notes discordant, filling her brain with a cacophony of noise.

When I was older my visits were fewer. Alone in her room in the home, 'visited' by her parents in horse-drawn traps and jingles. Listening to their voices in her head, she shrivelled up into herself. One day I did find out her age, but on that peaceful afternoon with a robin singing on a granite cross, there was no proud little lady to admonish me and press a florin into my perspiring palm.

Aerial Combat

SUMMER WAS THE season of the fly. Every day from dawn 'til dusk, the farmhouse tree was filled with an inane buzz of whirring, droning wingbeats. Each day their iridescent, distended blue-green bodies used every inch of available airspace for private flying routines. Their aerial manoeuvres turning each room into a battle zone.

Favourite of their devilish antics involved flitting from jam tart to cream sponge, and out through an open window, across the court to the steaming dungheap. After a brief sojourn spent bathing in a sea of thick brown ichor they returned to the home-baked delicacies. Here, they either dropped bombs in the form of white-dot pinhead egg clusters, or cleaned off their undercarriages. Each of their six legs being lifted in turn over their heads in a tongue-lick of delight.

In amazement, I watched as they flew head first into windows and walls in a ricochet of bodies without damaging themselves. A few however were intent on ending their days by diving head first into a pail of milk in a splutter of flailing limbs and bubbles.

As soon as this happened, war on all flies large and small was declared. Having tolerated their aerial antics with a certain indifference, my aged maiden aunt decided that enough was enough. A visit to the shop in the next village – Knowstone, affectionately known as 'town' because it possessed a church, chapel, pub and post office – resulted in the purchase of a variety of armaments which were supplemented when the mobile ironmongery walk-in lorry pulled up outside the gate. The farmhouse tree was going to be defended against enemy attack.

The weapons were laid out on the table for inspection, and over a cup of tea the two generals planned strategies and a method of campaign. Their artillery consisted of cardboard cut-outs which were suspended from ceiling hooks and were in the shapes of a basket of flowers, a parrot and a pair of lovebirds. Each cut-out was heavily impregnated with a chemical which gave off an odour causing the enemy pilot to be overcome by the fumes. Immediately, the aircraft went out of control, the six wheels spinning madly as it crash-landed belly-up in a bowl of food on the table, where the engines cut out.

The two generals were all for chemical warfare, but these weapons paled into insignificance when placed alongside the main piece of artillery. If by chance the enemy survived the outer ring of chemical cut-outs suspended in various branches of the farmhouse tree, the weapons encountered next ensured their downfall was permanent.

Costing 6d (2½p) the yellow cellophane flypaper was the nuclear bomb of the farmhouse tree arsenal. Removed from its cardboard canister, the two-inch-wide sticky paper ribbon was unrolled with extreme care to its full length of approximately eighteen inches. It was then given pride of place in the centre of the ceiling where it dangled above the dining table. Having set their weapons in strategic positions the two generals poured themselves another cup of tea and helped themselves to their rations – two Jacob's cream crackers each. Arms folded, they then waited for the enemy to fly in.

The aerial defence was soon breached, and the enemy aircraft came to a sticky end, the pilots made giddy from the fumes given off by the suspended cut-out shapes. The two generals nodded their heads in approval and exchanged self-satisfied smiles. Brushing the crumbs from the table they started preparing our one-o'clock dinner.

For the remainder of the summer each farmhouse tree branch was littered with tiny corpses, overcome by the chemical nerve gas. It was cellar, however, our dining room, which was the killing field, the main theatre of war. Each meal was watched over by the supervisory compound eye of the twitching aerial prisoner held captive in the sticky cell. Occasionally an enemy managed to escape, only to plummet legless and wingless into either a bowl of custard or a bowl of stew and dumplings where it sank slowly in a glurp of bubbles.

Whenever an escape took place during a meal, I tried not to giggle as the enemy began to sink without trace into the yellow sea or the brown swamp. Just as it disappeared from view into the ooze, my aged maiden aunt would tut-tut-tut, remove it with her fingers and holding it at arm's length drop it into the china sink where a quick gush of cold water washed it down the plughole. Returning to the table she would spoon off the small area where the plane had crash-landed, wash her hands and spoon, and continue with her meal.

The aerial enemy was being destroyed, the war was being won for another year. By the end of the summer campaign, the yellow flypaper nuclear bomb was almost blue-black with barely a space available for any more approaching aircraft.

Summer was the season of the cordon-bleu fly, and of fly-blown food.

Summer Carnival

THE SUMMER HOLIDAYS were always hot and stretched into infinity as I stepped off the school bus. And in those Corona pop-filled days, a carnival procession paraded through the village and entered the front court or fields of my farmhouse tree.

The first entrant jumped out at me at the break of dawn when I was searching for a willow warbler's nest in the deep hedge trough at the bottom of Lower Mead. The man, but not just any man, raced off across the dewy grass leaving me shaking but knowing that an encounter, such as this, would make me famous for fifteen minutes in my own dinner hour in the school playground. The man, a giant, was a legend in his own lifetime, sleeping beneath the stars or in tallets above the shippens and surviving on casual work as he roared through the villages.

He possessed the strength of a biblical Samson, having pulled machinery stuck in the mud to hard ground with ropes attached around his chest. He could lift a telegraph pole and carry a tree trunk on his shoulders. At the baker's he bought whole fruit cakes, and instead of cutting out a slice devoured the cake by biting huge chunks from it. Occasionally, he would be seen running across a field waving a wet shirt in the air. It was washday and he'd just washed it in the river. At least that was what my mates told me in the boys' lavatory at school. And now I'd seen him, I'd seen him for real.

The second entrant was Nameless, in his patched, string-holding-up-the-trousers suit. Tugging at his forelock he knocked on the front door where he asked for victuals and a billycan of tea. When my mother later discovered that I had briefly let him into the hall while she was filling his can I was told he had left us a legacy as she fumigated the hall.

I was left wondering what a legacy was, and why the tramp had told me never to divulge my name, adding cryptically as he tapped his nose that they were always listening. Who 'they' were I never discovered, but the flea inheritance left me itching for days, and when, the following week at school, I refused to tell the supply teacher my name I was made to stay in for all my playtimes and write out five hundred words.

In those never to be forgotten, one day slipping into the next, golden honey and golden cornsheaf days, I always enjoyed seeing the final two entrants. One feared; the other...

In mid-August a turban-suited gentleman entered the village brandishing a battered brown leather suitcase. Immediately high noon from a Western film descended, and the womenfolk deserted their outdoor chores and took refuge behind roller blinds and patterned curtains.

Once I plucked up courage and opened the front door to the bearded stranger. A cascading silk waterfall of scarves and blouses flowed over the threshold, to be quickly decanted back into his case by the travelling haberdasher Sikh salesman. All doors remained firmly bolted, no wares were sold and he left the parish a sad unwelcomed man.

On the final day of August the gipsy lady, her raucous infectious laughter from the bottom of the village heralding her arrival long before she opened the gate and entered our front court. In her wicker basket, sprigs of lucky white heather, tea cloths and home-made wooden clothes pegs. But it wasn't her basket of wares which fascinated and held me spellbound. Beneath her floral patterned voluminous summer frock were what I decided could only be two Christmas party balloons, which bobbed up and down as she laughed. But why, I asked myself, should she have Christmas party balloons hidden under her frock in the summer?

When asked to cross her palm with silver, my aged maiden aunt smiled and informed her that the tall dark stranger had passed through the previous week, but hadn't crossed the threshold. My mother also added that we'd been on a journey as well, because it had been the Methodist Sunday school outing a fortnight before.

The hidden Christmas balloons bobbed so violently that two buttons popped open, and in that instant the childhood summer holiday came to an end for ever.

Hay Harvest

HIGHER MEAD AND Lower Mead were our hayfields. In total about four acres with numerous species of grasses including Meadow Foxtail, Dog's-tail, Sheep's Fescue, Timothy and Sweet Vernal. In Sheep's Fescue alone there are approximately one and a half million seeds to every pound of weight. Flowers included red and white clover, daisy, orchid, lady's smock, trefoil and yarrow. They grew in poor soil, fed only by cow dung which had been spread in the autumn, and would not have survived in today's nitrogen-fed fields. At the edge of Higher Mead by the hay shed, there was always a bed of fragrant chamomile.

Around Derby Day, even though my father did not harvest with tractor-drawn machinery, he was always the first to make hay. He listened extra carefully to the wireless weather forecasts, tapping his barometer with an extra fervour as I listened for the words "Goin' up, set fair for a few days", and completed his ritual in the pound house. Here he checked the piece of seaweed, which I had brought home on the coach on the Sunday school summer outing to the seaside, and which was hanging above the cider press next to the hogshead barrels. If it was dry, the hay harvest could begin.

David's mum and dad, proud parents with little David in June 1948, in Lower Mead during the hay harvest

Cut into swathes on the first morning with the mowing machine, it was turned with the hay turner over the next couple of days and carried on the third or fourth. The best hay came from grass which had flowered, and before it had set seed, carried before the stalks had become brittle and brown. In this way vitamins were preserved, less sap had evaporated and the crop was heavier for harvesting.

Once the top of the swathe had dried it was turned two or three times, and when my father was certain it was dry enough to carry and would not combust in the stack it was raked into windrows with the iron horse rake. Higher Mead was then carried with the horse sweep which swept the hay back to the hay shed. Hay in Lower Mead was brought in with the horse and long cart.

The long cart was my favourite farm implement which was stored in the open linhay next to the butt-cart opposite the farmhouse at the top of front court. Crafted before the beginning of the First World War in the carpenter's shop opposite, it had taken several weeks to build and consisted of an oak framework, a floor and wheel hubs of elm and spokes and shafts of ash. It had cost approximately £18 and was used for hauling hay, corn sheaves, sacks and sticks when a hedge had been laid. When it was sold in the farm sale in 1966 it made half a crown (12½p).

That never to be forgotten, first-time ride on the final load with the instruction to hold on tight, as the first dew of twilight was damping the air. Exhilarating, frightening and sensuous, my small hands gripping the rope which held the hay between the lades, my knuckles white.

Lying out full length, flying above my farm's and fields' world. Head down, face buried in the hay stalks, my nostrils soaking in the scents of the dried grasses and flowers as they pressed into my face, the fragrances mingling with chamomile crushed by hoof and wheel. Honeysuckle with the first twilight moths fluttering over the flowers. Petals of the dog rose, pink and white falling into the hedge troughs. And the leaves of overhanging beech branches brushing my back.

To see and feel nothing except the three-day-dry stalks. Hearing only the sound of heavy hoofs, the jangle of harness, wheel stocks turning and iron-rimmed wheels jolting over ruts and pits in that first, never to be recaptured experience.

The load lurching and swaying beneath me, apprehension in the pit of my stomach. Approaching the hay shed, daring to sit up and take a look around, the feelings of fear disappearing, a smile filling my face. "Whoa, boy." Coming to a halt. The pause. A deep breath before sliding down the side of the load and into my father's safe arms. Crop and boy safely gathered in.

Our octogenarian farming neighbour helped out and my father reciprocated when he made his hay. He either pitched hay into the cart or he would tread and make the stack in the hay shed. Here, at the end of the harvest, the end of the day when the hay shed was almost full with the crop only a few feet from the galvanised iron roof, the heat was oven-hot and sweat poured from the forehead of the last man treading the stack.

Home bakes and bottles of tea, hot and cold, were brought out by my mother and aged maiden aunt for a feast drenched with the scent of hay and crushed chamomile, but not before Charlie the carthorse had been tended to. I helped out at the harvest by turning somersaults and cartwheels and pretending to be a farmer.

The Cider Bottle

IN THE RABBIT burrow in the far hedge of Higher Mead a glimpse of sunlight glinting on glass. A large brown eye gleaming in the blackness. A bottle, but no ordinary bottle. The cider bottle for those helping my father with the hay harvest. Hidden in a cool spot away from young prying eyes.

Pulling it out I held it up. Half full. I twisted off the rubber stopper and took a sniff. Suddenly my two imaginary friends appeared from nowhere and dared me to have a swig. "Go on," said Jim.

"Yeah, go on. It won't hurt you," echoed Derek.

Sitting down and putting it to my lips I took a long draught, pretending I was drinking my third-of-a-pint bottle of playtime milk without a straw when my teacher wasn't looking. The liquid from the brown bottle didn't taste as good as the cider straight from the apples when they'd just been pressed. I took another long drink, replaced the stopper and pushed the bottle back down the hole.

I stood up, and without warning my legs went from under me and I collapsed in an invisible tangle of twisted puppet-string limbs. My eyes crossed, my head lolled from side to side and all I wanted to do was giggle.

Crawling on all fours I burrowed into a hay pook. Once inside I began to dig my way through to the other side.

I blinked in the sunlight, and looked around for Jim and Derek, but they'd done their usual vanishing trick. Not for the first time they'd disappeared off the face of the earth at the first sign of trouble. Suddenly the view began to change. The harvesters seemed to double and, as I blinked, the second set merged back into the first. The hay shed began leaning over to one side and the beech trees rose up, only to drop back to the ground.

For the next couple of minutes I was transformed into a wizard, a magician, with powers of cosmic proportions. I could double the number of men harvesting hay with rakes and forks without saying the magic word Abracadabra. I could even make the sun bounce up and down across the sky like a gigantic rubber ball, and all through taking a couple of swigs from the harvest cider bottle. I could create a nightmare landscape.

Standing up to get a better view of my alien world, I immediately fell back into the hay, the strands pricking my bare legs. There was no pain from my fall. I stood up, only to fall back once more, laughing uncontrollably.

I suddenly felt very tired. I yawned a deep gaping yawn and rolled over and over on a beach of drying hay. The sea-sky washed over me and I drowned. As I fell asleep my aged maiden Methodist aunt's words filled my head: "Rots the body, rots the soul. Only for the heathen men."

Later, when I woke up, my bare arms and legs were stinging from the sun's rays and my bum was sore from when I'd fallen down. Rising unsteadily I ambled back to the farmhouse tree. "You're growing up," said Jim as he and my other imaginary friend re-joined me

"Becoming a man," echoed Derek.

If growing up is this painful I don't think I'll bother becoming a man, I thought to myself. All I wanted was water and gallons of it. In future I was sticking to fizzy Corona pop.

The following autumn when I was helping my father press the apples, he looked across at our octogenarian farming neighbour who was building the cheese, and winked. "A good drink for harvest time."

And then he looked at me and gave me his knowing look. I tried in vain not to blush.

The Once-a-Year Treat

WHEN I WAS a little tacker in the 1950s the Methodist chapel was the scourge of my young life. Dedicated in 1927, it was "built with bricks bought by our brothers and sisters", announced the lay preacher one Sunday. Why he was called a lay preacher, when he always stood up to preach, I never discovered; my question met by a shake of my aged maiden aunt's head: "Whatever will you ask next?"

As we walked home across Knowstone Moor and through Roachill my aged maiden aunt pointed out the spot where the original chapel, a wooden hut, had first been located. "Why did only brothers and sisters buy bricks?" I asked in all innocence. "Why not mothers and fathers and aunts and uncles?"

Mum, Dad and my aged maiden aunt exchanged their knowing glances, and my aged maiden aunt replied cryptically, "But they did."

Each Sunday I made the unwilling walk to Sunday school past summer hedges laden with raspberries red and yellow. Past the Masons Arms, crossing to the other side of the road to avoid the den of iniquity. Where, according to my aged maiden aunt, went only men who had nothing better to do of a night and ladies who were no better than they should be. Where, according to a mate, who had dared to look through a window, the men drank out of gert glasses the size of jugs and the ladies drank from funny-shaped glasses in which they had cherries stuck on the end of lollypop sticks. He added they also crooked their little fingers when drinking. I had another Methodist aunt who crooked her finger when drinking her tea. Perhaps she went into the den of iniquity when it was dark and she thought no-one was looking.

Me and my imaginary mates had dens, one in the hay tallet and another behind the 'ood rick in back court. We drank Corona pop and we never had any iniquity. When I asked my aged maiden aunt where I could get some, and whether she thought I would like it, she tut-tut-tutted and said, "Whatever will you come out with next?" Then she shook her head and walked away leaving me none the wiser. The only time I was allowed to be close to the Masons Arms was when I went with Dad to watch the Dulverton foxhounds meet.

Past the old schoolyard and the village shop, the front wall adorned with enamel advertising signs. Inside, glass jars with sherbet lemons, pear drops, chocolate buttons and wrapped barley sugars purchased by my aged maiden aunt: "Moreish and good for a journey."

And what a once-a-year magical journey it was in Venner's deluxe coach, boarded first by my elders and betters in mothball-scented Sunday best suits. The Sunday school summer outing treat trip to the seaside. A reward for reciting a recitation on Anniversary Sunday. A mass exodus from our tiny village.

I was awake long before the cock-crowing sun had risen from his eastern perch, and as soon as the feather-beams of warmth had tickled my chin I was tumbling out of my brass-and-iron double bed, stumbling over my po and fumbling into my red-and-white check short-sleeved summer shirt, grey flannel shorts, white ankle socks and sandals. Downstairs breaking into my Fort Knox blue-and-yellow plastic moneybox. A mountain of coins amounting to five pounds, fourteen shillings and sixpence-ha'penny (£5·73). "Back in the box with all of it except for half a crown..." (12½p) instructed my bank manager mother.

To which my aged maiden aunt added, "Put it in the leather purse Priscilla made especially for you. Don't lose it and remember a fool and his money are soon parted. And we'll put that ship ha'penny in the cardboard box with the others."

The dreaded ship ha'penny. An ordinary halfpenny piece, but embossed with the *Golden Hind* on the tail-side. Worth only one four hundred and eightieth of a pound it still bought two blackjacks. Whenever I received money from an aged relative in exchange for a kiss on a proffered check, caked in powder, or change from spending birthday and Christmas present money, it was checked by my aged maiden aunt. "Here's one!" she'd exclaim, barely containing her excitement.

Stored in a box which had once been a home to her new dentures, I collected them and once a month grudgingly handed them over to a Sunday school teacher great-aunt who totalled them up and put the number against my name in her notebook. I glowered as she announced, "The London Missionary Society *will* be pleased." When I'd collected a certain number, a coloured paper disc was licked and stuck on a large certificate and when all of the empty circles had been filled with coloured discs I was presented with it.

One summer on the annual treat outing, my aged maiden aunt pointed out to sea. "That's where all your ship ha'pennies go. They sail across the waves to help the little heathen children find God." At eight my geography was very limited but I knew which country was just across from Ilfracombe. Why were Welsh children heathens, and did God live in a coalmine? Yet again her logic had defeated me.

But never her kindness as she always gave me a silver coin worth more than the ha'pennies placed in her denture box.

The coach was a green-and-yellow magic carpet whisking us off to a sun-filled, sand-filled exotic land. Sitting behind my mum and dad wishing I could be at the back. Next to me my aged maiden aunt recounting tales of char-à-banc trips in the good old days, from an age long past when she was young. "We'll suck a barley sugar. Stop us having travel sickness."

"Will we see monsters and mermaids, Auntie? Will we?"

My question met with a strange look, and a shake of her head.

There was always a boy or girl who hadn't had a barley sugar and was sick over their new summer sandals.

"Will we soon be there, Auntie? Will we? Will we?"

My question greeted with "You be patient. Everything comes to him who waits".

At last the magic carpet landed, and there stretching as far as I could see, the deep blue shimmering sea. And everywhere lobster-red men, claw in arm with pink-fleshed ladies. Strutting lads in sailor suits. Charles Atlas men with hearts and swallows tattooed on arms and chests.

Stepping off the magic carpet, a shiny shilling pressed into my palm by a Sunday school great-aunt for regular and punctual attendance.

"Aren't you the lucky boy?" said my aged maiden aunt. "Put it in your purse and don't fritter it away."

Making our way to the beach. "This'll do us," she continued. "Out of the wind and away from the din and rumpus of that ole pier."

Changing into my bathing trunks behind a bath towel held up by my mum and aged maiden aunt. Rushing down to the water's edge. Falling forwards. A paddle and a piddle in the sea. The pee as quiet as the one in 'pneumonia' in the end-of-term spelling test. All around me ladies in party floral frocks rolled up and tucked into pink voluminous knickers, men with trousers rolled up to their knees, their stocking suspenders stuffed in pockets.

Taken out of blue-lidded sandwich tins, home-cured ham sandwiches soon becoming sand-speckled. A gulp of Corona pop followed by a belch. My father about to speak, stopped by a frown from Mum and Aunt. Sandcastle building and then the words I'd been waiting to hear. "We'll go to the pier now, while Auntie has a little nap."

Quickly walking across the sand leaving my aged maiden aunt knotting a handkerchief to ward off the sun. Past the red-and-white-striped "That's the way to do it" Punch and Judy tent. Along the promenade and into the slot-machine land.

Pennies rolling over cash-squared boards, always landing on the thick black lines between the winning shilling and half-crown squares. Six times I placed a penny in the slot and six times I worked the lever to work the crane and six times I nearly won the star-prize watch, only to see it drop it from the jaws and back down into the sawdust-strewn floor tantalisingly close to the hatch and my eagerly grasping fingers.

Leaving my magic end-of-the-rainbow land, having found no crock of gold but having made a sailor puppet in a glass case bob to and fro with loud guffaws of laughter. Leaving with my unzipped purse almost empty and my aged maiden aunt's words about a fool and his money ringing in my ears. Yet again she was right. Walking slowly back to the beach behind Mum and Dad, pausing to look through a café window. There behind the glass the biggest, bestest, most ginormous edible delight, with pears from New Zealand, peaches from South Africa, pineapples from the Gold Coast, syrup-sweet and golden, slipping and sliding into every nook and cranny between the strawberry, chocolate and vanilla ice-cream scoops in the tall glass dish. Between two gigantic wafers embedded in the top of the crown, a red ruby-sized glass alley marble – the biggest cherry ever seen, even bigger than the one on the Sunday school Anniversary Treat Tea meringue.

Licking my lips I pressed my nose against the glass wishing I hadn't frittered my money away. Wishing I could afford the knickerbocker yum-yum, pig's-bum yummy glory. Instead, a stick of rock with Teignmouth stamped on the end. Sucking and sucking. Breaking it in half, and yes, the letters went right through.

At the end of the Sunday school surf-spangled summer outing trip I boarded the magic carpet and sat gloating over my treasures: a piece of seaweed to hang in back kitchen or the pound house, my home-made barometer – damp for rain, dry for sun – a selection of pebbles, a gull's feather, and my richest treasure of all...

Meanwhile, in my mind, imagining the taste of that knickerbocker glory.

Stopping off at Exeter for fish and chips wrapped in yesterday's *Western Morning News*. "Never taste better than when eaten out of newspaper," said Dad.

"Greasy ole things," replied my aged maiden aunt, "but moreish. And look, a page from the *Western Morning News* with the wills on. Might be someone we know."

A sing-song: "Oh, we do like to be beside the seaside...", "Ten green bottles..." The driver's cap passed around and filled with coins. Another song: "For he's a jolly good fellow..." Trying to stay awake. Finding myself being half carried into my farmhouse tree. "And I've still got seven cows to milk, because they won't milk themselves," said Dad.

"Make sure you say your prayers," said my aged maiden aunt as I climbed the wooden hill to Bedfordshire.

"And I'll be up to tuck you in," added Mum.

Kneeling on my rag rug, words spoken silently, concluding with "And thank you, God, for a super day and making the sun shine. And please, God, make the next three hundred and sixty-five days go quickly, and I promise I'll be good and please make it be Teignmouth again with the pier. Amen".

Lying in bed with my richest treasure: a saucer-sized seashell pressed to my ear. Listening to the sound of the waves lap-lap-lapping in far-off magic-carpet land. Listening...

Clocks and the Summer Outing Clock

CLOCKS AND POCKET watches always fascinated me as a young boy. Every farmhouse had a chime of clocks in every room and men on market days and Sundays often had gold or silver hunters in waistcoat pockets, the chains stretching across the chest under which were often corpulent stomachs.

Farmhouse clocks came in a variety of cases – slate, wooden, marble, long and short. The grandfather clock's chimes were loud and quick but the tick, tock, tick of the Colonial clock in my mother and father's bedroom was sleep-inducing. A great-aunt and -uncle possessed a seven-feet-tall grandfather clock which wasn't wound up daily with chains (on which was attached an iron weight) but with a small handle inserted into the face.

My father had a dry joke concerning clocks which he told me on an annual basis. "What's the worst time to catch a train at East Anstey?" Shrugging my shoulders I would join in his fun by pretending not to know the answer. His smile: "Twelve fifty because it's ten to one if you catch it." His annual explanation with regard to betting odds.

On one Sunday school summer outing I lost my heart to the finest example of horology I'd ever seen. All other clocks ran down, never to go again after I'd witnessed the mighty edifice on Paignton promenade. Towering well over twenty feet above me and painted blue and white with doors, tubes, towers and turrets. Standing with my mother, father and aged maiden aunt I watched open-mouthed as the hands on the face approached the hour, and a mechanical extravaganza began to unfold. I stood entranced as, in front of my popping-out-on-stalk eyes, creatures and characters performed magical delights.

In a whirl of clanks a menagerie appeared through open doors and chimneys. A zookeeper rose up from under an umbrella, ringing a hand bell followed by two doors opening to reveal a pair of toucans pecking at a tree trunk. Next, a roundabout with marionettes opened out above the clock face, and an ostrich appeared from the top of a chimney. Finally the Mad Hatter popped up from a smaller tower and caught fish with a rod and line.

The clock struck eleven and one by one in reverse order the creatures and characters folded back into it until only the zookeeper remained, and then he too was lost from view.

As the alcohol-advertising spectacle ended, my aged maiden Methodist aunt tut-tut-tutted, shook her head and moved me along the promenade. Today in my memory, time stands still as I recall that morning, and five lost minutes of childhood are glimpsed again as I see the face of Guinness Festival Clock.

The Final Load

THE HAYFIELD EACH June was a shimmer of green waves, white with crashing surf, clover, daisies cresting the sea, ripening. That year the twilight, grey as mist, rolled across the still hayfield sea just as the final load lurched through the gateway. The old grey timbers of the shirehorse-drawn galleon creaking and groaning.

Spray hung on the air, wave upon wave upon wave. Chamomile, honeysuckle, meadowsweet and briar, each incense-sweet. Stacked on the quay, cargo from the voyages. The hay shed full.

The implement shed was a dark shadowland, day merging with the night, my father closing the galvanised door. The machinery, mower, turner and rake oiled and locked away. By the wall a scythe, its blade waiting to be honed; the final harvest.

Six Fields of the Farmhouse Tree

Lanefield

COATED IN MUD and dung chainmail they haul armoured bodies through Nature's war-torn landscape. With an oozing squelch of sludge and slime, sucking each leg free from the mire, weary and battle-worn they fight the elements. A slurry swamp of steers.

Bull's Mead

Green, black and white waves lapping swish-swash-swish over the sodden grass. Lift, plume, coil into a waterspout. Spiral on wind. Cone rising higher, tumbling towards the next grass continent. Field awash under a flood of pewits.

Higher Mead

Pulling the cart was a lumbering of strength. Heaving and straining, plodding hoof, head bowed. The creaking of wooden axle and hub. Iron rumble through pothole and rut, and the ground dust-dry.

The ton load lurching to the left and the right. Wisps in a straggle on beech branch and bramble. Swift wings scything the evening sky.

Pitchforks thrusting the air and the rick high. Final act in the annual ritual.

An oil slick of sweat staining the coat, flecking the flanks in foam. And the horse piss in a gush steamed, leaving a froth pool on the grass. Seconds later, small bubbles still bursting. In the hedges a twist of dog rose and honeysuckle. Underfoot the crush of chamomile. And everywhere hay, the scent intoxicating. Flutter of bat and it was no longer day. First dew of dusk and the twilight startling us.

Higher Down

Poppy, daisy and cornflower fluttering flaglike in the morning breeze, the fabric flimsy. The day unfurling in a corn shimmer-sheet. Stutter of clicking binder blades as I follow my father terrierlike, imitating him. Six sheaves in a stook. My arms, stalk-scratched and sun-scorched.

Lower Orchard

They grew in a gnarled twist of latticework. Nest clumps of lichen coating the branches. And the scolding holm-screech, a screaming saw blade serrating the air into jagged chunks. Through the foliage, a glimpse of fingertips eagerly grasping the first taste of autumn. The skins pockmarked. The anticipation flesh-sweet.

West Moory Mead

A clenched fist in a velvet boxing glove punches its way through the earth and grass, surprising the dawn. Driving summer from the ring, the first mushroom.

The Dungheap and the Mushrooms

IF THE GARDEN and orchards provided us with a variety of fruit and vegetables, and our seven cows gave us milk, butter and separated cream, it was the dungheap which provided sustenance for the soil and the mowing fields. "The cows'll be getting their own back in winter when they eat the hay," laughed my father as he flung a pick-load of dung over the grass.

Dung-spreading days were fun. Charlie the shirehorse backed up the butt-cart to the gigantic dungheap at the bottom of back court and next to the bull's linhay. My father filled it with the straw-encrusted dung and then Charlie pulled the load across to Higher Mead. Here my father pulled it out from the cart into equally spaced mounds with a specially designed dung pick, Charlie being controlled from the rear of the cart with "Move on", "Whoa" and "Back up".

At the end of the afternoon with the dungheap dug out, the cart was pulled home where it was swilled out with water from the stream running through front court, and returned to the open-fronted linhay.

Next day, with a long-handled five-prong pick my father spread the dung across the field to be broken down by the elements and the flock of starlings which always flew in during this period.

Once, the dungheap in the manner of Mount Vesuvius erupted, spewing out a molten lava of wriggling baby grass snakes from eggs which had been laid in the heat of the heap. Nearby Rhode Island Reds descended at speed and quickly devoured some of the snakes.

On another occasion in late August, horse mushrooms mysteriously heaved their way to the surface whereafter they were fried with bread and fat bacon in a sizzle of grease. Ten minutes later they were quickly devoured for breakfast.

The following week I was dispatched at seven o'clock in the morning to go and forage nearby fields for more bounty. But I had been beaten to it in our neighbouring farmer's fields. However, I was not to be defeated and half an hour later I emptied my satchel onto the cellar table where the sideplate-sized mushrooms were greeted with delight by my aged maiden aunt who set to immediately to peel them. "My, you have done well. We won't let anyone know where these came from, but where did you get them?"

When I revealed that I'd picked them in the churchyard her demeanour changed. "From the churchyard indeed. Whatever next? You don't know where they've come from. Take them out to the dungheap."

As I tipped them into the heap I was mystified – what did Auntie mean when she had said "You don't know where they've come from"? I knew where they'd come from and so did she because I'd just told her. Yet again her logic had defeated me.

Annually at mushroom time Dad would ask me his riddle – "What's the smallest room you can find?"

I'd pretend not to know the answer.

"A mushroom," he'd tell me with a smile, "because there's not *much* room inside."

Threshing Days

A HIGHLIGHT OF those bronze floating-leaf days was the arrival in the village of the Murch Bros threshing convoy. With no beating drum to herald its arrival it entered the village when I was asleep. Under the cover of darkness it took up its position beneath the beech tree canopy in the rickyard of a neighbouring farm.

Bellows of rage from the mythical creature of my bedtime-story and nightmare-filled sleep ringing through the air. An angry rhythmical throbbing, and the stench of fiery sulphurous breath. Like the warriors of old, two farm workers standing on its back thrusting sword-blade pitchforks into its back.

"A monster of a machine," boasted the foreman when he caught me skulking behind the bole of the biggest beech tree. As I gazed open-mouthed, he named the parts – "Creeper, blower, belt and drum. Smutters, straw shakers, sieve and spout. Collecting board, riddle and shut-off lid." Anatomically dissected, my salmon-pink and bright blue creature from its cave lair seven leagues away lost its magical sinews, wings and scales. Stripped down to iron and wood it became once again the thresher from nearby Umberleigh.

At the end of the day, their bounty regained, they pulled a tarpaulin sheet over it and hauled it away. Stacked against the barnyard wall, my dragon hoard of golden treasure. Two-hundredweight rough-spun hessian sacks to be carried on bent backs up stone steps to the granary. And how I enjoyed the tactile sensation of the newly minted gold-coin grains trickling through my fingers.

Time-Travelling

VISITS TO MY great-aunt were profitable excursions. Each time I left the venerable lady she would press a coin into my hand, fold my fingers over it and tell me it was a shiny new florin recently minted and that I was to put it in my money box.

From the age of five it was always a florin. Not a penny more, not a penny less. Gran also gave me two shillings when I visited her, until...

My mother, like many other children growing up in the early part of the last century, was 'farmed out' to live with another relative. In my mother's case she left the family farm at a young age, when her baby sister was born, to go and live with her father's sister and her husband on their farm six miles away.

In the early 1930s my mother married a farmer whose farm was only three miles away from her foster farm. Twice a year in the early to mid-'50s, when I was around seven, we cycled to their farmhouse. The visits taking place during my summer holiday and near Christmas.

A fatted calf was killed literally, and we feasted on roast sirloin, Yorkshire puddings and fresh vegetables from their garden. Afters was always home-made thick custard poured over a spotted-dick pudding crammed full of spots.

After the meal we sat around a roaring beech fire if it was Christmas, with my great-uncle seeing it as his duty to find out how well his great-nephew was progressing in his arithmetical studies. For the next fifteen minutes I was bombarded and bamboozled by a barrage of mathematical cannon-shots.

Puzzles which involved a hen and a half killing a cat and a half, while a rat and a half were laying an egg and a half in a day and a half. Great Uncle's conundra were much worse than the sums chalked up on the blackboard in school which involved a large iron water tank, five men with scythes, a half-inch-diameter pipe, a ten-acre field of grass, one hundred cubic gallons of water, two days, eight and a half minutes and one man and his dog.

As long as Great Uncle's hens were laying eggs and his farm cats were killing rats in the granary, I couldn't understand why anyone would be interested in how long it all took.

Apart from not being able to solve his problems I couldn't even understand them. How could half a hen lay half an egg and how could half a cat kill half a rat? What comprised half an egg? Was it the white or was it the yolk? And which half of the rat did the half a cat kill? The half of the cat doing the killing obviously being the head half.

When I questioned him about my dilemma, he replied that the menagerie of cats, rats and hens weren't real but imaginary ones. This only magnified the problem in my young head. How could imaginary hens, no matter whether they were whole or half hens, lay whole or half eggs? And how could imaginary half-cats kill unreal half- and whole rats? These were foul problems (or even fowl problems!).

When all of the eggs had been collected, the dead rats buried in the dungheap and the numerous other riddles solved, my mother would glance at the grandfather clock's brass face, smile and look at her wristwatch. Looking at any clock in my great-uncle's farmhouse between the end of October and the end of March was as pointless an exercise as attempting to solve his conundra. On his farm the grandfather clock, the black slate clock, the pocket watch and the wristwatch were always wrong for approximately five months of the year. On his farm it was always Summer Time. Even in the coldest months when there were six-feet-high snowdrifts against the field hedges, it was Summer Time. When everyone else put their clocks back, his metal hands remained rooted firmly in the future. For five months the isolated North Devon farmstead, approached by a half-mile rutted cart track, was a whole hour ahead of the rest of the country. A fact he relished.

"There's no-one ahead of your uncle and auntie," he announced, grinning broadly, "and that includes the queen."

Our afternoon visit concluded with my great-uncle's parlour trick, when he demonstrated his dexterity with hand–eye co-ordination with a pile of coins. Balancing the copper pennies on his right elbow he flicked his arm and caught the falling edifice in his right hand without a brick hitting the stone floor.

The pile was passed to my great-aunt who, acting as auditor, counted the coins announcing there were twenty-four. There were always twenty-four. Never twenty-three. Never twenty-five. Smiles were exchanged between the old couple which acted as a signal for my great-aunt to take out her purse from the drawer in the sideboard and remove a coin from it.

"There we are. A shiny new florin. Not as heavy as twenty-four pennies. But you must save it, mind." Always two shillings and always the same words about weight and not spending it.

On the following market day Thursday, my mother and I would

catch the weekly market day Western National bus to South Molton to visit Gran and Grandad. The visit to Gran's sister-in-law was discussed, and at the end of the conversation a two-shilling piece was placed in my hand with the words "Save it. Don't go wasting it".

A rift occurred in the family which led to my grandparents and great-uncle and great-aunt not being on speaking terms. Most farming families have feuds which invariable centre around money, land or wills or a combination of all three. Great Uncle's dispute came about when they sold their farm and moved twenty miles to a small hamlet near Tiverton where Great Aunt's bachelor brother owned a farm. His housekeeper had recently died and Great Aunt decided that they should look after him. This move ensured that they would inherit the farm and my grandfather and grandmother wouldn't see a penny.

Our first visit to see them, after the falling-out, took place in October. The fortnightly Devon General bus dropped us at Tiverton where we were met by their daughter who drove us back to the farm.

As soon as we had finished our roast dinner, a fatted lamb having been killed, my educational progress was once again put under the microscope. If I had hoped that a new great-uncle would mean the end of the conundrum ritual, I was to be sadly disappointed. The attack was now double-barrelled.

My new great-uncle began the assault by removing a small sheet of folded-up paper from the button tin kept on top of the Welsh dresser. Unfolding it he passed it to me indicating that I should read it out loud. I gave a silent gulp. As far as I was concerned it could have been written in a foreign language. I could barely understand any of it as I stuttered my way down through the page.

"The female of the bovine genus is a beneficent mammal. This ruminant quadruped is possessed of corneous protuberances projecting from her occiput. Her vision is binocular and she yields an edible nutritious lacteal exudation. She is herbivorous, assimilating her food in both the succulent and exsiccated state. Some of them chromatically correspond to the seventh colour of the spectrum and they are endowed with caudal appendages of exaggerated longitudinality. What am I?"

Shrugging my shoulders I handed back the piece of paper which was placed on the table.

Both men chuckled and my new great-uncle informed me that he was sure that I would have known the answer, bearing in mind that I was a farmer's son and well-educated. Too well-educated, to his way of thinking. Brawn not brains made for a hard-working farmer, to his way of thinking.

It was now his brother-in-law's turn to launch an attack.

"Two lookers. Two crookers. Four stiff standers, four dilly danglers and a swish-about. What am I?"

My heart sank. More mental torture. I gave his words long and careful thought. Suddenly in a flash it came to me. The answer had to be...

I called out the word and both men laughed and nodded. My new great-uncle then informed me that the answer to his problem was the same.

I nodded, none the wiser, hoping that he would enlighten me, but the sheet was folded up and replaced in the tin.

More anecdotes and riddles followed, and then it was time for more cups of tea. My two uncles having concoctions which they called tea sop. Their two bowls had pieces of bread broken into them onto which was poured milky sweet tea. The soggy end product was then supped with dessertspoons.

At this juncture Mum looked at the grandfather clock and then her wristwatch before smiling broadly.

My new great-uncle laughed. "Aye, 'e've brought his own time with him. 'E might 'ave moved farm but 'e 'aven't moved with the time 'n' the time 'ave moved with him."

More raucous laughter and the afternoon was rounded off with the tower-of-pennies-on-the-elbow trick. The total of twenty-four remained the same and I was presented with the traditional florin and homily.

Smiling, I gave my great-aunt the obligatory kiss on her proffered cheek which was greeted with the response, "We're saving our pennies for your nice Christmas present."

I smiled back. The nice Christmas present would be a pound note tucked inside of the card. An extra halfpenny stamp would be stuck on the envelope indicating the envelope flap had been stuck down instead of being folded into the envelope.

On the following Thursday my mother and I caught the market day bus to South Molton. After a roast pork and apple sauce dinner, Gran beckoned me into her tiny kitchen where she passed me the tea cloth indicating that I should dry as she washed up.

When the last plate had been put away in the cupboard she closed the door, and turning to me said, "I hear from a little bird that you've been on a little trip."

I nodded, wondering why it was always a bird and never another animal, and why the bird was always small. There was a slight pause and then she added, "And did she give you anything?"

I nodded again. "Two shillings."

Opening a drawer she took out her purse. "And what did she say?"

"She told me I was to save it."

A coin was pressed into my hand. "Well, here's half a crown for you. Enjoy it now. Go down to the square and treat yourself to some sweets and comics."

I could hardly believe my ears. A first. I was actually being told to spend money and enjoy myself. By the end of the afternoon I had fulfilled both criteria. My pockets were bulging with goodies and my hands were clutching copies of the *Topper* and *Beezer*.

Over the years the family feud continued, and my profitable exercise continued to be even more profitable as I travelled between the two time zones, a time lord in the multiverse of conundra and coin towers.

Curiosity and the Cat

IT TOOK THE stork sixteen years to locate the gooseberry bush in our top garden, and deposit me there on Michaelmas Day; perhaps a dragon would have found it more quickly, had it not been killed by my patron saint. My parents appeared old, to me, and many relatives even older in my young eyes; there was also a deluge of great-aunts, great-uncles, first cousins (removed) and second cousins. This caused confusion as many of the first cousins once removed were addressed by me as aunts and uncles. On my mother's side real great-aunts and -uncles were a thriving breed, but the species was extinct on my father's side.

The terms 'first' and 'second', when applied to relatives, mystified me. I had a second cousin I preferred to a first cousin, and I asked my aged maiden aunt one day why my second couldn't be my first. "What questions you do ask. She can't be because the first one is nearer to you."

The puzzle deepened. I didn't understand. My first cousin lived over thirty miles away, whereas my second cousin was only a mile away from the farmhouse tree if I took the footpath over the Crooked Oak; two if I walked the road to Knowstone and down the lane. Either way she was still closer. My aged maiden aunt knew this and her mental arithmetic was very good, so how come she was muddled over her distances?

One day my mother and I cycled four miles to a farm where a great-uncle and -aunt lived. I'd never met them before. Imagine my disappointment when I met them, only to discover there was nothing great about them. Both were shorter and thinner than average. In fact I had ordinary aunts and uncles who were greater in both stature and girth.

We didn't possess a car and the market day bus on Thursday was our main mode of transport. One great-aunt, whom I only saw on a couple of occasions, had really impressed me. She had driven down to see her sister in her own car, had bright ginger hair and was adorned in a fur coat. It turned out to be a very profitable first encounter, even if it was brief. Half a crown was placed in my hand with those rare words "Spend and enjoy. You're only young once". Such unheard words certainly deserved a kiss on my proffered cheek. But instead, lips met mine. For the first time I tasted lipstick, and the scent of perfume was not Devonshire Violets but one which was strong and heady. An exotic scent which had never assailed my nostrils before. Back at the farmhouse tree I heard my mother inform my aged maiden aunt, when they were discussing the visit, that my great-aunt had male admirers. No wonder, I thought to myself, if she gave them half a crown each time they met. I certainly admired her.

Another great-aunt, a very elegant old lady, came to visit us one Christmas and I was told to be quiet for the duration of her stay as she had recently lost her husband and didn't like noise. I don't think she liked children either, but a great fuss was made of her which I couldn't understand, especially when she gave us our presents on Christmas Day. Wills's Woodbine cigarettes for my non-smoking father and lipsticks for my mother and aged maiden aunt, neither of whom wore make-up except for powder and a dab of scent behind the ears ("Lipstick indeed. Only for ladies who are no better than they should be," said my aged maiden aunt when our guest had departed.) For me, an I-Spy book – *I Spy At the Airport*. Strangely, I never recorded one entry as there was little or no call for a runway in one of my dad's meads.

She left soon after the festive season and normal service, in the sense of noise in the farmhouse tree, was resumed. I never saw her again and no-one ever told me if she ever found her lost husband. When I asked my aged maiden aunt how you would lose a grown-up she gave me one of her looks, shook her head, tut-tut-tutted and went off to collect the eggs.

On one occasion we went to Tiverton to stay with a great-aunt and -uncle on my mother's side and once again my aged maiden aunt tut-tut-tutted when I asked whether it was her right or left side. The great-uncle impressed me because within an hour of our arrival he began beating the floor, touching curtains in the front room exclaiming, "Come on out! Show yourself! I know you're there!" The elusive stranger failed to materialise and I was eager to help him but was quickly ushered into another room and told to sit quietly while my mother and my great-aunt exchanged inaudible words. The unseen person failed to show himself, and during the night my great-uncle prowled the landing in his quest, rattling the knob of the door to our bedroom, which my mother had wedged tightly shut with a chair, while I snuggled into her in the double bed. Having two imaginary friends myself, I was impressed by this grown-up who was being pursued by an imaginary friend he'd obviously fallen out with. On a day visit a couple of years later he barely spoke or moved from his chair. No mention was made of his invisible friend. By the look on his face, the invisible friend was now his enemy.

Another great-uncle, a bachelor, farmed with another great-aunt and great-uncle. On a visit to see him he insisted on taking me out to his orchard where, he informed me, a tawny owl was nesting in a gnarled apple tree. I was very excited because I had never seen a tawny owl's egg and I was hopeful I might be given one for my collection. The nest's female occupant had other ideas and objected to the intrusion, showing her disdain by taking a chunk of flesh from between his finger and thumb. His hand quickly withdrawn, bleeding profusely, the wound had to be stitched up. On our next visit, exactly a year later, no mention was made of the owl, and from the safety of an armchair he pointed out the row of house martins' nests on the barn wall. I was hoping he would suggest putting up a ladder, but I was to be disappointed. Once again I returned home eggless.

On yet another occasion a visiting elderly great-aunt, with a feathery white moustache which tickled me when she kissed my cheek, referred to my aged aunt as my maiden aunt, the first time I had heard the term. Another mystery. My octogenarian hero described the village girls of my own age as maidens. When the visiting aunt had departed I plucked up courage and asked my aged maiden aunt what it all meant, and how could she be a maiden when she didn't go to school?

She gave me her knowing look. "I've never been married and that's all you need to know." I was about ask her why when she said, "You ask far too many questions for my liking. Just remember curiosity killed Tom cat."

None of our cats was called Tom. And why did she say the cat was dead when I'd just seen Mick and Grey Puss sunning themselves in back court?

I wanted to ask her why she called them both Tom and to tell her they were both alive, but the look in her eye made me think better of it.

The following week a great-uncle compounded the problem by informing me that curiosity killed the cat, but satisfaction brought him back to life again. Another mystery for my young mind.

A Toilet By Any Other Name Would....

THE WORD 'TOILET' never featured in the farmhouse tree vocabulary. Lavatory, little 'ouse, Elsan and po, yes, but toilet, no.

Integral to the lavatory were the house rules which had to be obeyed at all times.

"If you'm taken short, and it's only a pee, you go outside in the hedge or under a tree. But make sure there's no-one looking," instructed my aged maiden aunt.

"Raining, snowing, or the cobbled path is icy, you can use the Elsan indoors. Number twos and the weather's fine, you can go in the little 'ouse. Wet, then indoors," added my mother.

"And only use your po under your bed if you'm really took short in the middle of the night. Go downstairs before you go to bed and not too much to drink. Keep the po pushed right back under your bed where you can't see it. Out of sight, out of mind. Don't want you putting your foot in it either. If you can't see it, you won't think about it then, and you won't be tempted to use it," added my aged maiden aunt. "And try not to use more than two sheets of paper at a time. We've only got the *Western Times* and the copy of the *News of the World* from across the road when she's finished with it on Monday."

Squares of newspaper from the pages which had been drawn out, halved and quartered were left hanging from a loop over the nail on the back of the pine lavatory door with a nine-inch square cut out near the top of the door, to allow in the light when the door of the outside lavatory closed.

Affectionately known as little 'ouse, the outside lavatory was a six-by-four slate-roofed shed with a faded red-painted pine door with its cut-out hole – a primitive form of air-conditioning – and a glassless window. It was built over the stream which flowed down from Higher Orchard, along the roadside through front court, through the pond and through the fields to the Crooked Oak. This was the original lavatory, constructed before the indoor Elsan was put in, and it was a pinewood double-seater, one large hole for the menfolk and a smaller circular hole for the womenfolk and 'chillern'.

Beneath the two pine lids were two buckets balanced precariously on a plank. When the stream was running high in the autumn and winter months, the buckets were removed and put back in the spring and summer.

"Knock before you go in," instructed my mother. "Just in case both seats are taken, or if there's a woman in there. Even if you were to stand on tiptoe you won't be able to look in through the square hole. And remember if we have visitors you must use the little 'ouse and not the Elsan unless it's really pouring with rain. And use the newspaper squares, not the proper paper bought for visitors."

The indoor Elsan was installed in the early 1950s in a specially constructed small room next to cellar. It was a large dustbin-sized contraption containing a huge bucket which slotted down inside of it, and which was periodically topped up with Jeyes fluid. When full, my father would ceremoniously lift the bucket out and, if it was spring or summer, bury the contents in the garden next to the rhubarb patch. The whole routine resembling Act Four, Scene One from *MacBeth* when the charmed pot was carried bubbling along the cobbled path. Frothing gruel, thick and slab, oozing and slumping against the side of the big cauldron. Hubble, bubble, hubble, bubble. Fire burn and cauldron bubble. Double, double, toil *et* trouble.

In autumn and winter the bucket was emptied into the stream to flow either down to the Crooked Oak, or diverted to flow over Bull's Mead to fertilise the grass for the following spring grazing.

One fine day I asked my aged maiden aunt where my octogenarian next-door farming neighbour went to the lavatory, having just come back from having a pee behind a beech tree.

My mother and aged maiden aunt exchanged glances. "What sort of question is that?" put in my mother. There was a pause before she added, "He goes, and that's all you need to know."

"But..."

"No buts. Why do you always have to question everything?" added my aged maiden aunt. "Where he goes and does his business is his business. And it's no business of yours. Remember what I've told you before about the curious cat."

I left the room. I was going to make it my business. Cat or no cat. I was intrigued. I knew for a fact that he didn't have an indoor lavatory or a bathroom.

A week later and quite by accident, my curiosity was satisfied. Having spotted a pair of stock doves flying over his yard towards a shippen, I decided to see if I could find their nest on the rafters of his open-fronted shed. A stock dove's egg would be a fine addition to my egg collection.

I walked through our garden, through the gap in the dividing box hedge, which my father had cut out to enable my mother to have a short-cut when she took our neighbour his milk pudding or roast dinner on a Sunday, through his garden and into his yard. Within minutes I was standing by his 'ood rick. As I stood planning my next move, I became aware of a strange, grunting, straining noise. Perhaps a fox was sniffing around the corner of the rick out of my sight. Cautiously, not wanting to surprise it, I edged my way along the side of the rick and very slowly craned my neck around the faggots, only to withdraw it quickly.

Retracing my steps as quietly as I could, I left the yard, the stock doves' nest forgotten. I'd made it my business to solve the mystery and in so doing I'd caught my hero in the act of doing his.

Walking back through the garden I met Dad. "I hear you're interested in lavatories," he said.

I didn't know what to reply but he saved my blushes. "He've got one in a little shed with a pipe which connects it to his pond. Sometimes though, if he gets took short quick, well I leave it to you to work that one out. Good job there's a plentiful supply of fresh dock leaves. Don't be late for dinner. Your mum's stewing rhubarb to have with custard."

He walked off, leaving me with the image of my hero in a far from heroic pose. At the same time I thought of our Elsan and the thought of rhubarb for afters lost its appeal.

Hell

I'D JUST COME back from visiting my octogenarian next-door farming neighbour hero and I was recounting to my aged maiden aunt the naughty rude words he'd said when he'd hit his thumb with a hammer when knocking in a nail.

"Don't know why," she replied. "He's got no feeling in his hands. And don't you go repeating them or you'll end up roasting in the flames of hell. That's where all the bad people, those who swear and the heathens in the village, will end up, down in hell on Judgement Day when the last trumpet blows. Down in the fiery pit."

As she spoke I wondered where the entrance to hell was situated. On a recent schools' broadcast programme, *Travel Talks*, the man had told us about the hot regions of the world but he certainly hadn't mentioned hell. Perhaps the entrance was located in one of the hot regions, but how would my aged maiden aunt's bad people and the heathens get to a desert from the churchyard. Perhaps there were thousands of secret entrances all over the world. Perhaps even in a wardrobe like the one in *The Lion, the Witch and the Wardrobe*, that I'd just read. Perhaps one of the entrances could be in one of my father's fields.

I gave a gulp. Of course. That was why I wasn't allowed to go in the corner of Lanefield where there was a large boggy area. It wasn't the bog I had to avoid, it was the entrance, or *an* entrance, to hell. Also there was a tree in the hedge above the marshy area called a witch-hazel. Witches were bad people. Bad people went down to hell. The entrance to hell was under the roots of the witch tree.

Putting on my wellington boots I made my way to Lanefield, and kneeling down by the edge of the bog I pressed my ear to the ground because I'd read that in certain areas of the country where battles had taken place you could hear the sounds of clashing swords and neighing horses coming up through the earth.

I was certain that if hell was as hot as my aged maiden aunt had said it was, I would be able to hear the bad people and the heathens screaming in pain and torment as they roasted.

I listened. Nothing. I suddenly had a thought. In some parts of the world, day was night when it was day for us. Perhaps this also applied to hell. They were all asleep before going on their daily walk through flames.

Getting up, I made my way slowly towards the tree. As soon as I reached it I could see a hole in the hedge. It looked just like a rabbit burrow. I recalled how Alice had gone down through a hole, but how could I get through that narrow entrance? Lying down I pushed a stick into the hole. Suddenly I was slipping back down the bank. There was a loud squelching sound and I could feel an invisible hand tugging at my wellington boot. One of the bad, heathen people had woken up early. I'd found an entrance to hell and was beginning to wish I hadn't. It was me versus the bad heathen people.

"What are you doing down there, when I told you not to go near the bog?" Dad's voice.

Before I could explain, his hands were under my armpits and he was pulling me up onto safe ground.

"And don't you dare go down there again. Your wellington boot has been sucked under. Well, to teach you a lesson you can take money out of your money box and buy a new pair when the ironmonger's van comes next week."

I nodded shamefacedly. Once again he was angry with me, but not a real anger. No shouting, no sharp smack. He hadn't even raised his voice; it was just that look in his eyes, the look that told me I'd let him down. Just once I wished, and not for the first time, that he would raise his voice to me and smack the back of my legs, but he never would.

We returned to the farmhouse tree in silence, me hopping along as best I could.

That night as I kneeled at the side of my bed I thanked my all-seeing, all-hearing God, my invisible silent God, for sending my father along at just the right moment to save me from being pulled down into hell.

On the following Sunday, much to my aged maiden aunt's amazement, I put a shiny sixpenny bit instead of my usual thrupenny bit into the collection box and didn't dare look up into the magic eye as its owner passed the box down the row. Not only was I paying my all-seeing God for saving me, but also to thank Him for helping my father retrieve my wellington boot which I found next to my other one the following morning by the door in back kitchen.

My Octogenarian Next-door Farming Neighbour Hero

OUR OCTOGENARIAN NEXT-DOOR farming neighbour, the second oldest man in the village, was my hero. At milking time when he was driving his four cows into the shippen his voice bellowed bull-like over the rooftops.

"There'll be no need for a trumpet on Judgement Day," laughed my aged maiden aunt one Sunday evening as his words echoed over the farm. "Just get him to rise up first and shout, and the dead'll spring to attention in fear and trembling. Listen to the racket. Even the ole cuckoo have stopped calling."

Not only could my hero shout, but he also swore, much to my delight. My hero knew every swear word known to man. When things weren't going to his liking his voice forged swear-word links, varying in size, which he joined together to form a chain gleaming with rudeness. This chain was then coiled around anyone within earshot. Four-letter links, six-letter links, he forged them with relish, chuckling each time he cast his chain into the air.

One wet morning, after discussing the amount of rain which had fallen over the past couple of days, I went home and announced to my aged maiden aunt and mother, "The cows are up to their tits in shit."

My mother looked aghast and my aged maiden aunt almost dropped the cup she was drying.

"Go to the sink and wash your mouth out with a bite of soap and a beaker of water," said my mother.

"Whatever will you come out with next?" added my aged maiden aunt.

As I ambled slowly to the sink I wondered if I would be able to trade the words for aniseed balls in the boys' lavatory. A homily from my aged maiden aunt interrupted my thoughts. "Those are the sort of words used by the bad people in the parish – the heathens. They that know no better. Like that dreadful Kenneth Harris you mix with in your class."

My mouth began to foam as the soapy mixture began to work.

My aged maiden aunt's well-meant tirade, partially aimed at me, continued: "They that don't wash as often as they should, swear, and don't go to church or chapel as often as they should. They that goes into the devil's house. They'll be punished one day when they meet their Maker and get sent down to burn in deepest hell. You don't want to end up down there. Hell is not a nice place."

"Now spit out that piece of soap and wash your mouth out," instructed my mother.

"And I'll pour you a glass of Lucozade," added my aged maiden aunt in a softer voice. "A small glass, mind you. Auntie isn't made of money."

My hero also possessed an amazing pair of enormous hands. Split and cracked with age and wear, the thick stubby fingers resembled small cucumbers sticking out from the edge of a tea plate. On an icy winter's morning he would walk up to his open fireplace, crouch down and take out a couple of embers and juggle them around in his hands.

"Don't you ever try it," said my mother when I'd recounted what I'd seen through his kitchen window. "You'd burn your hands. His are made of leather. Tough as old boots. No feeling in them whatsoever. He does it to try and revive the circulation. You wear the mittens Auntie knitted for you and your hands will stay warm."

The leather-tough-as-old-boots hands were also iron-hard. On one occasion when he'd forgotten to take his mallet with him to drive a wooden fence post into the ground, he clenched his right hand into a fist and brought the fleshy part below his little finger crashing down on the top of the pole. Repeated thumps, and the post was wedged firmly into the ground.

An important ritual, before carrying out a task, was the spitting on the palms ritual.

"Always spit on your hands, little chil'. Gets the job off to a proper start."

I heeded his advice at school the following week before embarking on an arithmetic test and was rewarded with two strokes of the wooden ruler on the palm of my left hand.

My hero roared with laughter when I recounted my escapade. Taking me into his kitchen he rummaged in a tin and pulled out a sixpenny bit.

"There you are, little chil' Dreepence for each stroke. Get yersel' some sweets tomorrow."

On another occasion, I had to stay in at playtime because Kenny the Gorilla Harris had made a rude noise after baked beans for school dinner and I'd laughed when our teacher had asked who'd broken wind. It hadn't seemed a very sensible question to me, because I couldn't understand how anyone could break something which was invisible. I told my hero and once again a coin was pulled out from his tin and a thrupenny bit was pressed into my palm.

"There you are, little chil', and just remember the ole verse –

> Where ere you be
> Let the wind go free.
> In church or chapel
> Let it rattle, let it roar,
> Let it rip through either door."

I laughed because it was a rhyme my father said and I never got tired of hearing him say it.

He laughed until the tears rolled down his cheeks; when he had composed himself he added, "Boys always fart in school. And maidens too sometimes. Always 'ave done and they always will. Nothing ever changes."

I clenched the coin tightly in my hand. Not only had I got money to spend on sweets but my hero had said the rude word just as I hoped he would.

Chuckling, he gave me a gentle push. "Time you was off and time I had something for tea. Bread an' cheese an' a bowl of tea sop to wash it down."

My hero was lucky because he seldom seemed to have a bath. On Saturday as I was undressing for my weekly plunge into the soapy water I gave his bathing facilities a lot of thought. If he wanted a hot one in his tin bath he had to boil up water in the black iron kettle in front of the fire. That didn't appeal to me one bit. I envied my hero his swear-word vocabulary and his iron hands, but the idea of a tin bath of cold water left me feeling cold and it probably left him shivering as well.

Sparrows and the Barn Owl

MY OCTOGENARIAN HERO shot anything which interfered with his farming except the fox. "He belongs to the hunt, little chil'." Anyone under the age of eighty was called 'little child'.

One late-summer afternoon, feeling annoyed that a flock of house sparrows had been eating the corn scattered in his yard for his few hens, he placed a trail of corn on the ground directly opposite his back door.

As I came down into his yard with a freshly baked apple pie from my mother I caught sight of him getting down on his stomach in his kitchen with his shotgun in his hand. Hiding behind a barrel in the linhay I waited and watched. Suddenly there was the loud explosion of the gun going off.

The show over, I walked across and delivered his pie, barely taking my eyes off the ground in front of me.

Half an hour later when my mother was out in back court picking in the washing, a withe basket with a clean white tea towel over the top of it was suddenly thrust under her nose.

Lifting back the cloth she gave a gasp as the gory contents were revealed.

"Perhaps you could turn 'em into something, missus. Say for tomorrow's dinner. I know they'm no size to speak o', but there's enough o' the little varmints in thicky basket to make up a pie, I reckon." Pausing, he eyed up the contents before adding, "If you uses a lot o' pastry for the crust, that is. Go down a treat after thicky apple pie you sent the chil' down wi'."

"A pie indeed," replied my mother. "And who is going to pluck them?"

He laughed. "Cook 'em as they be, missus. Beak, bones, feathers, innards 'n' all. I'll pick the meat out 'n' spit out the odds 'n' ends I can't eat. Don't 'e waste time pluckin' and drawin' 'em. All I want for you to do is make a pie."

My mother gave an involuntary shiver as she recalled the event in the evening. "His basket must have been a quarter full with the poor little mites. Sparrow pie indeed."

"He shot right down through the flock when they were feeding in a line," added my father. "Blasted 'em with lead shot. I've buried 'em in the dungheap. He told me it was a terrible waste and that it had cost him a cartridge. I almost thought he was hinting I should give him a cartridge because you hadn't made a pie for him."

On another occasion my hero arrived at the back door on Michaelmas Day clutching a large cardboard box securely tied with binder-twine.

"A birthday present. Can't stop, little chil', but I'll have a piece o' your birthday cake tomorrow. Your mother bakes a fine fruit cake."

"Cut it on the knot," instructed my aged maiden aunt as I placed the box on the table. "Cord always comes in handy; shame to waste it."

Slicing through where she indicated, I passed her the string, pulled back the flaps and lifted out a black wooden display case with a glass front and sides. Looking into the case I found myself staring into the eyes of a barn owl.

"Well I never!" exclaimed my father as we tucked into my birthday cake. "He shot that one years ago when he was living out on the moor. It was in his tallet. Told me all about it soon after he moved in next door, when we were haymaking. Apparently one night it perched on his kitchen chimney and started hooting. He believes in the old superstition that if a barn owl hoots down your chimney it means a death.

"Anyway next morning he took his gun up to the tallet above his stable and shot it as it was roosting. Had it stuffed and mounted proper as you see it now. Some proud of it. Never thought he'd part with it. You'm a lucky boy. He must think a lot of you."

I gave my stuffed barn owl pride of place in my bedroom, on top of the chest of drawers. Each night I stared at him before falling asleep. On the fourth night in the light from a full moon...

Close my eyes.
Concentrate.
Must concentrate.
Close my eyes really tight.
Squeeze up my face.
Squeeze my lids tightly together until it hurts.
Form a picture of him in my mind's eye.
Gently. Gently.
Watch him wake up from his sleep.
Slowly release him from his glass cell.
Watch him flap slowly around the room.
A slow-motion flight.
Control the beat of his wings.
Project him through the closed window.
Gently. Gently.
Freedom to fly through the night sky.
Rising higher and higher.
Upwards into the stars.
My night bird.
My star bird.
My...
Out of the tallet above the stable
A brown and white hessian sack
Falls into the clear cool evening air
Billow of wind, opens into a flap of wings,
Slow-motion flight
Riding through twilight.
Ghost of the night,
Moon's white shadow
Cast over a spring tide
Of rippling green meadow waves.

In the morning when I woke up from the dream he was back in his glass case. A prisoner for another night, sleeping.

Tears

THE DAY EVENTUALLY arrived when my octogenarian hero had to retire from farming. As his way of thanking my family for the kindness they'd shown him over the years he sold his shirehorse Charlie to my father for much less than its market value.

Apart from his horse, his few hens and four cows, everything was put up for auction at his farm. A week before the auctioneers were due to make an inventory and number the lots, he had a massive clear-out.

Anything he considered to be rubbish, and which was small enough, was tossed into hessian sacks. These were then loaded on the horse-drawn butt-cart together with iron bedsteads, chairs and other old pieces of furniture. When full, the cart was pulled down through the lane, through a couple of fields to the edge of an old quarry, where the sacks were emptied out and the large items tipped into the quarry.

"Help yersel', little chil'," he said as he caught me watching him from the entrance to his implement linhay, where he was sorting out and bagging up. "Take whatever takes yer fancy and catches your eye. 'Tis all bliddy ole rubbish. Good riddance to it."

Rummaging through the 'bliddy ole rubbish' I became the proud owner of a pair of brass opera glasses, a drinking flask carved from a hollowed-out gourd with a silver cap, a brass candlestick, two copper powder flasks and a pair of stirrups.

"Bliddy ole rubbish," he laughed, when I showed him my treasures. "But if it makes 'e 'appy you 'ave 'em. Now you come along with me, little chil'!"

I followed him into his back kitchen.

"Bide there a minute and don't 'e go touching nort you shouldn't."

I didn't. I was almost afraid to breathe. His table was piled high with a Leaning Tower of Pisa. Constructed from glass- and chinaware, and porcelain objects, was a structure which had been built for the auctioneer to dismantle and number, and which threatened to topple over at any second.

A few minutes later he reappeared carrying a small circular black box.

David on a long cart during
haymaking, circa 1951

"Yer take un. 'Tis only ole coins. None o'em no bliddy good. All ole-fashioned ones. More bliddy ole rubbish. You 'ave 'em. But don't 'e go thinkin' you can spend 'em on sweets cos you can't. If they was worth ort I'd 'ave spent 'em years ago. Bliddy ole rubbish."

Placing the box in my hands he ruffled my hair. "Now we'll get all your rubbish together and then you must git on 'ome for yer dinner. There's nort else yer for 'e or for me neither."

In the privacy of my bedroom I tipped out the contents of my treasure-chest black box onto my eiderdown. There were over a hundred coins, many dating back to the late eighteenth century with one going back to the 1660s and a massive penny which my father later told me was a cartwheel penny. Even the box was old, with handwriting on the bottom which was so old-fashioned I couldn't work out what the words were.

The following afternoon, selected villagers trooped through his farmhouse and were given a private viewing of the numbered lots. As he guided the party around the rooms, he wrenched open drawers and tugged open cupboard doors to satisfy himself that he hadn't overlooked anything. Each tug and wrench resulted in an object crashing to the stone floor where it was either chipped or smashed to smithereens. Teapots lost their spouts, cups their handles, and porcelain figures either a limb or were decapitated.

"You'll have nothing left to sell at this rate," laughed a villager.

"No odds, 'tis all bliddy ole rubbish," responded my octogenarian hero. "Sooner 'tis all gone and all over, the 'appier I shall be."

Five minutes later the room erupted into laughter when he held up a set of false teeth which he'd overlooked in the back of a drawer. "Well, I never. They belonged to missus 'n' 'er bin gone years."

On the sale day, when a gilded clock, described by the auctioneer as Napoleonic, fetched ninety guineas – a clock which hadn't tick-tocked or chimed for over twenty years – the assembled villagers gasped.

"Must be even older than you," joked a villager as she gave him a friendly nudge.

"Not much," he replied.

Five minutes later the room became silent when a jug was knocked down for thirty pounds.

"Makes you wonder what the bits and pieces he broke was worth," whispered my aged maiden aunt.

"And what was in those sacks he dumped in the quarry," my father replied.

As the sale progressed and more lots were sold to dealers for unexpected sums, my hero showed his bewilderment. "Must 'ave been bliddy good-quality ole rubbish," he said to my mother as she poured him a cup of tea.

However, when a dealer asked if he had an axe he could borrow, to enable him to chop off the legs from a table he'd purchased, because he only wanted the circular top, my octogenarian farming hero, my swearing hero, took centre stage for one last starring rôle and swansong.

"I'll give you a bliddy axe, you bugger, and I'll cut off *yer* legs as well if you'm still 'ere in two minutes."

The dealer needed no second telling. Heaving up the table, he staggered and struggled his way through the back door while my hero was restrained by my father and a great-uncle.

At the end of the afternoon, when the final lots had been removed, he touched my mother's hand with a tenderness I never thought possible.

"Farm's gone. Furniture's gone, and I shall soon be gone. 'Tis all over, missus. 'Tis all over."

My mother squeezed his hand and as I looked at his face I could hardly believe what I saw. There were tears in his eyes. My hero was actually crying. And in that split second I realised that it was not only children like me who cried in moments of sadness, and I recalled the Sunday when my father, on our way to chapel, had dispatched with a hazel stick rabbits who were dying from myxomatosis. At the time he'd said he had something in his eye, but he'd been crying as well.

Later, we all stood by our yard gate in a rural guard of honour as he was driven past on his way to his new home, a couple of miles away, to live with his two nieces and their parents on their farm.

We all waved, and from the front passenger seat a plate hand came up and there was a slight movement of the cucumber fingers, but he kept his head bowed and I never saw his face.

Blowing my nose loudly, I wasn't going to be seen crying; I raced up to my bedroom. Throwing myself onto the bed I stared up at the ceiling, recalling past times with my hero. The large block of cheese on his kitchen table speckled with green bits which had a smell so strong it made me feel sick, and which vibrated on his cheese dish. "Maggots, little chil'. Maggots. Good job the block is movin', means they'm alive. Gives the cheese more flavour. Gives it body. Beautiful with a hunk o' bread and an onion after me bowl o' leek broth."

A smile crossed my lips as I recalled the one-and-only Christmas he'd treated himself to a Christmas cake. After an in-vain attempt at cutting it with a knife, he'd taken it, still on the plate, and placed it on the stone kitchen floor. He then attempted to 'cut it' with a mallet and chisel. The impact of the mallet head on the chisel causing both the iced cake and the china plate to shatter into cake fragments and china shards. How he had enjoyed squatting on the floor crouched over the remains, stuffing the lumps of cake into his mouth with both hands, his face a huge beaming smile in the leaping flames of the fire. I'd witnessed the whole event, unseen, through his kitchen window, and had rushed back home to recount the tale to my parents and aged maiden aunt.

Finally I recalled him at the end of his sale, defeated by age. With a loud sniff I reached into my pocket for a handkerchief. I became aware that the barn owl was watching me, the bird which he'd given me for a birthday present and which had watched over me since that day.

Closing my eyes and clenching my fists I concentrated, and for the last time I released my star bird.

My hero was gone.

The Passing of the Old Ways

IN DECEMBER 1961, a few days after I had arrived home from boarding school for the Christmas holiday, my octogenarian (now a nonagenarian hero of ninety-three) died peacefully on the shortest day.

On hearing the news I went up to my bedroom and cried, glad that I had not heard the news at boarding school where no-one was ever seen to cry.

Looking across at my chest of drawers I stared into the eyes of the barn owl. My old Stone Age man was dead. I had lost a hero and the village had lost a man of the old ways, the country ways. Ahead, a new age.

The Charmer

I ALSO HAD another hero in the village and he was an octogenarian as well. This hero was a smallholding, cobbling, chimney-sweeping charmer.

Well into his late eighties he rode his white mare Sally to the Masons Arms a mile away. At closing time he would be helped up on her back, her flank slapped and he would be transported back to his tiny cottage. When Sally stopped, he knew he had reached his destination.

On fine autumn afternoons, muttering and mumbling to himself, he lurched up the road to glean his harvest of fallen branches from the russet field of Beerclose Copse. As twilight crept across a poppy-crimson sky, he hauled his final stick harvest homewards. On the ground, his faggot sheaf left runic squiggles in the dust.

When proposing to his wife, he promised that if she was true to him, he would cobble her shoes for the rest of her life. It was also said he boasted that the double number of their children equalled the number of times he'd shaved during his married life.

At one time he had owned an Aunt Sally stall which he erected on fair days. By climbing an apple tree in one of our orchards I could see into his attic window. Through the dust and dirt on the glass I could see old tarnished fairground props from bygone days. On rubbish-collecting days he would put out an old tin bath containing piles of baked bean and rice milk pudding tins.

My octogenarian hero was also a charmer who, through touch and incantation strange, could conjure out and charm away the ringworm, wart and festering sore. In my nine-year-old eyes this wizened, walnut-brown, white-stubbled face belonged to a wizard, a shaman who possessed magical powers. "His face needs a good wash," said my aged maiden aunt, "but he has got the old ways, the old power."

One afternoon when I had been attempting to retrieve my kite from a tangle of blackthorn branches, a spike embedded itself in my heel. I was taken to see my hero in his dark, smoke-filled room. There he was crouched over the open wood fire, stirring a concoction in an iron crock suspended from an iron crook. My mind filled with words from the school playground, where classmates had told me that he cooked a stew of beetles, frogs, lizards and worms, and these creatures, when eaten, meant that he lived on and on for ever.

Beckoning me to him, he muttered inaudible words, and passed his hands through the air above my foot. Next he told my mother to take me home and to put a hot poultice on it. I hobbled, crying, from the room, believing he had told her to put a hot poker on my heel. That evening my foot was bathed with hot water, dabbed on with a wad of cotton wool. The following morning my foot was healed and there was no sign of the thorn, either in my heel or in my bed.

He didn't live for ever as my school mates said he would, and when he died a way of life died with him.

A Bus-driving Hero

MY PRIMARY SCHOOL bus driver owned a red-and-cream ramshackle rust-bucket bus, and he was another of my heroes, along with Zorro, the Lone Ranger, Dan Dare and Robin Hood. The paintwork was so dirty that it resembled a page in my aged maiden aunt's autograph book, without the clever verses. We scribbled our names in the grime, and Kenny the Gorilla Harris wrote rude words which he couldn't spell properly, such as 'wily' and 'bom'.

Some of the seats had holes where mice had pulled out horsehair stuffing for their nests. One day, Kenny found an old nest with mouse droppings in, and rammed it down the back of the girl's dress in the seat in front of him. She screamed so loudly that Mad Fred the driver nearly drove into the hedge. He was not amused; neither was Kenny when he was given a cuff around his ear which went red.

The rust-bucket bus belched out blue smoke, and so did the pipe which Mad Fred always seemed to have in his mouth. If he wasn't smoking it, he was chewing on the stem of it. He was clever because he

David, aged 8, the Robin Hood
of Beerclose Copse

could light it without letting go of the steering wheel. He manoeuvred the wheel with his elbows, and his fingers lit his smelly old pipe. Next to his seat was a brown glass bottle of cider from which he occasionally took a swig. After a few quick gulps of cider the rust-bucket bus always went faster around the country road corners to Bishops Nympton.

It shook, rattled and rocked, and rolled along. One evening, for no reason the sliding door fell off; fortunately the glass didn't break. Mad Fred knew the same swear words as my octogenarian next-door farming neighbour hero. He lifted the door into the rust-bucket bus and placed it between the seats in the aisle. The following morning when the rust-bucket bus pulled up, a black curtain, where the door should have been, was flapping in the breeze like a rook's ragged wing. "Best sit one seat back. Don't want any of you falling out. No need for a door monitor cos there isn't one to monitor," he laughed.

On another occasion we were going downhill when we were overtaken by a rear wheel, and the bus juddered to a halt as Mad Fred managed to steer it gently into the hedge. He used words my octogenarian hero used, and more besides. I bet none of them was in the spelling test we missed because we had to walk the last mile to school.

Occasionally he did some thatching, and there would be a long ladder in the gangway between the seats. "Walk carefully. Don't want you breaking any of the rungs," he instructed.

Each summer term we collected wild flowers, to write in our flower notebooks each morning. If, on the way to school, we saw a flower we hadn't got, Mad Fred would stop the bus and we'd all pile out to pick one each for our collection. If there was any traffic behind, Mad Fred would laugh and say, "Do 'em good to wait."

Primary school trips in the 1950s were almost unheard of. The nearest I got to the Swiss Alps for a skiing trip was running down the coal heap in the playground when we'd had a fall of snow.

One day, royalty visited nearby, and a school trip was arranged. It cost a shilling. Kenny the Gorilla Harris wanted to stay behind and spend his shilling on sweets, but he quickly changed his mind when the teacher told him he would have to copy out a blackboard full of problems, do them all, and learn fifty spellings.

Mad Fred even cleaned the rust-bucket school bus and hung bunting over the front of it. Other schools lined the route to see Princess Margaret plant a tree and unveil a plaque by the side of the road. I was on the end of our row, and a boy from another school couldn't stand still. He kept hopping up and down from one leg to the other. He just couldn't stop fidgeting and he looked as if he was about to burst into tears. It spells Trouble (with a capital T) if you're standing next to a boy who cries, because you automatically get the blame. Suddenly I saw a puddle by his sandals. When he saw me looking at it, he crossed his legs and told me that his orange was leaking. He added that if I didn't say anything, he would give it to me. I was quite happy to accept it, because why should I tell anyone about a leaking orange?

When we got back to school Kenny the Gorilla Harris got the ruler on the palm of his left hand for being disrespectful in front of the monarchy. We didn't know what it meant, because all he had done was to say that he didn't understand how she could be a princess because she wasn't wearing a crown, and that she was short like one of Snow White's dwarfs. Mind you, he did say it in a loud voice.

I couldn't find a leak in the orange. It was sweet and juicy, and it was a beaut.

By the end of the week the rust-bucket school bus was dirty again and we scribbled our names in the grime again. School journeys were never boring with my hero Mad Fred at the wheel.

The Leonine or Bisecting Rhyme

MY FATHER KNEW two poems off by heart. One written by Thomas Hood and the other by Robert Southey, which he had learned as a schoolboy in the early 1900s. Each August he would recite them to me while we were digging the late potato crop in the garden.

"Good rhymes and rhythms. That's what I call poetry."

One morning, only a week after he'd recited his words, I heard a line which contained two rhyming words, had a good rhythm to it, but certainly wasn't composed by Hood or Southey.

The day had started badly. No matter how much I shook and rattled my blue-and-yellow plastic money box, the result was always the same. It was empty, the final coins having been used to buy my father a jar of Brylcreem for his birthday. I was destitute; no money for either comics or sweets.

Replacing my money box on the top of the cupboard, I climbed down from the chair and pushed it back under the table. This was a serious matter; it would be another six weeks before half-term, six weeks before I'd be able to catch the Thursday market day bus into town.

My thoughts were interrupted by my father's voice. "Bill's on holiday this week. They'll be sending a relief driver, so it's best if you stay inside the court gate when the lorry comes this week. No going out in the road. Stay in the court."

Before I could ask why I had to remain in front court, he'd left the room. At least I could still watch from behind the gate. The Ambrosia lorry from Lapford, over twenty miles away, collected our full churns of milk each morning. Lifting the metal churns was heavy work and I enjoyed watching Bill swing them off the wooden milk stand next to the farm, and up into the turquoise lorry. Replacing the full ones with two empty ones was easy work and Bill usually whistled as he clanged them over the side of the lorry.

Fifteen minutes later I was standing in the open-fronted cart linhay and the milk lorry arrived. Perhaps I'd find out why I couldn't leave front court and go into the road.

The man who climbed out of the cab was red-faced; with a heave and a gulp the first churn was hoisted off the milk stand. A space was cleared and the second churn was wedged into position. Seconds later the two replacement churns clanged onto the milk stand. Having completed his task he wiped the sweat from his forehead with the back of his hand and breathed out deeply. It was at that moment he saw me.

"Morning, boy. Show us yer knob for a bob."

For a second I was stunned. Why should the relief milkman want to pay me a shilling to see my... I was about to run off and tell my father when an image of my empty money box flashed into my head. A shilling represented twelve liquorice bootlaces, or a box of aniseed balls, gobstoppers and the *Dandy* and *Beano* with change left over.

A plan, followed by another, quickly formulated in my mind. "You throw the shilling over the gate first."

Licking his podgy lips, he thrust his hand into his pocket, and the next second the early-morning sun was glinting on the silver coin as his finger and thumb sent it spinning through the air and over the gate where it landed a short distance from my feet.

Heads I win, tails you lose, I thought to myself as I bent down and retrieved the coin. The day was certainly getting better. With the coin clenched in my hand I was turning and running towards the safety of the farmhouse tree. As I ran I heard a swear word which I'd heard my octogenarian hero use. Next the cab door slammed and the lorry was revving up.

I headed for the shippen where I knew my father was brushing up the dung.

"Dad," I called out as I entered the cob-walled building.

Placing the broom and the pick on the wheelbarrow, he turned towards me.

"Dad. Guess what the milkman said?"

He frowned. "You haven't been outside the gate?"

I shook my head.

"Well. Go on. What did he say?"

"He said... he said... He'd give me a shilling if I showed him –" I paused – "a shilling if..." I paused again. Saying the word in the boys' lavatories at school was fun. But this was different. This wasn't Kenny the Gorilla Harris and my mates. This was my father. "A shilling if I showed him... if I showed him my willy. But he didn't say willy, Dad, and I didn't. I didn't show him anything."

His explosion of words smashed through the air. "He what! You wait here."

With a speed I never knew my father possessed, he was out of the shippen and sprinting across front court to the gate.

A couple of minutes later, and he was back again and slightly out of breath. "Missed him. Lorry's left the village. I'll make a telephone call. Soon put a stop to his little game. Here, this is for you."

From his pocket he pulled out something and pressed it into my hand.

I stared at my palm. Another coin. But this was a better coin. A two-shilling piece. "Thanks, Dad. Super."

Making my way back to cellar I smiled to myself. The day was getting better and better. The second part of my master plan had been even more rewarding than I had hoped for. Pulling out the chair again I stood on tiptoe and reached for my money box. Coins placed in the slot would make the little plastic man rise up to the top. I had second thoughts. On Thursday I'd be taking it out again. The little man would have to wait until the end of the month when it was my birthday and I could give him loads of money.

The following morning it was wet, and I watched from my bedroom window as the milk lorry drew up outside of the gate. At the same instant my father stepped out from behind the cart where'd he'd been standing, waiting.

Now there'd be fun. The milkman jumped out from his cab. No fun. It wasn't the red-faced milkman I'd described to my father. Bill's relief had himself been relieved.

I turned away from the window, and taking the two coins from my dressing-table drawer began spending them in my head.

Eighteen *Dandy*s or *Beano*s. Thirty-six planet-sized gobstoppers. Thirty-six liquorice bootlaces. One hundred and forty-four blackjacks. Almost as good as a birthday or Christmas. Hundreds of inches of liquorice bootlaces, and I hadn't shown anyone anything.

I began licking my lips in anticipation.

Oh yes...

> I remember, I remember,
> The farm where I was born.
> It was on a summer morning
> The milkman's work was done.

A Penny for Five Hours of Entertainment

THE DARK CHOCOLATE-BROWN Bakelite cabinet was a fixture on the window shelf in cellar. Set into the large Caligari cabinet was an oblong window which lit up and illuminated a world of strange-sounding place names in green and orange letters – Hilversum, Budapest, Allouis, Motala and Lahti – when the set was switched on and had warmed up. In 1956 it was replaced with a portable wireless set. The modern age had arrived at the farmhouse tree. The size of a small vanity case, it cost the sum of almost twenty-three pounds inclusive of delivery and the first battery. It was a princely sum, bearing in mind that the profit on the farm on which we had to live was barely seven pounds a week.

"We shall be able to listen in any room now," said my aged maiden aunt. "A proper treat. Us'll be able to have the ole wireless on in front room on Christmas Day." With the advent of portability, our in-house entertainment knew no bounds, in theory. But in reality the vanity case seldom travelled far, staying put for most of the time in the manner of a corpulent uncle at Christmas ensconced in the best armchair, who moved only when the call of nature dictated.

"Costs a penny for five hours," announced my aged maiden aunt as she read the instruction pamphlet, her eyes looking in my direction as she continued: "About two hours a day, that's roughly fourteen a week. Best say we'll listen to it for fifteen a week to be on the safe side."

I sighed. I had been set a mental calculation. Fifteen hours a week. Four weeks in a month. Sixty hours. A penny for five hours. Twelve fives are sixty. A shilling a month, that makes twelve shillings for forty-eight weeks. Plus four more weeks to make fifty-two. "Thirteen shillings, Auntie, for a whole year."

"Don't forget extra programmes like the Derby, Grand National and the Boat Race," put in my father.

"And my *Children's Hour*," I added quickly.

"If we say fifteen shillings, that should cover everything," said my mother.

"And a lot of pleasure it'll give us too," said my aged maiden aunt with a smile.

I was slightly mystified. We listened to these programmes on the old wireless, so what was going to be new?

When the first battery had "run out of juice", as my father put it, it was ceremoniously cremated on the open fire in kitchen.

"Enough left in it to squeeze out for a firework display," laughed my father as he gave the burning mass a good prod with the poker. Immediately a peacock tail of orange-blue-green-turquoise feather-flames and sparks plumed and fanned out, before the firebird took wing and flew up the chimney leaving a skeleton of black charred metal rods and the acrid smell of burning flesh. For years to come, spent batteries were treated with the same reverence.

The 'a lot of pleasure' consisted of a diet of vitamins in the form of the Home Service, with the Light Programme providing a certain amount of roughage. Each Friday the local baker delivered a copy of the *Radio Times*, two crusty loaves, a currant loaf and occasionally, as a treat, fancy cakes. In the evening I read it through and picked out all of the programmes I would enjoy, providing they weren't on a Sunday. My mother and aged maiden aunt censoring the programmes, with many being considered as totally unsuitable, too much roughage which was far too coarse and fibrous for my tender digestive system.

Certain programmes in particular caused both women, especially my aged maiden aunt, to grimace as soon as the titles were announced and certain voices heard.

"*The Goons* indeed! Do you know a family called Goon? Green, yes, they live over town, but not Goon. No, certainly not Goon. They want to learn to speak properly as well. Childish gobbledegook. And I ask you, whoever heard of anyone called Eccles and Bluebottle? Cakes and flies, yes, but not people. Won't waste the battery on that nonsense."

Does the Team Think incurred her wrath. "Think! Think! They don't even know the meaning of the word. Well, they won't be doing their so-called thinking in this house, especially on the Lord's Day. Whatever next? *Top of the Form*, now that makes you think. A chance for you to improve your general knowledge. And *The Brains Trust*, they think, but not this lot. Not this team."

The navy never larked around because their antics took place on a Sunday. Not only because their antics took place on a Sunday – not only because it *was* Sunday – but it was when we were eating our roast beef before setting out for chapel.

"Meal times are for eating quietly, not for listening to that din, especially when it's a lot of nonsense. Enough to give you indigestion. They wouldn't have behaved like that in the war, or we'd have lost. Churchill wouldn't have allowed it," said my aged maiden aunt. "The Sabbath is for *Chapel in the Valley* and *The Sunday Service*, but not if it's Roman Catholic. No need for waving tins of smoke around and choking everybody. Leastways, that's what I've heard goes on."

Beyond Our Ken was certainly beyond her threshold of tolerance, and Kenneth Horne was instantly banished to outer space with her words of disdain ringing in his ears.

Another comedian, another Ken as his bad luck would have it, always annoyed her when he 'popped' up on *Workers' Playtime* in the morning. Opening his act with the catchphrase which in his case was very prophetic – "I won't take my coat off, I'm not stopping" – meant he was quickly silenced and banished even before he attempted to remove the garment.

"Very true, my lad," she chastised. "You keep it on, because you're not stopping in this house a minute longer, and it's raining so you'll

Eastacott, the farmhouse tree, 1960

need it. Workers' playtime indeed. You don't play when you're working. Whatever next?"

Ken Platt was left to roam unheard airwaves and realms with the other Ken, while the workers found their playtime coming to an abrupt end, having to return to their work benches and chores with their mugs of tea remaining unfinished.

In 1960, after much soul-searching as to whether she should be spending a part of her personal savings on what she termed a luxury, my aged maiden aunt at the age of almost seventy purchased a state-of-the-art Roberts radio for her own enjoyment in her bedroom... "A birthday present to myself."

In the evenings, after my father had hand-milked his seven cows, we sat listening to the wireless and discussing the programmes while we played cards, read or, in the case of my mother and aged maiden aunt, knitted, sewed and darned socks or replaced missing buttons.

We had a go with Joe, shared embarrassing moments, and got into a pickle with Wilfred and Mabel. We investigated crimes for thirty minutes with Inspector Scott and Sergeant Bingham, occasionally solving the case in the short time allowed at the end of the programme. We marvelled at the vocal dexterity of Percy Edwards as he walked down a country lane frightening the birds and other animals with his impersonations of them. Peter Goodright made us laugh with his impersonations of people. "What a good take off," laughed my father. We asked Freddie Grisewood any number of questions, but Gilbert Harding restricted us to twenty.

We took whatever was on offer from here, tried to become top of the form, moved in for a life with the Lyons family, who in turn invited us to meet their friends the Huggetts, and enjoyed a life of bliss with the Luscombes.

From Monday to Friday at a quarter to seven we enjoyed an early-evening beverage with Dan and his son Jack, the only time we ever entered a pub. Occasionally we danced in the Palm Court to a very posh orchestra. We endured the hardships of a desert island and I tried to fathom out how a shipwrecked person had managed to salvage seven records, the Bible and a luxury item. My aged maiden aunt and my mother kept a daily diary with Mrs Dale, both women constantly worrying about Jim's health.

I helped Carlton Hobbs and Norman Shelley to solve elementary crimes while my father attempted to compose odd odes with Cyril Fletcher. My mother went into town for the night and was entertained by a variety of theatrical acts in the playhouse compèred by Vic Oliver with mini dramas starring Jack Hulbert and Cicely Courtneidge.

In 1963, when electricity entered the farmhouse tree, we rented a seventeen-inch black-and-white TV set from Rentaset. We'd moved with the times, and we took our pick of what to watch, but our evenings were never really the same again. Knitting and darning were put to one side, the newspaper folded, and my library book remained closed. Watching television was a passive, impersonal exercise and could never be compared with listening to the wireless.

Classical Music, Men with Two Christian Names, and Different Weather Forecasts

CLASSICAL MUSIC WAS seldom heard in the farmhouse tree. On one occasion in 1959 my father sampled a new programme which came on at nine o'clock on the Light Programme after we'd been listening to *Sunday Half Hour*. Normally on a Sunday it would have been turned off at this time, but when the announcer gave the title of the programme my father's interest was aroused, and *The Hundred Best Tunes in the World* briefly entered our world.

At the end of the programme he announced, "We shan't be having that one again. Either I can't count, or they use a different number system from us in their part of the world. Not only weren't there a hundred, but even the ones they did play wasn't the best. Not in our part of the world anyway."

To which my aged maiden aunt added, "Well, what do you expect from a man with two Christian names and no surname? A Sunday night and not one hymn. It won't last. Mark my words. Showy business people. Always got to be different."

The presenter may have played symphonies, arias, duets and concertos; he may well have popularised serious music across the land, but his less than a hundred tunes were never heard again in our small part of the world.

As to what my family would have thought of Stravinsky or Schoenberg, I never found out because the needle in the illuminated tuning dial never stopped at the Third Programme station, and no-one embarked on a journey of musical discovery. There was an unwritten maxim – 'We knew what we liked, and we liked what we knew'. Modernism was an unspoken word, a blasphemy in the farmhouse tree. We were strictly roast beef and Yorkshire pudding – Home Service and Light Programme. As my aged maiden aunt said, "Why have rice when we like potatoes?"

Even Alberto Semprini didn't serenade us each week, his melodies not loved. Old and new ones alike, all were neglected. A foreign Johnny wasn't allowed to cross over the threshold of the farmhouse tree.

Sing Something Simple with the Cliff Adams Singers was however much enjoyed when it was first aired in 1959. Even though the presenter had (more or less) two Christian names, his choir was much admired. We knew a Methodist family called Adams, but it was assumed by my aged maiden aunt that the Cliff Adams Singers were Cliff Adam's Singers, the apostrophe counting for little in our part of the world, let alone the positioning of it. Besides, Adam was a strong Old Testament name and this would have worked in Cliff's favour, in her eyes.

David with his parents and a pet rabbit in front court, 1958

Another presenter with two Christian names who was banned was Brian Matthew. This, however, could have been down to the fact that his choice of music in *Saturday Skiffle Club* in the 1950s was considered unsavoury, raucous and a din. Even though he had an apostle's name, it counted for little, especially when I informed my aged maiden aunt that the skiffle groups used washboards and thimbles.

"Huh. Washboards are for washday Monday and thimbles are for sewing nights. Pianos are used for proper music. And call that singing? More like a pig stuck under a five-bar gate. Whatever next?"

It was renamed *Saturday Club* in 1957 and my aged maiden aunt certainly didn't agree with the description in the *Radio Times* – "the best of today's pop entertainment". For her, pop was a fizzy drink in a Corona bottle and certainly not an entertainment.

"Paul Robeson. Now there's a singer for you," said my father as the strains of 'Swing Low, Sweet Chariot' resonated through the gauze speaker. "A voice as deep as our pond. Not from our part of the world, but a grand voice all the same." The strong biblical Christian name also stood him in good stead, in my aged maiden aunt's eyes, but later that week when a Sikh haberdasher salesman with his battered case containing a rainbow of exotic materials entered front court, our doors remained firmly bolted, my aged maiden aunt wanting to have nothing to do with a tall dark stranger from another part of the world.

Although not linked with music, a comedian who in her eyes had two Christian names was Ted Ray. His programme, *Ray's a Laugh*, which ran until 1961 always annoyed her. "I'm not laughing. He doesn't raise a laugh in this house or anywhere else, I shouldn't wonder," she said one day, obviously relishing a good pun.

Strangely, Kenneth Williams who could have possessed two Christian names, but didn't quite, was greeted with delight when occasionally heard by mistake. His trembling camp voice always made her laugh and he was never told to stop messin' about.

But one man who was always welcomed into our house and who also possessed two Christian names and no surname was Billy Graham. When he made a rare visit to Britain, his voice coming through the gauze speaker, he was welcomed with open arms in our part of the world – "A great man. A great man." I rather think she would have liked me to have become a missionary, but donating my ship ha'pennies towards overseas missionary work was enough for me.

When we took delivery of a portable wireless for the princely sum of twenty-two pounds, fourteen shillings and sixpence, my father chuckled as he tuned it in for the five-to-one weather forecast. If classical music was seldom heard, the forecasts each day were considered essential listening. Their prognostications, linked with the barometer reading each morning, were essential for the running of the farm.

After we had listened to the forecast and all decided that the tone and sound were much better on the new set, my father turned it off and said, "Here's a little story for you. We were the first in the village to have a wireless set. Sam who helped out at harvest time when he wasn't hedging and ditching for the council couldn't stop admiring it. After a long, long time of saving up he proudly told me one day that he'd bought his own set just like ours. Well, a couple of days later there was a knock on the back door at ten to one and there was Sam, cap in hand, asking if he could possibly come in and listen to the weather forecast.

"I asked him if his had broken down. He fiddled with his cap and he said that he and missus had been talking it over, and they both reckoned that because I was the master I'd get a more accurate forecast on our wireless than what he was getting on his."

Thirty years after my aged maiden aunt's death, *Your Hundred Best Tunes*, having undergone a name change in 1960, and having moved to the Home Service and back to the Light Programme, was still going strong and was still being presented by Alan Keith who still hadn't got a surname. "Showy business people. Always got to be different."

Jimmy, Norman and Henry (and Patricia)

"THAT YOUNG JIMMY'S a little scamp," chuckled my aged maiden aunt as *The Clitheroe Kid* finished on the wireless. "His mother's got her hands full with that one. He's always getting into scrapes. Needs to feel her hand on the back of his legs."

"He's a very good actor," I replied in a know-it-all voice.

But she was not to be deflected. "A bundle of trouble all the time. I wouldn't want to be his teacher. Good job he's not in your class. He'd be in the dunce's corner every day of the week. Worse than a cartload of monkeys."

Trying to visualise what a cartload of monkeys would look like and where she could possibly have seen one, I persisted with my argument. "But he's a grown man, Auntie. Jimmy Clitheroe isn't a boy." I was keen to air the knowledge I'd gleaned from Kenny the Gorilla Harris, who had added other personal details which had made us snigger in the boys' lavatory.

"Funny sort of man, if you ask me," she continued.

"He's a man who's short," I added. "Less than four feet nine. And he looks just like a boy, but he isn't."

She gave my revelations a few seconds' careful thought before giving her pronouncement. "A dwarf, eh? A midget. Well he can't help that, but he should grow up and act his proper age. Can't help being small but there's no need going around pretending he's a boy. Whatever next?"

Another of my favourite programmes was a *Children's Hour* series – 'Norman and Henry Bones the Boy Detectives'. The two teenagers, who were cousins, experienced adventures unlike those experienced by any other children except for the Famous Five and the Secret Seven.

Both boys lived in the same Norfolk village, went everywhere on their bikes, knew everyone for miles around and had the peculiar knack of finding a mystery to solve as soon as they went on holiday. And gosh everyone was a frightful blackguard. Henry was fourteen, Norman sixteen, and they employed detective skills of which even Sherlock Holmes would have been proud.

One afternoon at half past five, my aged maiden aunt came in just as they had solved their latest case.

"Henry is actually a lady," I announced.

There was a slight pause as she took in this groundbreaking statement. But she quickly responded to my latest revelation. "Funny name for a girl. Short for Henrietta, I suppose. Like that George in your Enid Blyton books that's short for Georgina."

"No, Auntie, the person who plays Henry in the play is a female. Henry Bones is a boy like me. The actress who plays him is called Patri –"

Before I could complete the name she interrupted me – "Pass me the *Radio Times*."

I watched her nimble fingers leaf through the pages, her tongue moistening the index finger every couple of flicks. At last she reached the relevant day and the cast list. After scanning the names she made her pronouncement. "Your Henry Bones isn't played by a woman. The *Radio Times* has made a printing error. It should read Patrick. A woman pretending to be a boy indeed. It's not wholesome. Whatever will you come out with next? They'll correct it next week, you see if your auntie isn't right. It'll be Patrick, you mark my words."

I checked the copy of the *Radio Times* when the baker delivered it on the Friday.

"Well, what does it say? Auntie was right, wasn't she?"

I shook my head. "It still says Patricia."

She gave a snort. "Well they'm wrong again. That's all I know. Need to have a word with their printers."

They were still making printing errors and getting it wrong in 1971 when I watched Jeremy Sandford's *Edna, the Inebriate Woman*; Edna was played by Patricia Hayes and not by Patrick Hayes pretending to be a woman.

As to what my aged maiden aunt would have said, I can only guess. Something along the lines of "Showy business people. Always got to be different. Whatever next?"

A Gottle o' Geer

MY AGED MAIDEN aunt, who frowned on the wireless set being switched on during our Sunday roast beef and Yorkshire pudding dinner, was in bed poorly. Outside, the rain was pouring down and we wouldn't be able to walk the mile to chapel for Sunday school and the afternoon service. For once my all-seeing, all-hearing, invisible God had answered my prayer. And with my aged maiden aunt in bed, Sunday for once was going to be a fun day. *Educating Archie* – a wireless treat.

"Of course Albert Saveen was the first ventriloquist to appear on the wireless," announced my father after we had listened to the programme and the Bakelite wireless set was switched off. "He had a show on the Light Programme called *Midday with Daisy May*. That was the name of his girl dummy. Odd really, a male ventriloquist and a girl dummy."

The show we had just enjoyed featured Peter Brough and his dummy Archie Andrews. It revolved around Archie, a young schoolboy who was having private education at home with a personal tutor, and each week a guest on the show would attempt to make him clever.

The guests were performers who were to become stars in their own right in the world of entertainment, and included Tony Hancock, Max Bygraves, a teenage singer Julie Andrews, and Beryl Reid who was Archie's girlfriend.

"I could never understand how you can have a ventriloquist on the wireless," continued my father smiling broadly. "For a start you don't know if his lips are moving. Anyone can be a ventriloquist on the wireless. For all we know when Archie says 'a bottle of beer', Peter Brough is moving his lips. A strange breed, wireless ventriloquists and their dummies. Do their lips move? That's what I want to know."

The chance for me to solve the mystery, in the manner of Norman and Henry Bones, occurred in the late 1950s when Peter Brough and Archie Andrews appeared on stage at the Regal Cinema in Barnstaple for the first week in January, in a Christmas extravaganza entitled *Archie Andrews' Christmas Party*. The guests at the seasonal bash included Edward Victor who was to provide handmade humour, George and Lydia who would thrill fellow partygoers on an unsupported ladder, the Four Montis who were equilibrists and Archie's girlfriends. Musical entertainment was to be provided by Rey Overbury and his tinkling feet, or were those the feet of his assistant Suzette? There were also Cy Pagos and the Poodle Boys featuring Bambi the only record-miming poodle in the world. Margery Manners was going to sing, while Goga and Partner were going to juggle, and Jack (Tarzan) Lambert was going to provide a comedy trampoline act.

My father could barely contain his laughter. "A miming poodle. Listen to the wireless and he'll be on *Children's Favourites* next."

Saturday the seventh of January arrived, and my mother, aged maiden aunt and I were driven by a family friend in her Morris Minor to the cinema. Tickets costing four and sixpence each were purchased, and a sixpenny programme. During the interval I was treated to an Orange Maid ice lolly.

As soon as the final curtain came down I was allowed to go to the stage door where I hoped to meet my schoolboy hero. After a few minutes a uniformed doorman, with a matching shiny peaked cap, emerged and informed the small queue that Mr Brough and young Master Andrews would not be receiving guests. Our autograph books were taken away and returned five minutes later signed in pencil.

"Looks like all his education paid off," said my father as I showed off my autograph book. "'Good luck from Peter Brough and Archie Andrews'. A neat little writer. I expect he'll be using a fountain pen soon. Writes his name just like Peter Brough as well."

"Peter Brough wrote it, Dad," I laughed.

"Is that so?" he replied, winking at his sister, my aged maiden aunt. "Now then, the answer I've been waiting to hear. Did you see lips move? Peter Brough's, that is."

"No," I replied.

My father looked crestfallen, and waited for me to enlarge.

I took a deep breath. "Peter Brough had a very bad cold. As soon as he came on stage with Archie Andrews he told us that he didn't want to spread his germs around the audience."

My father was mystified. "Are you telling me he never said anything else? I hope you got your money back."

With a mischievous twinkle in her eye, my aged maiden aunt enlightened him. "He talked right enough, and the ole dummy kept moving his lips and fluttering his eyelids right enough. But Mr Brough held a handkerchief with one hand in front of his mouth the whole time, while his other hand was working the dummy's doings around the back. His head swivelled around and his mouth kept gaping open and his eyelashes flicked up and down."

My mother joined in. "Great big white handkerchief the size of a tablecloth. Hardly see his head let alone his mouth."

My father slapped his leg in delight. "That proves it. His lips were moving all the time, I'll bet."

My aged maiden aunt laughed. "And he looked some smart in his blazer with navy and light blue stripes and a matching handkerchief and scarf. And that was just the ole dummy."

"All I can say is that it was a good job you didn't meet him. Think of the germs you'd have brought back with you. We'd have had colds until Easter."

Many years later I discovered that Daisy May had originally started her wooden life as a boy. The first sex change operation on a ventriloquist's dummy in radio and medical history, and probably the last. I also read that Beryl Reid actually dressed up as a schoolgirl in her old school uniform and black stockings with a handkerchief tucked into her knickers, to get into the part of Archie's girlfriend.

What my father would have made of such revelations I shudder to think, but he would certainly have spluttered into his gottle o' geer.

Jelly, Jam and Chutney

WINTER TEAS WERE jam-, jelly- and chutney-filled. A greaseproof paper lid removed, and summer was released in a pouring out of memories.

Always around Derby Day, the first cut of hay – mower, turner, rake, sweep and cart. Cascading stalks, dry and intoxicating, filling the air with the sweet scent of harvest. Running, rolling, skipping through the swathes. Salt, mustard, vinegar and pepper. As twilight came down on a flutter of bats' wings, I turned my last cartwheels over the mead as iron-rimmed wheels turned up the lane. Harvest home and the hay shed full.

Always in summer the drone of light aircraft, prospectors of moorland, hedgerow and orchard combing for gold in gorse bush, apple tree and honeysuckle, returning to hangars weighed down with bounty. In May a load of hay, in June a silver spoon, in July not even a fly. On a china dish on kitchen table, wax cells of sticky treasure.

Always in summer the sun flowed honey-thick across a red sky at night or morning, delighting or warning an unknown shepherd's days. My question as to where this unknown shepherd lived greeted with a laugh and a ruffle of my tousled hair. Golden corn with a scattering of poppy, bindweed and cornflower waving gently in the breeze. Call of the cuckoo, skim of the swallow, minnows in a jam jar, birds'-nesting days. Summer treats. Chocolate, strawberry and vanilla flavoured ice cream between wafers or in cones, melting into the memory days.

The bramble patch was a wild beast of a shrub, its barbed tentacles ensnaring my unwary bare arms, and snagging my red-and-white check short-sleeved shirt. This was my multi-eyed mythical monster; its compound orbs rage – black in the sunlight. Plucked from their sockets they were placed in an enamel bowl wedged in my withe basket. Occasionally the beast lashed out, attempting to trap my hand in a writhing of thumb-thick coils.

Tipped into a saucepan on the Calor gas stove the orbs bubbled into a boiling purple pulp, and maggots danced a dance of death. Swollen and taut as a cow's udder the stained muslin bag bulged pendulous from the back kitchen beam, dripping. Next morning, the blue-rimmed enamel bowl on the flagstone floor was almost full of blood-thick strained juice. A mirror locking in the sun-filled carefree summer days.

Placed next to the pots of chutney and jam, jars of strawberry, raspberry, gooseberry, plum, greengage, damson, beetroot and bean in the dressing room attached to my parents' bedroom. A shimmering kaleidoscope of dancing patterns in a shaft of sunlight, when the door was opened.

The teatime pot resealed and replaced in the pantry cupboard. In the hearth of the open fire the apple logs blaze sun-hot. At the edge of Beerclose Copse my mythical hydra stirs in his winter sleep.

Betraying the Pet Pink Pig

THE PET PINK pig was an important member of my two Sunday school teacher great-aunts' family. Snorting out its day in the tiny lean-to pigsty at the top of the small paddock, the pet pink pig grew fat.

"Fat pigs should never lie on warm straw," stated a great-uncle. "They should lie wet in mud until they're coated in it. Warm litter melts their fat, and they shouldn't burn off energy moving about too much either. A good fat pig should weigh between fifteen- and twenty-score."

But my great-aunts' pet pink pig enjoyed a bed of warm golden barley straw and every Saturday I went up through the garden path to lean over the stone wall enclosing the paddock, to rub its back and tickle its ears.

"You make sure you keep your hands well away from its mouth," warned my father. "The teeth could bite your fingers off. Chomp through anything, a pig's teeth. A mincemeat machine on legs. They even say there's some who give 'em dead rats to chew up."

"Yes, keep your fingers well out of the way," added my mother. "There was a chap not far from here lost a finger to a pig." She laughed. "He was a short little chap and people said it was a good job the pig wasn't hungry or it would have eaten all of him for dinner."

My aged maiden aunt added a warning: "And they also say there was a little boy who was very, very naughty. His dad put him in the pigsty as a punishment, and when he came back to let him out, all he found was his pair of boots." As she finished speaking she looked at my pair of shoes which I hadn't polished that morning.

But my great-aunts' pet pink pig continued eating the household scraps, crusts of bread, potato peelings and the best barley meal. And it grew fatter and fatter and fatter.

"Why's the pig been given extra milk in his trough for the past fortnight?" I asked one November morning at the breakfast table.

There was a brief pause and glances were exchanged.

"Needs to get even fatter. Winter's coming," replied my father before quickly changing the subject.

Early one frosty morning the following week, I was mooching around front court when the brittle silence was shattered by a high-pitched squealing which appeared to be coming from the bottom of the village.

It was the same sound I'd heard the previous year, and it was also about the same time of the year. On that occasion my mother had suddenly appeared, whisking me off to complete a selection of chores which she suddenly decided needed doing. The following Saturday when I'd gone down to see the pet pink pig, the paddock was empty and no-one wanted to answer my questions.

This year I would investigate. Leaving front court I ran down the road in the direction of the sound. It was definitely coming from the direction of my great-aunts' house. The drawn-out squeals and screams smashed into my head, lodging in my memory. Just as I thought my skull would explode, the squealing stopped.

Entering the small yard at the back of their house I stopped in my tracks. A dozen yards ahead of me was the pet pink pig.

It was lying out on a wood rack, and under its chin across its neck was red...

Running off I found a spot in my great-aunts' garden hedge where I could watch without being seen. When I had plucked up courage I looked across into the yard. Buckets of boiling water were being poured over its back, the steam billowing into the cold air. A man, a stranger, was standing over it with what looked like a piece of tin in his hand and he was scraping it across the pet pink pig's back. He was shaving it, he was removing the hair and bristles.

I gave a gulp. This was too much for me to take in and understand. Turning slowly I retraced my footsteps to the farmhouse tree.

But curiosity as usual got the better of me, and next morning I sneaked back quietly to the yard and opened the outhouse door. There, hanging from an iron hook, strung up by its hind legs was the pet pink pig.

I stared at it. A long incision had been made straight down through its belly and the innards had been removed, kidneys, liver, heart, lungs and even the head were all gone. It was hollow and opened out like a hardback book, its belly part propped wide apart by a wooden bar. Walking up behind it I poked my index finger into the flesh. It was cold and solid. Quickly withdrawing my fingers, I clenched my hand into a tight fist.

Thump, thump.

I clenched my other hand into a fist.

Thump, thump, thump, thump.

My fists pummelled the solid flesh.

Thump, thump, thump, thump.

My own flesh punchbag.

Very slowly it began to swing towards me.

Another flurry of punches and it moved slowly away from me.

Stepping back I walked around to the front of the punchbag, and I suddenly realised I'd been punching the pet pink pig.

The pet pink pig I'd fed apples and acorns on Saturday afternoons. The pet pink pig which had never once tried to chew off my fingers or eat me up. The pet pink pig which had given off gurgling grunts of pleasure every time I tickled its ears.

I winced as I recalled the events of the previous morning, and the red line across its throat was now a mocking grin in my memory.

Blushing, I stuffed my hands as deep as it was possible for them to go into the pockets of my short trousers, and stared down at my black shiny wellington boots in an attempt to escape the small accusing eyes in my memory.

Looking towards a corner of the shed I saw a wooden tub covered over with a sack. Once again curiosity got the better of me and I lifted a corner of the coarse material.

"Intestines," said one of my great-aunts who had entered unnoticed. "About sixty feet of intestines."

I gulped at the thought of all the tubes and coils and loops squirming around inside of the pet pink pig. How could they all possibly fit in? Did I have that amount of intestines inside of my body?

"We'll turn 'em inside out, scrape 'em, cut 'em into small pieces and clean 'em in hot salty water. Then we'll chop 'em up, mix in small bits of stomach fat, and fry it all up with some onions."

I nodded, feeling my knees begin to tremble.

"Now you'd better be getting back, because the butcher'll be here in a minute to cut and joint it so we can salt it down. We'll have gammons, hams, flitches and shoulder hams. Hard work. We've got to rub the salt well into every joint and every crevice together with brown sugar and saltpetre."

Before I could make my exit the butcher was there. Unnoticed, he was standing in the doorway. The stranger I'd seen yesterday with a long-bladed knife in his hand, the stranger I'd watched from their garden.

He leered at me. "Butcher. Pig Sticker. That's me. Head first, cut it into halves. Cut off the ears. Remove the eyes. Then I'll take out the brain and cut up the rest of it. Trotters is me personal favourite. Mind you, there's they that don't like the feet. But when they've been cooked and allowed to cool they'm full o' jelly." Licking his lips he chuckled. "Not your party jelly, mind you. Not red or orange. But still sweet to my way o' thinkin!"

Without waiting to hear any more I ducked between them and bolted from the shed, his laughter snorting in my ears.

Back in front court I was greeted by my father. "You'm looking pale."

"Hungry," I mumbled. "Forgot all about breakfast."

"Must have been something pretty exciting to forget your breakfast," he said in his knowing way, adding, "There isn't much worth knowing about pigs that your two aunts don't know. And in a day or two I'll have a present for you. One you'll have fun with. A present with a difference."

Over the next couple of days I pondered his cryptic words. A present with a difference, and it wasn't even my birthday or Christmas.

At last the day of the mysterious present arrived.

"There you are. A football for you."

I fingered the strange object. It was certainly the shape and size of a football, and it was almost as round. But there the similarities ended. It wasn't made of leather. It wasn't laced up and it wasn't brown. It was made from a sort of transparent material. It was just like looking into glass, but it wasn't glass. The material was very light and I'd never seen or touched anything like it before.

"Thanks!" I shouted as I ran off in the direction of Higher Mead, the ball at my feet.

For almost a week in my spare time, I kicked it around the fields. It was great, because I never knew which direction it would go when it bounced. It had a mind of its own. I was Manchester United and I was top of Division One and I also won the F.A. Cup final. Eventually I got fed up with playing football and I tied the strange object on the end of the tail of my green-and-yellow kite.

A few weeks later at the breakfast table, a Willow pattern plate piled high with fried eggs, bubble and squeak, fried bread, fried bacon, fat and streaky, and sausages was placed in front of me.

The grease slipped down my chin, and at the end of the meal I watched my father slide the blade of his knife across the surface of his plate. It arced like a silver rainbow as it scooped up the remains of the gold yolk. With a smile and a wink he slowly extended his tongue over the blade to savour the final licking.

I was about to emulate him, when out of the corner of my eye I saw my mother slowly shaking her head. Foiled again, but one day I'd manage to copy him. He replaced the knife on his plate and wiped his mouth with the back of his hand, a loud smack of his lips and the ritual was complete. "There's no doubt about it. You can't beat home-cured bacon."

My eyes went wide as what he had said sank in. He continued, "Nothing wasted when you kill a pig." With a laugh he added, "Only the tail and the squeak, that is. And even the tail makes a good fly-swat."

My mother and aged maiden aunt joined in the laughter, but I recalled the squeal-scream.

"The secret lies in what it eats, and the quality of the barley mash," said my aged maiden aunt.

As I sat staring at my empty plate they proceeded to give me a comprehensive list of the edible delicacies.

"Brawn from the head, bones and ears and the odds and ends," announced my mother, "not forgetting Bath chaps from the cheeks."

"Pudding from the chittlins with groats and currants added to sweeten it," put in my aged maiden aunt.

And the list continued.

"Sausages, rashers, fat bacon, dripping and lard."

"Chops, ribs, joints and ham."

"Faggots, from the minced-up liver and heart with a bit of sage and onions. Beautiful."

"Like I said, you can't beat a pig," concluded my father, "and a flitch hanging on the wall is prettier than any picture, to my way of thinking." Pausing to take a good swig of tea he gave his final addition to the list. "Why even the bladder makes a good football."

I gulped as he continued.

"I was about your age when I had my first bladder ball. My father, the grandfather you never knew, made it for me in... let's see... must have been nineteen hundred and ten. Cut it out, cleaned it and blew it up. Got one every year just like you will."

I could feel my face beginning to turn red. Not only had I been eating the pet pink pig, but I'd also scored goals at Wembley with... with his naughty part.

I blushed even more.

In my memory, the echoes of the early-morning squeals and screams and the red grin across its throat. But worst of all, the memory of the eyes on a Saturday afternoon as I fed it apples and acorns. Two small eyes looking at the boy who was going to betray the pet pink pig.

High Days and Special Treat Days

TWO NOT-TO-BE-MISSED SUNDAYS in the Knowstone calendar of chapel services were Summer Anniversary Sunday and Autumn Harvest Festival Sunday. These were followed by the Monday celebrations which were secular and frivolous, rather than spiritual and serious. The summer Sunday celebrated the harvest of young souls nurtured on texts, prayers and knowing right from wrong. The autumn Sunday celebrated the harvest of produce nurtured by farmer, villager and God. Both Sundays were special enough to warrant a visit from the High Priest – the Methodist minister from the manse, rather than a lay preacher from his farmhouse; farmer during the week and religious orator on Sunday.

Anniversary Sunday was a celebration of Knowstone chapel being built on its present site in 1927. A month before the great day, us little tackers were presented with our Sunday school recitations to learn.

Two cousins (removed), old in my young eyes, whom I was brought up to believe were great-aunts, ran the chapel and the Sunday school. Linked with the fact that my father, aged maiden aunt and their parents and grandparents before them were staunch followers of the faith meant that I had little choice but to attend the "pretend school", as one of my non-participating mates called Sunday school. There was no escaping the ritual, and I had spouted my first recitation, parrot-fashion, by the age of four... "Two little dicky birds sitting on the wall, one named Peter, one named Paul. Fly away Peter, fly away Paul. Come back Peter, come back Paul." The names relating to two biblical apostles.

By the age of nine I had

David's paternal grandparents, probably on their wedding day in the early 1890s. He never knew them; both died many years before he was born.

progressed to a ten-verse epic of *Iliad* proportions concerning a boy who stole an apple from a tree, dropped it, followed it as it rolled down a hill and into a field where it was eaten by a horse. My aged maiden aunt was most impressed when I recited it to her on a run-through before the great day. "Good words, telling you that crime never pays and a thief never prospers. You'll do well to remember that recitation."

The Anniversary service was an ordeal which had to be suffered with a stiff upper lip which invariably trembled in front of a congregation of assorted relatives and Methodists from other chapels in the circuit, keen to see the standard of other village Sunday schools. We sat on wooden forms on either side of the altar, pink scrubbed legs crossed in the hope that we wouldn't wet ourselves as we waited to shine like golden stars in front of the congregation. Invariably the heat and solemnity of the occasion proved too much for one young initiate and a small yellow pool flowed across the polished floorboards. After an outflowing of tears the young disciple was united with his parents, his ordeal put on hold for another year.

On Monday, after real school, a repeat performance when our headmistress was in attendance, and Treat Tea. And what a Treat Tea it was with the trestle tables set up by parents, groaning under the weight of goodies contributed by villagers. Bread and butter cut in posh triangles, cut rounds overflowing with cream and jam, paste sandwiches, and the bestest of all, the fancy cakes delivered on a large wooden tray by Chanters Bakery from Bishops Nympton. These were the finest delicacies in our feast, the finest fancy cakes that had ever been served up – angel cakes, butterfly buns, chocolate-and-cream éclairs, jam tarts, lemon curd tarts, coconut pyramids, macaroons, slices of fruit cake and Battenberg, and the crowns of the royal feast – tennisball-sized, cream-filled, cherry-topped meringues. Treats of the highest order, seldom seen and eagerly devoured. Firstly by half-closed eyes during grace and then by mouths. Mouth-watering delights. Rewards for reciting our recitations. Edible rewards which caused our eyes to pop out on stalks, mouths to dribble in anticipation as we waited for the off.

Every year when I sat at the tea table I was aware of my mum and aged maiden aunt watching my every movement as they served the beakers of lemonade. Although it was meant to be a fun tea, for me it was a serious occasion. Every year my eyes flitted over the delicacies and the dreaded fish-paste sandwiches, and the even more dreaded bread-and-butter triangles. Finally my eyes were drawn to the crowning glory – the yum-yum, pig's-bum with the alley-sized scarlet cherry.

I'd never had the meringue, having been brought up by my mum and aged maiden aunt to always begin with a slice of bread and butter. Fellow Sunday school members who hadn't heard of etiquette grabbed the best fancies, including the meringue, and I was left with the jam or lemon curd tarts.

One summer it was different. As soon as grace had been said and "Amen" had barely left my watering lips, aged almost ten, I put into action the scheme I'd been planning for days. My left hand made for the bread and butter, while my right hand dived at the fancy cakes. Success. I had perfected the two-handed prong attack. Between the fingers of my right hand, the prized meringue. "Thank you, God," I whispered, not daring to look at my mum and aged maiden aunt. Repercussions could wait until I was back at the farmhouse tree.

After Treat Tea, games outside where we searched for shiny pennies hidden in grass tussocks, under stones and clods of earth by our two Sunday school teachers. On a good hunt, enough coppers for a comic, aniseed balls and a gobstopper. At the end of the evening, walking wearily home with my mum and aged maiden aunt while my dad was finishing off the milking.

"You've been a good boy, and we'll overlook the meringue this time. A lot of lines to learn, and you spoke up well. We'll see if Auntie has enough change left over when she gets her pension on Thursday for a little treat – a little book." And she did.

When the final shooked sheaves, cut and bound by the binder, had all been safely gathered in, and ricked ere the winter storms began, Knowstone chapel held its Harvest Festival service and auction celebrations. On the preceding Saturday afternoon, six lady followers of the faith including Mum, and the two great-aunts who weren't, worked as one, harnessing their decorative talents to turn the chapel interior into a cornucopia filled with floral and vegetable delights. On window ledge and altar rail, a plethora of potatoes, parsnips, turnips, cauliflowers and carrots. A jubilant chorus of bunched asters and chrysanths. Each item of produce tended and grown by cottager and farmer in garden and field, all except for one bunch of black grapes…

Crowning the display, a collection of corn dollies, crafted by members of the Women's Institute, or Wild Indians as me and my mates called them, in the wooden hall at Roachill, which were hung with pride on the wall behind the altar. Echoes of the last neck of corn

The ladies decorating the chapel for the harvest festival in the mid-1950s. David's two Sunday school teacher great-aunts (who weren't) are far left, his mother next to them.

which had always been nailed on the barn door of the farmhouse tree by my grandfather half a century ago.

On the Sunday afternoon when Sunday school had ended, I joined my parents and aged maiden aunt on our uncomfortable wooden plank-backed seat designed to make dozing off during the sermon impossible, as the congregation filed in. A gathering of parishioners who had come as thankful people – farmers who had ploughed the fields and scattered the good seed on the land and who wished to sing to the Lord of the Harvest and thank Him for feeding and watering it with His almighty hand. All had come rejoicing after bringing in the sheaves.

Instead of sitting and calculating numerical permutations on the hymn board during the sermon, I marvelled at the bounty on display, feeling a sense of pride that my mum had contributed to the overall effect, and that my dad had grown some of the vegetables. As one, we sent our rousing harvest hymns heavenwards, and I sang as loudly as the grown-ups, but my mind was jumping ahead to the auction of produce on the following evening. A treat time – being allowed to stay up late on a school night.

"I'm not sure they should sell things in the house of God," said my aged maiden aunt as we crossed the road to avoid walking on the same side as the Masons Arms. "Remember Christ casting out the moneychangers in the temple."

What fun it was as the produce was auctioned off by a local farmer whose fifteen minutes of village fame had arrived, with all proceeds going towards Sunday school funds – the summer seaside outing treat, the Anniversary Treat Tea, book prizes at Easter and the Christmas party treat with a visit by Father Christmas giving out gifts from his hessian sack. An evening filled with innuendos about the size of farmers' cucumbers and marrows, jokes which went over my young head but which were greeted with raucous laughter.

The bidding reached dizzy heights, well above the true value of the lot held aloft as the villagers were determined not to be outbid by a neighbour. A marrow would often make over ten shillings (50p; spending power today of approximately £20). It would then be taken home, hollowed out, stuffed with mincemeat, sage and onions, roasted and served up as *mock duck*. The purchaser in all probability having a glut of marrows in their own garden out the back, sometimes even buying back their own marrow.

My own marrow, with DJH scratched on with a pin by the garden fairy when I was asleep, which as if by magic grew bigger until the letters were almost an inch tall, selling for twelve shillings (60p). The purchaser – my mum.

During the auction my aged maiden aunt had kept her purse firmly shut and her hands in her lap until the final lot was held up. The bidding was brisk but she knew what she wanted.

"Sold to Miss Hill, Eastacott." Nods and smiles.

"I dearly love black grapes, but the pips get under my false teeth," she said, plucking four from the one-and-only bunch in the auction and passing them to me. "A little treat, and the money is going to a good cause." A pause for reflection. "Mind you, 'tis more than I really intended to bid."

A Little Something

THE SOUND OF Sheffield steel on the granite pump trough in back kitchen was another scream-squeal in my brain; Christmas was beginning. Parcels hanging from a beam in the outhouse. Wrapping paper, white and brown. Deft movements of the knife. The parcels all of a-shudder and a-judder. A flutter of feathers. A crimson stain on the outhouse earth floor.

In the evening, the white top hat on a plate on the cellar table became the centre of my attention. Sitting on the edge of my chair waiting and watching, willing the conjuror to begin her show. Abracadabra. A hand thrust into the top hat, and then withdrawn. No white rabbit, but ribbon after ribbon of intestines. Small objects – heart, liver, crop and gall. Occasionally a small yellow balloon egg accompanied by a musical flesh symphony of slurps, gloops and glurps. The flourish of the conjuror's hand. "More, Mum. More!"

An encore. My mother's sleight of hand, a finger flick and a rubber band was fastened into position. My mother's party piece completed, we enjoyed the shared experience. The chicken drawn and trussed. To come, the Christmas roast and the wishbone, and the sixpence-in-the-pudding ritual.

On the Thursday before Christmas, the market day shopping expedition and a visit to Gran's. A treat fish-and-chips one-o'clock dinner with a slice of bread and butter. Unwrapped from the newspaper and greaseproof paper, my mouth watering as the momentous meal slipped onto my Willow pattern plate.

Sitting back on the settee, Gran approaching with a smile on her face. "A little something from us both for Christmas." An envelope pressed into my palm.

Opening it excitedly. The little something was a big something. My annual five-pound note, a paper fortune. Giving her a kiss, every gift has its price. Gran leaving the room. Grandad asleep and full in his chair. Fingering the note, I begin to daydream of the spending power I possess.

Sweets, sweets, sweets and more sweets and an excess of other goodies. Three hundred Mars bars, a whole field of potatoes turned into four hundred packets of crisps hopefully with blue twists of salt, or six hundred packets of K.P. ready salted peanuts. One thousand, two hundred packets of chewing gum making up four thousand, eight hundred white sugar-coated pieces to chew. One piece a day. I could be chewing gum for over twelve years. Six hundred packets of pink lump bubblegum. Goldfish bowl-sized bubbles bursting back in my face leaving my cheeks coated in a thin sticky gauze.

My mind beginning to boggle as sweet-boggling facts begin to melt and flow through it. One thousand, two hundred gobstoppers almost as big as ping-pong balls. Lick, lick, lick. Take it out and check the colour change. Purple to pink to lurid green to white. Put it back in my mouth, wipe my fingers on my short grey flannel trousers. Lick, lick, lick again.

Four thousand, eight hundred liquorice blackjacks or strawberry-and-banana chews. Enough to build a tower a hundred feet high.

Six hundred sherbet fountains. Sucking too much up through the black liquorice straw and coughing violently. Blowing a powder snow blizzard over my mates. Six hundred boxes of aniseed balls. Thousands of tiny orange ball bearings to suck and suck until your tongue and lips turn orange. Finally biting into the aniseed. Six hundred packets of sweet cigarettes with six hundred cards, hopefully all different. Can there be that many different sets to collect? My aged maiden aunt tut-tut-tutting, thinking her dear little boy is smoking a real cigarette.

Six hundred packets of lovely Love Hearts. If only I had the courage – 'Be my love' or 'Always sweet' to give to ...... with the beautiful long corn-yellow hair. If only.

Two hundred Fry's Turkish Delight bars. Three hundred Crunchies. Two hundred Bountys. Two hundred bars of Dairy Milk chocolate. Six hundred packets of Polo mints. Suck, suck, suck. Wedge the tip of my tongue through the hole in the middle. Hundreds of Wagon Wheels to keep me rolling along through the year. Yum, yum, pig's bum.

And finally, the liquorice.

A shilling for a boxed set of liquorice assortment, including a pipe with a red dot jelly sweet to make it look real, to smoke after the sweet cigarette and make me look like Fred the driver of the rust-bucket red-and-cream school bus. A hundred boxes, a hundred pipes. One pipe a week for almost two years.

And how many liquorice bootlaces? A quick mental calculation. One thousand, two hundred, each measuring approximately thirty-six inches. WOW! Over forty-three thousand inches of liquorice. Would the village shop have enough room for all that liquorice? Remembering my measuring table. One thousand, seven hundred and sixty yards to a mile (or five thousand, two hundred and eighty feet). DOUBLE WOW. Over half a mile with each bootlace put end to end.

My daydream becomes mobile in my mind. Out of Gran's front door, over her daily scrubbed step and onto the washed-down pavement. Down the street to the town square. Under the clock and into the pannier market and through to the auction ring. About turn, back past the Western National bus stop and the barber's shop and retracing my steps back to Gran's, following the black bootlace trail.

And if I didn't want to buy sweets I could always buy two hundred black-and-white I-Spy books or one hundred deluxe colour pages in the middle I-Spy books. Were there that many I-Spys I could buy or even make?

Thirteen Famous Five hardback books with the colour picture on the dust-jacket. But had Enid Blyton written thirteen Famous Fives?

Twenty super-duper 3D View-Master reels in glorious Technicolor; one hundred and forty pictures of dinosaurs just like the ones I imagine when I listen to *How Things Began*, at school on Monday morning. Pictures of royalty and coronations, exotic flowers and Florida parrots, Robin Hood and Tarzan. More than enough to buy the brown light attachment and a battery to fit on the View-Master, to enjoy it in bed at night.

Finally, comics. Six hundred weekly copies of the *Beano* or *Dandy*. WOW again. Twelve years' worth of either comic. I can be reading them until my twenty-first birthday. Will I still want to read them when I'm that old? An easy one, that. Yes. Twelve years of Desperate Dan adventures. Would there be enough cow pies? Would he even live that long?

My mind returns to books. Twenty Observer's Books to go with my Birds, Butterflies, Birds' Eggs and Flowers. I'll be able to observe everything in the world.

Gran re-entered the room and burst my daydream bubble. "You're to put that in your money box, save it and buy savings certificates in the post office for when you're older. Your mother knows you've got it. You're not to go frittering it away on sweets and comics."

TRIPLE WOW! Gran could read my mind and she wasn't even in the room.

A happy liquorice pipe dream while it lasted.

Christmas

THE FINAL MARKET day visit to South Molton, the lead-up to Christmas. This was my final chance to shop in the pannier market, and I'd seen just the present for my mother, but it cost half a crown (12½p) and I'd only got two shillings (10p) of my pocket money left.

"Don't worry," said the stall-owner as I explained my predicament. "I often see your mother and the old lady. I can trust you. Give me your florin and after Christmas you can give me another bob. That's a couple of coppers for me lending you the extra money you need."

It seemed fair to my nine-year-old brain; he was doing me a favour. All went well until I met my aged maiden aunt. "What's in your brown paper bag?"

I showed her the gift and was immediately interrogated. On learning what I'd done she grimaced. "A form of H.P. You come with me, young fellow my lad."

My bag was banged down on the stall. "Give him his money back. Don't want him picking up bad habits at his age. You save up and only buy it when you can afford it, in my book."

He hesitated but, seeing the look in her eye that I knew so well, reimbursed me, leaving me wondering what a gift for my mother had to do with brown sauce.

My aged maiden aunt smiled at him. "And here's a tip for you."

The stall-owner returned her smile, but it quickly changed to a frown when she added, "Never a borrower nor a lender be."

Taking my hand she guided me to another stall where there was an identical cushion cover. "Only two and thrupence (11p) here," she said. "Always check other stalls before you part with your money, You'll have a happy Christmas now, knowing you haven't got a higher purchase debt."

The 21st of December heralded the start of Christmas; it was the day my father and I set out to cut our Christmas tree. Every year he knew which holly tree would give us the best branch. Having sawn off a five-feet top branch, we collected sprigs of holly and ivy with berries.

Back at the farmhouse tree, the holly tree was positioned in the window alcove of front room. With a thrill of excitement I removed the decorations from the sideboard and began decorating the tree. Baubles, bells and multicoloured silver spangled birds with feather plume tails adorned the holly-leaf sprigs, together with twelve pink, blue, yellow and white miniature wax candles. One candle for each of the twelve festive days.

After a brief stop for a Christmas treat – a beaker of Corona orange pop and a home-made mince pie and separated cream – I sat and made paper chains from gummed paper strips. Next they were stretched from corner to corner of the ceiling. Huge red, white and blue crêpe paper balls and bells and brightly coloured cut-outs of Father Christmas, Mr Punch, Judy and a policeman, and two Chinese lanterns, were suspended from ceiling hooks. Finally family photographs were draped in greenery, and then my father took time off from his farm work to help me blow up a dozen balloons. The festive scene was complete.

"Lovely," said my aged maiden aunt as she made her annual inspection. "We'll enjoy being in here just for the special days. You've earned a barley sugar."

On Christmas Eve in the evening, when my father had finished hand-milking our seven cows, we visited an auntie and her brother and played card games and sang carols around the organ. The three-mile walk home just after midnight was always exciting. The stars seemed brighter and nearer, and glinted like icicles in the frosty night sky, and the bag of presents I was carrying always seemed heavier than the one we had delivered. As we walked along I saw my mother and father link arms and smile at each other. I took my aged maiden aunt's hand and was rewarded with a squeeze of my fingers.

Back at front court my father would recount how, as a young boy, he had joined his father in the shippen, where once they had seen two Ruby Red cows kneel as the clock struck midnight. He had never seen it again, and I never witnessed it. As we stood in silence watching the haloes of breath rise to the raftered roof in the beam of torchlight, I even forgot about my bag of presents and in those precious seconds Christmas really began.

I had a great fear of Father Christmas. Our kitchen chimney was very wide, and if Father Christmas could climb down it, so could anyone else. I was also frightened by a man in a robe which completely enveloped him, and a beard which covered all of his face except for the nose and eyes. For these reasons I made it very easy for my mother and father, by asking them to ensure that Father Christmas left my presents at the foot of their bed.

At half past six I would run from my bedroom along the landing into their room and examine my presents – one big gift, one medium-sized gift and a stocking full of small goodies. The stocking contained a bag of sugared almonds, a tin of toffees, a bar of chocolate, pink and white sugar mice, a yo-yo or a gyroscope, a bag of glass marbles, a couple of I-Spy books and a big juicy Jaffa orange. The medium present was always a Rupert Annual.

Big presents over the years were a Bayko Bakelite building set. A Bakelite View-Master and half a dozen 3D reels. A Magic Robot game – your questions always answered by his wand. A remote-control driving game where I steered my car around a town street plan and parked it up after avoiding obstacles. A Meccano set of red and green pieces. The crane on the lid looked magnificent; all I could build was a park bench. Trade Descriptions, where were you when I needed you?

The main gift would have cost about two pounds, the Annual seven and sixpence (37½p) and the small ones about a pound altogether. In total, three pounds and ten shillings. In today's money, about sixty-five pounds.

I never asked why there were no presents from parents; I was just relieved that they'd allowed the red-cloaked stranger to leave his gifts in their bedroom.

One Christmas my Rupert Annual had pages missing and had to be exchanged by my mother at Moules newsagents in South Molton. Father Christmas didn't call the following year and I was no longer afraid of him.

Christmas Day dinner, the bestest dinner of the year. The golden eagle-sized roast chicken. Pulling the wishbone, either on the day or a couple of days later. The St Paul's dome Christmas pudding and the silver sixpence. Into front room with damp-patch continents not charted on any atlas. My father leaving: "The cows won't milk themselves. Not even on Christmas Day."

Tea around the beech and applewood fire. The home-made Christmas cake decorated when I was asleep. My mother so proud of her achievement. The room bathed in candle- and firelight.

Carols around the piano. The footsteps of Good King Wenceslas lit by the two candles in two brass holders attached to the piano. My eyes straying to the top of the polished sideboard. A large glass bowl with four brown bags. Almonds, brazils, filberts and walnuts. My father's party trick with two walnuts. His clenched grenade fist exploding open to reveal cracked shells and kernels. A bowl of sugared almonds, figs and dates. Icing-sugar-dusted cubes of pink and white Turkish Delight, New Berry Fruits. A bottle of Stone's ginger wine. The Methodist family giving into temptation just once a year. My aged maiden aunt singing her Christmas ghost story song – 'The Mistletoe Bough'. Me frightened that my aged maiden aunt might topple into her oak blanket chest and never be found until she was a skeleton.

Old photos and black-edged funeral cards removed from a drawer matched with each other in a bizarre game of happy families.

The cold chicken and pickle supper: "Just this once," said my aged maiden aunt. "After all, it is Christmas, but I expect I shall be up half the night with indigestion."

Up the wooden hill to Bedfordshire. Christmas Day over for another year.

Cracking a Nut

TWELFTH NIGHT SAW the end of the Christmas celebrations and we spent the evening around the open fire in kitchen playing cards and asking riddles, as the faggot and the apple log burned down.

Four brown paper bags placed on the polished dresser top. Four chairs pulled up around the fireplace. The chieftain and his tribe begin their winter ritual. My aged maiden aunt chooses her words carefully and quotes from the Holy Bible – "Out of the eater came forth meat. Out of the strong came forth sweetness." We sip our hot honey-and-blackcurrant cordial, as she relates how with a ass's jawbone the lion Samson smote down thirty men to gain their spoil and garments.

My mother, ever mindful of my mental powers, makes her riddle a mathematical one as she adds more honey to our drinks. "If a hen and a half lays an egg and a half in a day and a half, how long will it take twelve hens to lay a dozen eggs?"

My father laughs. "The old ones are the best." I stop myself from shouting out eighteen; half-guessing it is wrong. My father, mother and aged maiden aunt exchange a knowing glance. He laughs again. "The cow gave birth to it, it grows in the wood, but the smith creates it."

With a nod my aged maiden aunt thrusts the bellows between the glowing sticks and begins a rhythmical pumping, her action steady and unhurried. "The more I feed it, why then 'twill grow most high, but if I give it water why then 'twill surely die."

Flickering red and orange streamers dance up the chimney. She removes the bellows. My father nods. "That's what I call a fire." A shared smile passes between them. I feel excluded. He adds, "A hole full, a sky full, but you won't fill a bowl full."

A blue billow of smoke blows back into the room. We cough. My mother laughs as she unhooks the brass toasting fork from the mantel. "What flies for ever, and yet rests never?"

My father chuckles. "When the north wind doth blow –" breaking off, he adds – "'Round the house, 'round the house the lady dances and on the latticed windowsill she drops her white gloves."

Holding the bread against the fire, my mother completes the first rhyme – "Then we shall have snow, and what will the robin do then, poor thing?" The shared smile passes between them. Again I feel excluded. Turning the slice she adds, "Into the stable goes the white horse, only to come out bridled and brown."

Their smiles broaden, heads nod. "Reflection time," my father says as we stare into the flame. The silence broken only by a spitting spark and the hiss of bubbles from a green log.

My aged maiden aunt rises from her chair. "I'll fetch the butter and more bread for toast." At the door she turns and smiles. "A white barn, two roofs are there on it, but no door is there to be seen."

This acts as a cue for my father who gives an exaggerated wink, "Which is correct? The yoke of an egg is white, or the yoke of an egg are white?"

I recall my first Christmas riddle ritual as I munch my piece of toast, battling with is, are, are, is. Only one egg, it had to be singular and not plural. I took a deep breath and gave my answer.

My aged maiden aunt re-enters the kitchen and we relive that first shared event as my father slowly repeats my words from that winter's night. "The yoke of an egg is white. White indeed; whatever next?" Raising his hand he conducts a chorus and we all join in: "The yoke of an egg is yellow. The yoke of an egg is yellow."

As I chant the words, blushing once again, I suddenly realise how long it takes twelve hens to lay a dozen eggs.

I shout out my answer. Immediately their shared smile passes between us; I am included and my father laughs. "We'll lay your eggs to rest. Your turn. I think you've earned it."

My aged maiden aunt butters more toast.

I take a deep breath before uttering the riddle I've been saving from my comic. "What's black and white and red all over?"

They appear to be perplexed, each glancing at the other. A gentle shake of heads acknowledging defeat.

"A newspaper," I shout. "A newspaper is black and white and *read* all over, because people read it."

A nod of heads. Applause. Another smile. My father says, "Well done."

My eyes wander towards the paper bags; my father tracks their route. "Time for nut-cracking. You choose first. Filbert, almond, walnut or brazil?"

He knows my choice. Our private celebration. "A walnut, please." I anticipate the event. Rolling up his shirtsleeves he takes out two nuts, places them on his left palm, slowly clenches his fist and smiles. I silently will him on.

The veins in his forearm become steel hawsers threatening to sever his skin. I hear the crunch of shells from within his grenade fist.

"A little brown house within a little green house. A little white house within the little brown house. Within the white house there dwells a sweet heart."

The final riddle cracked, our ritual is completed, catechist and initiate sharing the age-old lore. His hand explodes open; I accept my reward. Twelfth Night draws to a close; the log burns down. The twelve days are over. Christmas is done for another year.

Snow

THE FIRST FALL always came when it was dark, never during the daylight hours.

"On the last stroke of midnight," my father said, "stay awake and you'll see the first flakes."

Riding through the night, my northern dream warriors smothering the sky in a swirl of arrow shafts tipped with ice crystal barbs.

And in the morning, white on the windowsills, white on the slates, white on the 'ood ricks, white on the meads, white on the haystacks, white on the hills. White on white on white.

The phosphorescent glow of the snow-filled light, from the snow-filled world, filled my bedroom world in an eerie glow. Snow on snow on snow.

The winters were white when I was boy. Icicles of the sabretooth tiger's white sharp pointed fangs hanging from the slates and guttering. Gigantic Christmas cake haystacks with icing running down the sides. The dungheap a cream-encrusted pudding. The waterfall a frozen crystal palace. A white coal heap, and camouflaged sheep. The snow as soft as the froth on a newly filled pail of milk.

Home-knitted woollens for winter days, always blue, green or grey. Pull-overs, jumpers, mittens and stockings fastened below the knee with elastic garters. A balaclava-bank-robbing-helmet, and constricting my neck a striped boa scarf. Reared by my aged maiden aunt from leftover scraps, its tasselled tail trailed on the ground behind me. A bright orange overcoat handed down when a fat cousin had exploded out of it. Minus three buttons, it transformed me into a walking circus big top. Finally short grey flannel trousers, very thin in a certain place.

The scream of a gleenie, sharp and shrill, shattered the silence in a shower of shards. "A guinea fowl," announced my father with a chuckle. "Cost you twenty-one shillings to buy one of those. A guinea a fowl." Another laugh at his annual dry joke.

> Boys and girls come out to play,
> The snow had come this winter's day.
> Leave your sorrows and leave your sleep,
> The snow is white and crisp and deep.
> Come with whoop, or come with a call,
> There's tons of snow for one and all.

Flying across my unexplored winter wonderland, two Jack Snipe zig-zag-zigging. In Beerclose Copse, Mole and Ratty digging in their search for Badger's stately home. Daring myself to enter the wooded wonderland. In my memory, another of my father's dry jokes. "How far can you walk into a wood?" Playing along with him, pretending not to know. "How far, Dad?" His laugh. "Halfway, because then you start coming out again." Frightened by the eerie silence, running quickly out again.

Over the meads and into Quarry Field. Making a snowball to roll down the slope. As big as a house, as big as a castle, as big as the universe. One, two, three, push. My shoulders heaving, my muscles straining. At last it rolled away on its own. Faster and faster, magnetising the snow. Pressing the grass flat, it gathered speed. As big and as round as the silver winter sun. Wishing my teacher was being pressed flat and the Methody man who shouts in the pulpit. And the aunts who sent me Christmas present ties with stripes on, yet more home-knitted stockings, handkerchiefs with my initial embroidered in the corner. Why couldn't they have sent me stink bombs, a catapult, a year's supply of gobstoppers, a comic token, a horror mask or indoor fireworks?

But then catastrophe. Hurtling towards the Crooked Oak my snowball struck a tree. A million billion, trillion, zillion snowflake fragments. My winter sun totally eclipsed.

Sitting down I stuffed my mouth with snow. Ice-cold candyfloss, acid drops, pear drops. Soft-white-snow-white-snow-marshmallows, winter mixtures striped and round, snowflake sherbet fountains.

Building a snow octogenarian hero farmer snowman right outside of his back door. Bombarding it with large white cannonballs, watching it collapse in a heap. My hero exploding into the yard, wrapping the air up in a link-chain of swear words, glittering and sparkling with rudeness.

Quickly fleeing the brushing-up snow scene, running up the road and climbing over Orchard gate. Running across the snow-covered grass and clambering up the hedge. There in the middle of the adjoining field, Farmer Down's bull standing in splendid isolation – his ruby coat blazing in the sunlight, his brass ring glinting bright. Jumping down in mock bravado I walked across the white sawdust, the toreador in his orange cape entering the bullring.

Closer and closer. Suddenly the docile bull turned and faced me head on as my snowball hit him on his side. The scene quickly changing from bullring to Ice Age. A hairy mammoth ten feet tall, eyes blazing beneath his shaggy coat, padded the ground in a white-hot fury. Lowering his curved-horned head he lumbered slowly forward and charged the caveman hunter. Thud, thud, thud, thud, thud, thud. Retreating, I clambered back up the hedge. There was only one casualty. The grey flannel trousers snagged on a hawthorn branch and ripped in the thinnest place.

Time for peeing my initials in the snow. The downward stroke of the letter D. The snow turning Corona lemon-pop yellow. A sharp gust of wind blowing the pop against my leg and into my black wellington boots, scorching the skin, turning the flesh red and swollen in a bad attack of frostbite.

In the afternoon, sitting in the kitchen window seat listening to the excited whoops, calls and screams of the bottom of the village children sliding down the road. "Listen to the little savages," moaned my aged maiden aunt. "Best you stay where you are."

How I wished and wished I could be a little savage, if only for just half an hour.

Listening to the voices of David Davis, Carlton Hobbs and Norman Shelley, Dennis the Whistling postman, Jennings, Norman and Henry the boy detectives, Clara Chuff, Larry the Lamb and the Midnight Folk from my wireless box of delights.

Towards the end of that happy-go-lucky-go-carefree-go-day, more snow tumbled through the air filling in every imprint, hoofprint, bootprint and hole, to be followed by the wind. Whipping around every stable, shippen, shed and sty a phantom sculptor carved out vast billowing shapes – white seashells curved and scalloped; pale ghosts with outstretched arms beckoning at me through the twilight. Each hour they grew taller and taller against walls and hedges and gates. By the end of the night the farmhouse tree lay under the shadow of ghostly guards and sentries.

This was the winter when I was a boy. To some it lasted a hundred years, but for me it was only a hundred seconds. Then came the Sorceress, creeping quietly through the night, her cloak of warmth billowing over her shoulders. Through moor and dale, over hill and vale she roamed, waving her magic wand, conjuring the snow away.

Water drip-drip-drip-dripping into overflowing water butts. The ice melting from the haystack cake, the cream running down the sides of the pudding dungheap, the crystal waterfall palace melting. And just as the dawn was breaking, the sabretooth tiger lost its fangs and became extinct.

This was the end of my three-day Ice Age dream, and in the morning I awoke to the reality of grey slate roofs and meadows glowing green.

In the hazel copse, catkins whispering gently of Spring the Sorceress.

Ancient Crafts

HIS BANDSAW WAS a shimmer-shine of speed, mesmerising and hypnotic, drawing me across the road from the security of the farmhouse tree and into his carpenter and wheelwright's shop. Window frames, doors, stairs, garden tools, handles and, in the distant past, carts both long and butt. The scent of sawdust, fox-track sharp. A volcanic heap three feet high.

And everywhere timber. Ash, elm, and beech. Plank upon plank of various lengths and thickness. Planed and shaped. Length upon length upon length. Stacked in readiness. In a corner, timber not yet prepared. Old Fred catching my eye. Addressed by me as Mr Newton and his son Mr Gordon. The saw switched off, the silence loud. "Best oak and elm for the job they'll all require me to do, but the one they'll never ask me to do, and for which they'll never pay me or thank me personally." A throaty chuckle.

Running my fingers along the grain. Counting the rings, feeling the age. The bandsaw switched on. The scream of the blade growing louder. Sawdust spitting out, the scent growing even stronger in my nostrils.

Once in a while, a light in Old Fred's shop burning into and through the night. At breakfast our fried breakfast eaten in silence. His cryptic words creeping into my head. Three days later, the sound of a tolling bell.

The music from the smithy was hypnotic. Metal on metal. An echoing chime. An ancient beat ringing through the cob-walled building and into the village. Nailed to the door, a rabbit's paw. The throaty bass of the bellows. Wordless chants composed of spark and flame. The hiss of hot metal hitting water.

The blue smoke hanging from rafters and slates was filled with the incense of singed hoof. Lining a wall an assortment of tools – cross-peen, ball-peen and sledge hammers. Hoof parers, pincers, knife tongs and rasps. Relics for the future. Horseshoes and horse-drawn iron machinery repaired.

Robed in an apron of leather and grime, Charlie forged his links on a primitive altar of iron resting on a block of elm. Wrought from the shadows of blackness, he brought forth a bright yellow light. His strength silent, his touch gentle. Iron, fire, air and water, the ancient elements.

In Memory: Death of a Farmer

WHEN YOU DIED, the sap drained from my cob-walled tree, and it became simply another farmhouse. No more, no less. An economic entity revolving around the balance sheet. Next, a two-act drama began to unfold. Act One – the sale of the farm. Setting – the public guildhall. Act Two – sale of household effects and dead stock. Setting – farmhouse, yard and mowing field. Theatre in the round, unscripted, unrehearsed. An improvised drama of rural life with relatives, friends, would-be buyers and hangers-on making up the cast and audience. Plot-line – the end of an era. Subplot – memories. Lead rôle and villain of the piece – the auctioneer.

"On instructions received from Mrs Hill we are proud to be able to offer up for sale the excellent stock-rearing farm known as Eastacott in the hamlet of East Knowstone, situated equidistant from Tiverton and South Molton off the A361. Vacant possession on completion on Lady Day. This is a freehold property, ladies and gentlemen. All details to be found on your instructions of sale sheet.

"This is the first time in its three-hundred-year-old history that the farm has come onto the open market. It has been in the hands of the present family for over a century. It is now up for sale, owing to the death of that well-respected farmer Mr John Hill."

The opening soliloquy before the main action of the drama.

"Right then, ladies and gentlemen, this is a most substantial property of sixty acres. Who'll open the bidding at, shall we say, twelve thousand. Properties like this don't come onto the market every day of the week... Eleven thousand, five hundred then... Come on then, who'll start me off?"

'Midst a haze of sweat and tobacco smoke, the drama slowly unfolded. I sat there numbed, as like the drowning man my life flooded in front of me. The wave of emotion drawing me under in a tide of sad nostalgia, while the memory bubbles exploded in my face and I floundered in the depths.

I saw your hands reach out towards me. Saw in your eyes reflections of the farmhouse tree and its many branches.

Back kitchen with its washday copper, granite trough and long-case pump. The swivel beam gallows where noosed by either neck or legs, pheasant, rabbit, snipe or woodpigeon dangling. The pig hung, drawn and halved, swinging, ready for curing, salting down, jointing and frying. When not working on the land your hands constructed a wooden board swing for wet afternoons. Palms pushing me higher and higher. My toes touching the wooden raftered ceiling.

Front room branch, my favourite branch where tongue-licked multicoloured paper chains stretched across the limewashed ceiling. Hanging from hooks: red, white and blue crêpe paper bells, Mr Punch, a policeman, snowman, Father Christmas and Chinese lanterns. In the window alcove for the twelve special days, the holly tree. Flicker of yellow, white, pink and blue candles casting wax-spattered shadows over baubles, bells and silver spangled birds of paradise. On the mantelpiece, a small framed rural scene with the words 'A boy's best friend is his mother, the best the world's ever had. The poet says there's no other, but what about dear old dad'.

On the sideboard where photos and funeral cards were stored, holly sprigs, tangerines wrapped in foil and tissue paper. Bluebird toffees, string-tailed sugar mice. A box of Tom Smith's crackers and a glass bowl full of nuts. Your hand a clenched fist grenade exploding open to reveal a cracked walnut. The front room branch. My favourite branch, until...

The swallow-raftered barn where every year mud-saucer nests of the swallow sprouted mushroomlike in the dark daylight above the chaff-strewn floor. Outside in a dotted line beneath the guttering, thirty miniature upturned beehives made from mud; summer residence of the migrant house martins.

Adjoining the barn, the engine house barracks, home of the stationary Titan. Body beautiful of iron, brass and steel, oil dripped from the black bronzed sweating form. Huge revolving wheels and pistons, muscled cogs flexed for fighting action. Once his battle-cry echoed through the barn summoning an army to obey his command – chaff cutter, cake cracker, mangol chopper, thresher. But now, defeated by the marching gods of progress he sits in a sultry stance surrounded by his fellow fallen soldiers, each one brooding on glories from the past.

The implement shed branch with it's cobwebbed props from bygone days – mowing machine, hay turner, rake, sweep and scythe. The lingering scent of chamomile crushed by hoof and boot, a wisp of hay. In the hedgerow, meadowsweet, briar rose and honeysuckle.

The pound house branch with empty firkins and hogsheads, cider press and crusher shrouded in webs. Echoes of the autumn pulping and pressing. Cob walls drenched in the scent of juice and golden barley straw.

Ammonia acid-filled stench of the stable branch. Horse brass-, harness-, saddle-strewn walls. The hay-lined wooden manger, kitten-filled. The pitiful mewing of the mother cat. A hessian sack draped in the corner on a heap of straw.

Whitewashed, dung-stained shippen branch walls. The stone floor with it's golden straw. Sandpaper tongue rasping the curly chestnut coat of a finely dressed marionette, its strings tangled. A spring calf. Your hand on mine as I gripped the teats in my initiation ceremony.

Rambling rose-covered woodshed branch filled to the brim with moots, logs and faggots. The eight-feet-high 'ood ricks with faggots of kindling and pea-sticks for the garden. In the courtyard the wood horse, billhook, cross-cut and bow saw. Here the child acting like the man.

Under the flowing laburnum tree, past the outside lavatory, a glimpse of the Welsh poppy. Through the moss-coated creaking gate above the stream, running into the box-hedged garden. A withe basket of vegetables and flowers. A flittering butterfly.

Finally the fields of the farmhouse tree, the patchwork quilt of browns and shades of green. The squares and rectangles stitched together with beech hedges. And as the bidding reached its climax the names flooded through my brain – Long Halls, Little Close, East

Furze Close and Lower Down. Lower Orchard, Higher Orchard, Lower Meadow and Bull's Mead.

Here through spring, summer, autumn and winter, the journey through my childhood. The returning cuckoo, the first robin's nest. Each year our search for the leaf and moss cup. Your hand delicately removing the mottled egg. A shared delight, the egg replaced with reverence and care.

The hedgerows' wild riches. In Higher Orchard, banks of wild strawberries. Tiny rubies dropped into my treasure-chest jam jar to be eaten with sugar, milk and cream. In Little Close, wild raspberry canes, common red and the rare yellow. Gold ingots, the precious fruits hanging like pendants in the beech and hazel hedge. By the gate at West Furze Close, wild gooseberries, some as big as alley marbles. The skin stretched taut, splitting to spill their coloured veins over my chin.

For the second time the auctioneer's voice interrupting my thoughts: "Do I hear eleven thousand, ladies and gentlemen?"

In the hay shed your hands gripping the iron knife, slicing out wedges of summer. A lingering scent of harvest days. Harsh trek through ice and snow with hay in a roped bundle on your bent-over back.

"For the third and final time, ladies and gentlemen."

CRASH

The gavel came down.

SOLD   SOLD   SOLD

Ten thousand and nine hundred pounds.

Your hands drew back, and in your twinkling eyes reflections dimmed and slowly disappeared as the tide surged in.

And the farmhouse tree and the patchwork quilt of textures, shades and hues was wrenched from your clawing fingers.

End of Act One. Intermission.

Act Two. Sale of dead stock and household goods. The sound of the hand bell ringing. Summoning.

"Right then, ladies and gentlemen, if I may have your attention. It's eleven o'clock and I've got almost two hundred lots to auction off, so I suggest we make a prompt start. Implements and tools first, and then we'll move indoors.

"Lot One. A fine wooden five-bar gate. A fine gate. Keep stock in and strangers out. Two pound anywhere?"

The ancient gate encrusted with lichen. Each year your hand scratching out my height with a nail mark and your annual dry joke – "Growing up, not down. That's good."

For the second time I sank beneath the waves as grey faceless figures peered, and fingers prodded at the items floating on the tide.

"Sold for ten bob."

Lot 31. Cross-cut saw... five bob

Lot 24. Cream separator... five bob

Lot 56. Cake cracker... half a crown

Lot 66. Cider press... half a crown

Lot 68. Thresher and belts... seventeen and six

Lot 110. Willow pattern dinner service... forty-five bob

Lot 188. Butter churn... a bob.

In my head the dairy rhyme. "Come butter come. David stands by the farmyard gate, waiting for a buttered cake. Come butter come." The dairy a whitewashed North Pole. In winter my breath rose like a balloon to the ceiling where it hung, suspended. A muslin bag above the fruit-filled slate shelves. Turning the handle to revolve the cogs in the whirring machine which separated the cream from the milk. Your hands on mine providing the power. Once again the child acting like the man.

For the third time the waves washed over me as once again your hands reached out. The works of Nature's art created by the season's brush strokes. Flesh canvases viewed at arm's length. Pigments of earth and sweat, the mixing of summer dyes. Brown paste from the sun's palette flowing across the paintings. Gouged straight line. Winter's mad flourish. Crazed master drawing harsh patterns, the primitive elements with depth and texture etched deep by the sweep of time. Hands calloused and rough, and yet possessing qualities portrayed by Dürer.

For the second time, reflections in your eyes, this time mirroring the passage of the seasons. A random sequence of events unintentionally created at the whim of the auctioneer.

"Lot 24. Three pails, various sizes. Half a crown."

Milk-pail handles sticking to iced hand, pulling pith and fibre from numbed fingers. The cruelty of winter.

"Lot 61. Horse-drawn plough. Five bob anywhere? Half a crown then. Good scrap iron. I'll take a shilling."

Hands guiding the share. Eye on marker object. Straight furrow in a harsh landscape. The autumn pattern of your life.

"Lot 132. Two glass vases. Who'll give me a shilling?"

Hand-picked snowdrops, violets and primroses accompanied by the self-conscious kiss on my mother's lips. The ceremonies of the annual spring ritual. In summer the hand-picked sweet peas.

"Lot 150. Collection of old nature books. Bob anywhere?"

Hands gently caressing the tracery on a painted shell carefully lifted from the nests of chaffinch and warbler. The tenderness of summer.

Lot 158. Garden tools and a butterfly net. Two bob start me off?"

While you toiled with the fork I chased white butterflies for bounty. At the end of one hunting safari day you gave me your simple philosophy – caterpillar, butterfly, life, death.

"Right then, ladies and gentlemen, we come to the final lot. Thank you for your attention and may I just remind you that all lots can be paid for at the table by the front door. A Windsor chair. Never wear out. No woodworm. As good as the day it was made. Start me off at five bob."

This was your chair, where at the end of a weary day you fell asleep, the cat dozing on your lap. A contented smile playing on your lips. This was your chair.

"All done at ten bob then

"Going... going......"

One hundred and ninety-six lots up for sale and sold. Accompanied by the barbed remarks. *Fancy putting that up for sale. I wouldn't give it houseroom. Fancy they'm still usin' that. And still usin' a horse.* The coarse laugh. The spit on the ground. The final intrusion into privacy. The final violation of grief.

His gavel came down for the final time and appeared to hang in the air. The farmhouse tree creaked and groaned as the final bubble exploded.

One day a sharp-pointed barb of frost penetrated the heart of my farmhouse tree. Instantly the warm red sap ceased flowing through the limbs. With no time to cry out against the attack you sat, the frozen model in your pose. Legs still crossed, the glass of Stone's ginger wine in your hand. The toast barely completed. And on your face a look of cold surprise at the suddenness of winter's fury.

I quickly left front room, the wrestling on I.T.V. turned off, racing out to back court scattering the hens. By the 'ood rick I kneeled on the ground blindly mumbling a jumble of words. Running back indoors, hoping.

I never understood why you had to die. Wrapping paper not yet thrown away. Boxed crackers from Christmas Day. The Stone's ginger wine bottle half empty, or was it perhaps half full?

Chains and Chinese lanterns hurriedly taken down, the holly tree stripped bare of tinsel, baubles, bells and candles. Yours was an untimely exit with the wishbone still to pull.

For a split second the impression of a smile on your lips. A spring breeze dancing. How I wished. How I wished. How I wished.

Across the road from the carpenter and wheelwright's shop, loud in the clear night sky, the sound of hammer and saw splintering the silence. From their bedroom the sounds of my mother's sobs punctuated on the hour, every hour, by the chime from the grandfather clock.

The undertaker's secret art transformed the face I knew into a framed still-life canvas. Too peaceful, too serene. A grotesque death mask with the primitive qualities destroyed.

And did your eyes still twinkle? And were those eyes still blue? Under the candlelit silence in the window alcove I placed my final kiss on your lips.

How I wished. How I wished. How I wished.

Outside of the gallery in the hall the cat sat on the mat. For three whole days, until the crated exhibit was carried out by the uniformed attendants, the cat waited for a final viewing. Not eating, not sleeping, just waiting, just waiting. But the curators would not let him in.

The 1st of January. No seasonal greetings exchanged. Tears mingling with silver raindrops. Blurred grey faces against a grey background of grey walls, grey stones and a grey sky. Firm handshakes from worn-once-a-year dark suits. Distant relatives seen only at funerals.

The public well-worn vocal intrusions into a private grief.

"We know how you feel. He was much respected. He'll certainly be missed. No age really."

And everywhere a profusion of flowers – lilies, chrysanths and carnations. But all too grand for the one who loved the simple primroses, violets and snowdrops.

Dust to dust. Ashes to ashes. I scattered my hot tears and the cold earth swallowed them up.

The caterpillar. In the earth a seed. Blossom floating on the breeze. The butterfly awakes.

Gone.

As the sale ended your hands reached out for the third and final time. But the tide could not be turned back.

And part of me drowned on that day, on the day that you finally died. And the last drops of sap drained out of the farmhouse tree as the final curtain came down on the rural two-act play.

John Hill, born 6th September, 1901. Died 28th December, 1963. Farmer and Custodian of the farmhouse tree. RIP. Crash. The gavel came down for the final time.

The goodbye wave to childhood and the boy became a man.

Summer Song

EACH YEAR IN mid-to-late April, he greeted its call with delight. "Bringing back the sun and warmth. Our turn to have the summer now." A rare sighting greeted with a smile.

Seldom seen, the glimpse foretold a bumper crop – sweet hay, golden grain and juicy cider apples.

We never attended his cremation. The church service, and back to the farmhouse tree for the long wake. Over a cold beef buffet around the beech-log fire I overheard a farmer say, "Just like sweet pork, so they tell me. Smell it in the smoke, so they say."

Late in the afternoon under a silent January sky his ashes were laid in the ground. In the evening I conjured up his face, watching it rise through the flames.

Each spring the sun song rises and sets, igniting the sky over meadow and hedgerow. While swallows and swifts skim the beams, my phoenix is unseen. But felt.

The Pair of Hobnail Boots

I

INSIDE THE FARMHOUSE tree back door, crafted in the carpenter and wheelwright's shop, seldom bolted with the iron bar forged in the smithy, both buildings opposite front court, a pair of boots. Leather hobnails soled with studs carefully tapped to form a symmetrical pattern plus iron toe-pieces and horseshoe iron heels. Leather protected by the coats of dubbin regularly applied, wax oil and tallow to waterproof and soften.

To make me chuckle with delight, he'd perform his party piece. Striking his heel on back kitchen stone-flag floor, careful not to slip and slide; sparks in a shower-spit of tiny petal flames.

Leather laces looped through eyelets. An old one saved, his fingers knotting and threading it through a conker, the hole bradawl-bored, oven-baked for the playground championships.

Marching along the road. The two of us playing at soldiers. Chest out. Shoulders back. Swing those arms. Left, right, left, right. His boots clicking out the rhythm. The sergeant major leading from the front. Left, right, left, right. Squaaad halt. Stand at ease. Stand easy.

Through the gate into Lower Orchard, where cider apples grew on lichen-coated branches bowed down by weight and age. Filling hessian sacks, stored overnight in the stone- and cob-built pigsty. Stacking them against tree trunks to be carted back to the pound house in the afternoon.

Striding through lank tussocks, his legs a pair of geometrical dividers, his hobnails leaving indentations into which I placed my sandalled feet. Step out, pull up the other foot. In sunlight razor-sharp the robin's autumn song serenading the footsteps of the follower as the two campaigners return to their base camp.

II

One January night the first snowfall of winter, in the blizzard-blitz unheralded, bombarded my farmhouse tree, coating courts and fields in its cold white mantle. In the morning we went to the corrugated iron-roofed hay shed, tar-coated in July by summer visiting gipsies, encamped on moorland where villagers held commoners' grazing rights.

Watching him kneel, and with his hay knife, the blade fifteen inches long, honed to a silver sharpness, slice out a wedge of summer with which to feed his five Red Ruby steers.

Watching his shoulders heave and shudder with the strain, hands plunging the iron blade deep into the stack releasing the scent of sun-filled days. In a blast the sweet intoxicating aroma awaking memories of tossing grass stalks high into the air, turning cartwheels and rolling in the windrows raked ready for the sweeping. And all through the harvest his hobnails tramp forward, turn and back again. Forward, turn and back again.

The summer bundle roped and carried on his back. Trudging through snow to the middle of the mead. His stock haughty with a head-toss of impatience. Half stumbling by his side, eager to keep up. Small impressions of my wellington boots almost level with his prints.

The cattle fed, we turn and head for home. Carrying me piggyback. Almost losing his balance with the exertion and my weight. Dropping me onto the stack, breathless. With a laugh his finger pointing at two sets of footprints outward-bound, but only one set returning.

For several weeks after his death, the hobnails remained in a corner on the flagstone floor inside the door where he had cast them off. When last we'd stepped out together I covered and filled his prints in the mud but I could never fill his boots. Always the follower, never the farmer.

Returning

AFTER AN ABSENCE of twenty-five years I returned on a hot summer's day to the once-owned family farm. In an instant the air, sun-scorched, shimmering in ripples, dissolved time and place. For a fleeting moment the view across the vegetable garden – the 'ood ricks eight feet high, built of beech and hazel faggots, wire-bound like sheaves of corn when meadow hedges were cut and laid by hand. The scene drenched with the scent of sweet pea and neatly trimmed box hedges.

The orchard, where ripening fruit hung heavy. Listener, Quarrenden and Duck's Bill. Greengages, damsons and victoria plums dripping honey-golden, wasp-sucked flesh. My childhood linhay, its painted iron roof a toad's back oozing tar black bubbles. Inside, four open-fronted wooden boxes where light Sussex and Rhode Island Reds came each day to lay their eggs in nests of barley straw. The bantams strutting out, their heads held high.

The after-summer ritual. An Iron Age assortment of paring hooks, wood hooks, scythes and axe blades lying next to the oakstand-mounted grindstone. Small hands turning the wooden handle, eager to please. The wheel revolving slowly. Iron pressed against stone. Water droplets hitting rosy cheeks, leaving rust freckles. Laughter at his annual joke of wetting the dry whetstone.

Leaving the linhay, he walks towards a tree, picks a plum and places it on the outstretched tiny palm.

The mirage melts, the figures disappear. My fingers close on thin air. Again the bungalow where once my orchard grew. In my memory, the setting sun glints on a sharpened scythe blade, never to be used again in summer fields thick with thistles.

The Village Shop

THE VILLAGE SHOP in the next village was burned down in the winter of 1963. Following a hard frost, the owner, so it is said, went up into the attic with a blowtorch to thaw out the pipes beneath the thatched roof. The snow was deep, the fire brigade was unable to get through and the shop was destroyed. My pleasure palace of edible delights was no more.

Today when I return to my roots I stand by the railings which front the old schoolyard and look across the stretch of grass. Momentarily the new village hall is replaced by the shop. I glimpse a small boy with his mother, her brown shopping bag by her side, climb the couple of steps and enter the confectionary paradise. Through the open door I watch the boy rest his chin on the counter, while standing on tiptoe, tapping his thrupenny bit, given to him by his aged maiden aunt, against the wood. He takes a step back and stares expectantly at the array of glass jars filled with winter mixtures, sherbet lemons, pear drops, dolly mixtures, liquorice comfits, gobstoppers and barley sugars.

His mother completes her purchases and passes something to him, and he replaces the thrupenny bit in his pocket. They turn and leave the shop, the small boy carrying the shopping bag and sucking a sweet, a small white bag containing four ounces of sherbet lemons in his other hand.

They look straight at me. A shiver runs through me and I return to the twenty-first century.

Knowstone old schoolyard, village shop and church, mid-1950s

EPILOGUE

ON LADY DAY in 1966, a traditional quarter day when farms change hands, we left the farm. For my aged maiden aunt, especially, leaving the family farm was the biggest wrench in her life. When she walked slowly out of the front door for the final time, her small weekend case clutched tightly in her hand, she left a part of her spirit behind, and although she lived for another six years, life was never the same again.

Her final days were spent in hospital, and one day when I visited her I recalled the wet afternoon in the 1950s when I had shared my secret thoughts with her about the farmhouse tree being the name I had given our farmhouse and outbuildings, because they were so old.

Squeezing my hand she replied, "Our little secret." Her eyes filling with tears as she continued, "I wanted so much to die on the farm where I'd lived over seventy years. Your father was lucky; born and died in the same room. But it isn't to be. In His wisdom, He've decided otherwise."

Drawing her to me she kissed my cheek. "Close the door quietly as you leave – others are trying to sleep – and help yourself to a sweet."

Turning quickly away I heard in my mind the policeman's laughter echoing out of the gramophone. She had kept her promise. Our little secret. Just between the two of us. A backward glance. On her bedside cabinet, an unopened bag of barley sugars. She was asleep and I never saw her awake again.

I'll never know what she would have thought of a children's book about dragons published in Great Britain, Australia, New Zealand and Canada, and translated into Italian. "Whatever will you come out with next? You and your fanciful notions."

ENDWORD

I N THE AUTUMN of 2010, Eastacott was put on the market for £695,000, having last been sold in 1965. Before that date it hadn't changed hands, for money, for almost two centuries. Originally 59 acres, 3 rods and 12 poles, the current size is seventeen acres, and the seven fields which made up the seventeen acres are now three. Gone from the original acreage are the three orchards, plantation, and fields with names such as Long Hall, Higher Orchard, West Furze Close and Little Close, and the hedges where the wild gooseberries and yellow raspberries grew.

Higher Mead where hay was harvested with a horse and sweep now contains a huge cattle-shed complex, which is far removed from the whitewashed shippens where my father hand-milked the seven horned cows.

In the early 1930s, when my father bought out his brother's half share, the farm was valued at £920. Ten years previously, when their father had died, livestock and machinery had been valued at £830. In 1953, after all out-goings had been accounted for, the annual profit was £354.

Mark Twain, when asked where money should be invested, suggested buying land as it was no longer being made. The financial advice still holds good, bearing in mind that when the farm was sold in 1965 it made £10,900. The equivalent of approximately £160,000 today.

In the summer of 2011, I returned to my roots, staying with a second cousin, who in the past organised strawberry-and-cream teas, with meringues, fruit cake, cut rounds of jam and cream, cheese straws and bread and butter for £3 a head, much of the baking done by herself, in aid of the church. The mouth-watering teas have gone into annals of local history.

The peace and stillness continues to pervade the parish, and in many ways life is similar to that which I knew as a child in the 1950s. The pace of life moves with the pace of the earth. The Masons Arms is now a pub restaurant *par excellence* with a reputation linked with stars; not the star of the Golden Star Brigade of my childhood, I hasten to add.

On a walk between Knowstone and East Knowstone, I was delighted to find red raspberries growing in the places in the hedgerows where I had picked them on my unwilling walk to Sunday school.

On another walk across the fields between Eastacott and Owlaborough, the farm where my grandmother was a child, I was rewarded with a splendidly crafted wooden bridge over the Crooked Oak. This was far removed from the wooden plank I fell off when pretending to be a pirate walking the plank.

In both villages I met up with villagers and farming families I knew as a little tacker, and the new young owners and their father greeted me at Eastacott with the same warm welcome my parents and aged maiden aunt extended to visitors.

In front court, house martins pitched on the concrete yard where once they gathered mud from the stream; hopefully they will one day build again on the barn wall. Linnets flitted on thistles in Bull's Mead; the first time I had seen them there. Perhaps my father scythed the thistles too early in the summer.

Inside the farmhouse I was given a guided tour and the attic, the mysterious place of my childhood, is now a superb bedroom with panoramic views over the surrounding countryside. Front room is now combined with the dairy and again a panoramic view is experienced from the new window.

Back stairs and the Elsan lavatory have disappeared and back kitchen is now a state-of-the-art laundry room.

Finally, I went into the room which had been my aged maiden aunt's bedroom. For the first time, I strayed into the attached dressing room where I had never entered as a child. In my mind's eye as I looked across her bedroom, the glimpse of the oak chest, and on it a bag of barley sugars and the glass of water with her false teeth in.

I came away from my short stay spiritually refreshed, content in the knowledge that the old farm has passed into safe hands and that it will be cherished as I loved it as a child over fifty years ago.

Is Writing Prose and Poetry Real Work?

THE PARLOUR CONVERTED into a bedroom. My grandfather growing smaller and smaller in a shrivel-stick heap of protruding bones with each passing day. "Trouble down there with his privates," said my mother. I wanted to ask his private what, but her tone implied no further questions. And I was told quietly to give him my hand to shake.

From beneath the sheet a tremble of spider's legs crept out, ensnaring my fingers in a gentle grip. Strength sapped, his hand fell back in a tightly rolled ball of frustration. His eyes a memory web of shining strands.

A fist flick, and a two-hundredweight hessian sack of corn lay in the back of the shirehorse-pulled blue butt-cart. Another twist of the knotted wire-veined wrist heaved the long-handled prong-load of hay high into the summer sky. Hands guiding a plane to shape the planks to create a fine five-bar wooden gate.

Grimacing, he heaved himself up in his single bed. "Not a line on your hands," he chaffed. "Soft and pink. They'll never make a real man's hands. Never done a real day's work, and never likely to. And you a farmer's son!" Coughing, he collapsed back into his bed.

Today I sort ears from the chaff, each sack carefully weighed before being placed on the cart. A harvest nurtured with due love and care.

Today I guide the tool to shape and form, from raw materials, a sound and solid structure. These hands, a man's, still soft and pink, place words upon a crisp white sheet.

Today as I compose my lines I think about his words, and I ask myself the question... Is writing poetry and prose real work for me, a farmer's son?

APPENDIX

The following pieces, although not directly linked with
my childhood, grew out of a country childhood

Foxgloves and Beech Leaves

(In memory of Ken Vercoe, Craftsman and Friend)

KEN WAS A craftsman in wood who lived in our Cornish village, to
where my wife and I moved in 1984. Everything he made was
crafted to the highest standard – sash windows, porches, kitchen
cabinets, doors and furniture. Just like Boxer the carthorse in *Animal
Farm* and Charlie my father's carthorse, he was always there to give of
his best. I see his mark throughout the village and his skills and spirit
live on, having been passed down to his nephew Alan Solomon from the
age of twelve.

In a phalanx of blooms, foxglove spikes thrust upwards, flowers
for the countryman. In the same vase a spray of beech leaves, wood for
the craftsman. The unfurled leaves as soft as the lips of our farm
shirehorse. A ton of flesh, a hogshead barrel of a belly, leather-staved,
sweat oozing from every pore. Clasping his mane I sailed green seas, a
young captain exploring new worlds.

The seven sash windows in our house replaced. Fitted in the style
of a suit, Savile Row, bespoke. Hand-stitched in mahogany. Each tool
an extension of his hand. Chisel, hammer, plane and saw.

Taken for granted, seldom praised, reliable. Always there to work.
From dawn 'til dusk, the measured plod of heavy hoof in a lurch-
lumber, hauling the sheaf-laden long cart over stubbled field and
stone-rutted lane. Harvest home.

My memories interrupted by a sniff, a muted cough. Watching
the crimson curtains slowly closing. Enfolding. A flower falls on the
windowsill. A leaf unfurls. In the stable the shirehorse unbridled.
Sleeping.

The Gardeners

NO MATTER WHAT time of the year I visit the Lost Gardens of Heligan, I always come away refreshed. What finer way to experience Nature's changing seasons than to wander through lovingly tended vegetable and flower beds and the exotic jungle gardens. My father was one of those rare farmers who loved gardening, and this makes a visit even more poignant.

No matter how many other visitors are experiencing the delights you can always find your own quiet space for a spot of contemplation – a rare delight in today's busy world which is seldom hushed.

As you wander around you can see the gardeners at work. All taking pride in their various chores which include working in the melon house or tending plots. In October, the Harvest Festival display of fruit and vegetables, a reminder of my childhood Harvest Festival Sunday in the village chapel. In November, a visit to one small room is essential. Here I pause to reflect on those gardeners who never returned to Heligan in 1918. Leaving the gardeners' lavatory of the past, I recall those young men who lifted the lids of the forcing pots to check the melons, who hoed the rows, earthed up the potatoes and provided the flowers and vegetables for the big house.

Gardeners who were suddenly soldiers in trenches, where there were no King Edwards or Majestics and where the scent of the ripe melons back home was replaced by the stench of death.

Young lads who never returned to become men and see the fruits of their labours. A lost generation, but one whose spirit still lingers in those quiet places which are forever Heligan.

Prologue

On the evening of 5th September, 1998, the sculptor Heather Keir Cross unveiled five ice sculptures which had been commissioned by Tim Smit for an exhibition at the Lost Gardens of Heligan.

One of the figures – Vine Man – lost his legs as he was being removed from the fibreglass mould, but he was on guard in the vinery in the evening. Four other figures – the Dreamer, Hoe Man, Scythe Man and the Kneeling Boy – were situated in strategic positions in the gardens where moonlight reflected on clear ice, and ice which had been coloured with blue/purple dye.

The following morning all that remained of the exhibition – *The Ghosts of Gardeners Past* – were the legs of Scythe Man, a part of Hoe Man's upper body and pools of muddy water. In the melon yard, Kneeling Boy's shape could still be seen in front of a tray of onions.

I

Sun-scorched, the earth is iron-hard, but even so the weeds continue to grow. A gardener's work is never done; I have to reap where the wind blows. Finding a wounded linnet in the flower garden, I nursed it in a wooden cage, its voice pure. The singing at chapel was strong on Sunday. How sweet the name of Jesus sounds in a believer's ear. It soothes his sorrow, heals his wounds and drives away his fear. My big happy family praising our Lord.

If I had a hundred pounds I'd buy a cottage with a garden, fill it with hundreds of flowers and the sound of my harmonium. Scent of the box hedges strong. Underfoot, crushed chamomile. And everywhere lavender. The air still, filled with insects' whirring wings. A blue sky and the storm broke. I never knew that sound could be so loud. 12th April. Aged 23.

II

Summer was hot this year. July melting into August. A trickle of juices, melon and peach. In the bee bole wall, straw skeps, honey-filled. Sweetener, mead and wax. In the vegetable garden, rows in straight lines, every sort a man could wish to eat. "Like soldiers lined up for inspection," my girl said. I'd hoed them that morning. I felt so proud.

Picking a peach. Skin as smooth as a mole's coat. She rubbed it gently against her cheek, bit into it. The flesh sun-golden, juice dripping from her chin. I brung her a bunch of flowers – sweet peas, rosemary and boy's love. The scent filling the glass house. Through a pane, a glimpse of bats flitting in on the twilight.

"They might get tangled in my hair," she laughed. I pulled her to me. Holding her tight. Shivering, even though the night was hot. Our last peach was honey-sweet. So very, very sweet. I never knew the earth could be so muddy. 30th October. Aged 19.

III

Not a thistle or a dock to be seen. My whetstone is almost worn away. I carved a John Gilpin doll for our little daughter. She is the pride of my life. The potatoes are well earthed. Majestic, Duke of York and King Edwards. My tubers are fit for royalty. They'll be well pleased in the kitchen.

The nearby cornfield is almost ripe, more golden than I can ever remember. And poppies, so many poppies. Can't say I've ever seen so much scarlet there before. Soon be time to praise our Lord again. They say I sing like a nightingale at chapel. All is safely gathered in, ere the winter storms begin. I never knew that trenches could be so deep. 3rd April. Aged 42.

IV

I'm proud of my work this year. In charge of lifting lids to check the forcing pots, and how I love the scent two days before they're ripe. Oh, yes, I know my melons. Soon be time to bend the tops down, wrench the bulb, disturb the roots. Cook will be well pleased with me. "He knows his onions too," she'll say. The roses so pink and fragrant. During crib time I bury my nose in American Pillar. And the sun so hot. So very, very hot. The air a shimmering mirage.

Heavenly Father, hear my prayer. Day and night I'm in Thy care. Look upon me from above, bless the home I dearly love. Bless all those with whom I play, make us better every day. God bless my family and make me a good man. Amen. I never knew that blood could be so red. 24th May. Aged 35.

Epilogue

We never knew that it could be so cold.
We feel so numb. So very, very numb. No-one ever told us.
No-one ever told...
No-one ever....
No-one...
No

Barely discernible etched into lime, names in pencil on a thunder-house wall. A month, a date, a love heart.

William Guy

Percy Carhart

Charlie Ball

Charlie Dyer

August 1924. A seven-word line inscribed for all time: 'Don't come here to sleep or slumber'.

They are back in the garden again. Sowing, hoeing, weeding, earthing up, scything, planting, harvesting, pruning.

"Back where we belong… Unseen."

ACKNOWLEDGEMENTS

(People, places and things in no particular order)

Miss Robbins my primary school teacher, and the wonderful nature table. My grammar school English teacher Mr Wadey who introduced me to Jacques Tati and *Moonfleet*. D.C. Thomson for the *Dandy* and *Beano*. William Wilson the barefoot runner. The lead accumulator wireless set and Archie Andrews. The library books which arrived in chests at school and at a neighbour's house. Corona pop, sherbet fountains, aniseed balls, gobstoppers, liquorice bootlaces, yo-yos and marbles. I-Spy books and Observer's Books. Yellow and red raspberries, wild strawberries, hazelnuts and blackberries. Brooke Bond tea cards, transfers, scrapbooks, Rupert Annuals and William books. Ken Vercoe, a true craftsman. The fields, orchards and hedges of the farmhouse tree. Beerclose Copse, Rock Copse and Knowstone Moor. Doctor Syn. Ted Hughes for telling me a farmer's son could be a writer and whose poetry-reading led me into the world of poetry. Miss Bucknell and her Morris Minor car for taking me to Wheaton's Booksellers of Exeter and Smith's of Barnstaple. Jill Pirrie who has encouraged me since 1987. Paul Nagle who provided the original score for a stage dramatisation of *The Farmhouse Tree*. Jennings and Derbyshire who were instrumental in getting me to know my imaginary friends Jim and Derek. Michael Moorcock for the multiverse and more things than were dreamt of in my philosophy. John Davey for friendship and support. Dave & Moira Shoesmith and Phil Rogers of Compact Disc Services. Pink Floyd. Maggie Burt for deciphering my handwriting. The skylark and the curlew on Knowstone Moor. Charlie the carthorse and the scent of chamomile around the hay shed in Higher Mead. Haymaking. The King James Bible. My octogenarian heroes. Gail Penston the London editor who believed in my dragon book. Philip Bowern my Devonshire editor who had faith in my childhood memories and who always answers my e-mails. Migraines which opened the portals back into my childhood during an attack. The Crooked Oak. My two great-aunts and their bookshelves of books. My mother, father and aged maiden aunt who gave me the best childhood possible. Priscilla who introduced me to *The Wind in the Willows*. Colin who showed me there was another world beyond my farmhouse tree. Kathy, my wife of over forty years who has been with me all the way with encouragement and love.